SANCTIFICATION AND THE LIFE OF FAITH

SOTERIOLOGY AND DOXOLOGY

Kent Eilers and Kyle C. Strobel, Series Editors

Atonement and the Life of Faith
by Adam J. Johnson

Glorification and the Life of Faith
by Ashley Cocksworth and David F. Ford

Sanctification and the Life of Faith
by Kyle C. Strobel with Kent Eilers

Union with Christ and the Life of Faith
by Fred Sanders

SANCTIFICATION AND THE LIFE OF FAITH

Kyle C. Strobel with Kent Eilers

Baker Academic
a division of Baker Publishing Group
Grand Rapids, Michigan

Published by Baker Academic
a division of Baker Publishing Group
Grand Rapids, Michigan
BakerAcademic.com

Printed in the United States of America

Library of Congress Cataloging-in-Publication Data
Names: Strobel, Kyle, 1978– author | Eilers, Kent author
Title: Sanctification and the life of faith / Kyle C. Strobel with Kent Eilers.
Description: Grand Rapids, Michigan : Baker Academic, a division of Baker Publishing Group, [2026] | Series: Soteriology and doxology | Includes bibliographical references and index.
Identifiers: LCCN 2026013578 | ISBN 9781540961679 paperback | ISBN 9781493455911 ebook | ISBN 9781493455928 pdf
Subjects: LCSH: Sanctification—Christianity | Holiness—Christianity | Christian life
Classification: LCC BT765 .S87 2026
LC record available at https://lccn.loc.gov/2026013578

Italics in biblical quotations have been added for emphasis.

Baker Publishing Group publications use paper produced from sustainable forestry practices and postconsumer waste whenever possible.

26 27 28 29 30 31 32 7 6 5 4 3 2 1

For John Webster (1955–2016),
whose generous hospitality to us
was a formative gift.

Contents

Series Preface

And Moses said, "Here I am."
Exodus 3:4

IN THE WILDERNESS, Moses stumbles upon a burning bush that somehow goes unconsumed. As if the scene is not arresting enough, the God of his forefathers bellows forth from that crackling, glowing bush: "Moses, Moses!" The response of Moses is simple and yet so evocative of a faithful response to God's call: "Here I am." Holy Scripture pictures that response time and again. So many other encounters with God are unmistakably echoed and foreshadowed here: those of Samuel, Mary, Jesus, and of course Adam. To Adam, God calls, "Where are you?" and he hides, and his hiding is paradigmatic of us all, sadly (Gen. 3:8–10); *but* Moses, Samuel, Mary, and Jesus *offer themselves* in response to the gracious calling of God: "Here I am, Lord." Their proclamation inspires what this series humbly attempts to accomplish: theological activity that bears witness to God's work in time and space to redeem and restore by following the doxological pattern of Moses. Addressed by God and fearful to look upon God's face, Moses finds himself suddenly shoeless in God's holy presence.

Said more formally, the volumes in the Soteriology and Doxology series offer specifically theological interpretations of the Christian life through the lens of various features of God's gracious activity to save, in which doctrinal activity is suffused with and held together by praise. The *gracious acts of God* are the contemplative aim of the series, advancing Christian rationality in grateful response to the redemptive, restorative, and transformative work of the Father by the Son and the Spirit. Focusing on soteriological loci, the topics addressed follow a twofold inclination: that God is the ever-present, captivating reality of all theological work, and that this focus awakens a doxological response that is intrinsic to the proper mode of theological reflection. As such, the orientation of each volume is both dogmatic *and* doxological: Each particular doctrine is located within an attentive retrieval of the Christian confession, all while demonstrating how theological reflection springs from worship and spills over into prayer and praise. Seeking to be catholic and evangelical, this series draws upon the richness of the whole church while keeping the sufficiency and singularity of the gospel at center.

The books in the series are designed for theologians-in-formation, meaning that the pedagogical aim of each volume is to train student-readers in a form of theological reasoning that unites what often remains painfully separate in Christian theology: doctrine and spirituality, theology and prayer, the church and the academy, the body of Christ and the individual theologian. This series' approach to theology is exemplified by men and women across the Christian tradition, from Athanasius to Benedict, Ephrem the Syrian to Anselm, Bonaventure to Catherine of Siena, and Aquinas to Calvin. However, with the inclusion of theology in the academic disciplines of the modern university, the expectations and norms of theological reasoning have been altered in many quarters: Exegesis is sequestered from theology, and dogmatics from doxology. This series offers something different. It seeks to retrieve forms of theological reflection unapologetic about their home within Christian worship and celebratory of their place within the entire Christian tradition.

With the sight of God as the proper aim of theological contemplation—trembling before the descending fire that calls us to bear witness to his presence—each volume seeks to constructively articulate soteriological loci through the broad range of biblical, historical, and contemporary issues with an eye to expositing the Christian life. While the different authors will vary in how they approach these tasks, the overall flow of each volume will follow a broad fivefold movement: (1) creed, (2) scriptural range, (3) comparative soteriology, (4) constructive theology, and (5) the Christian life, along with a doxological prelude and doxological interludes throughout. Having approached the doctrine from the standpoint of the *regula fidei* through creedal reflection; looked to Holy Scripture for the doctrine's content, scope, and form; and measured diverse traditions of biblical interpretation and theological reasoning, each volume offers a contemporary restatement of Christian teaching that shows how this theological locus directs doxology and Christian living. The *lived* reality of Christian existence, often far from the purview of theological reflection, remains the focused end of articulating the saving acts of God.

> O the depth of the riches and wisdom and knowledge of God! . . . For from him and through him and to him are all things. To him be the glory forever. Amen. (Rom. 11:33, 36 NRSV)

Kent Eilers
Kyle C. Strobel
Series Editors

Acknowledgments

I (KYLE) WOULD LIKE TO THANK Biola University for providing a sabbatical to work on this project, and more specifically Talbot School of Theology, which works so hard to make these things possible. To my dear community at the Institute for Spiritual Formation and Redeemer Church, you are a profound gift to me. I am grateful to many folks who listened, read, and engaged with me on this, including Jamin Goggin, Ryan Peterson, Tim Pickavance, John Coe, and my students. Above all, my family is a continual source of support and encouragement and is, alongside Redeemer Church, the main "place" of my work. Thank you.

I (KENT) WISH TO THANK Huntington University for providing a sabbatical to work on this book and Emmanuel Community Church for lending me a quiet space for writing (with a fantastic view of towering trees). I'm also deeply grateful to those generous readers who accepted my invitation to offer their feedback and reflections on my writing: Tammy and Hannah Eilers, Trevor Maggart, Tim Hallman, Zen Hess, David Buschart, and Mark Vincenti. And finally, of course, this project would never have been possible without my family. Thank you a thousand times over, and to Sam: for laughter.

FINALLY, WE WOULD LIKE TO THANK Elliot Ritzema for his thoughtful and engaging feedback, as well as everyone at Baker Academic for helping bring this book to fruition.

Our Hope for the Reader

THE CALLING OF A THEOLOGIAN is to stand before God with your whole person and your whole life, bearing witness to the triune God of the gospel from before his face. The theologian beckons, like Philip before them, "Come and see" (John 1:46), and our invitation comes from within a life shared with God. This invitation calls us as whole persons and not merely one aspect of our psychology (e.g., intellect, will, affect). While this fact is obvious for the Christian life, it appears less obvious for theology. But what becomes clear through the lens of the doctrine of sanctification is that theology, as *sanctified* reason, demands drawing near to the one who has drawn near to us in Christ Jesus.

Our hope is to model a work of collaborative theology that moves beyond mere intellectual speculation or polemical posturing and instead serves as an invitation to abide in Christ Jesus. We hope that you will draw near to God with mind, heart, and body to present your life to God by faith. Our hope for you, in other words, is that you would praise God for his faithfulness as you share life with the God who is the Holy One. This means that the intellectual, spiritual, and affective demands of this book are not segregated but need to be integrated into your person as you draw near to your Lord, not only reasoning with him but also presenting the fullness of your life to him.

What follows is a collaborative work of sanctified reason that integrates Scripture and tradition, mind and heart, intellect and spirit, inviting you to reimagine your own calling to think along the contours of the gospel to understand our distinctively Christian calling in Christ Jesus. Integration of this sort was largely the norm for theology throughout the history of Christian thought until the modern era. Now, unfortunately, we often segment these things into hermetically sealed categories, disciplines, and methodologies, leading to bifurcation between intellect and affect, doctrine and life, and the work of theologians and the work of the church. We have written this book in such a way as to facilitate a more integrated sort of engagement. One key element of this approach is doxological interludes, spaced throughout the book, that call you to pause, reflect, and pray.

One might see doxological interludes as a nice reflection after doing the hard work of theology, but we don't see it that way. These reflections should feel discordant with a mode of theologizing that is primarily academic (that is, in service to the academy), because we are orienting our theology for the life of the church. This means that the goal is not simply knowledge, but praise, prayer, and learning to love God with our whole heart and love our neighbors as ourselves. But theological training is not often constructed for that kind of engagement, and so these interludes are meant to shake us out of our academic slumber to set our sights on the truth of who God is and what he has done *for me*.

The broad goal of the doxological interludes is to engage your imagination in ways that invite contemplation and self-reflection about the main themes of the book: God's presence and hospitality and the dynamics of divine and creaturely holiness. Each interlude centers on a scriptural scene in which God is intensely present. We provide a work of visual art, relevant Scripture for each scene, a brief invitation to prayer, and space for written reflection. Each of these moments is a call to draw near to God in the truth of your life. Each space is an invitation to enter into the rest that he has provided you in Christ Jesus—to be with him as his own.

Hear the words of Jesus as an invitation not only to learn from him but to learn from him as a mode of entering his rest: "Come to me, all who labor and are heavy laden, and I will give you rest. Take my yoke upon you, and learn from me, for I am gentle and lowly in heart, and you will find rest for your souls. For my yoke is easy, and my burden is light" (Matt. 11:28–30).

DOXOLOGICAL PRELUDE

Public domain

Andrei Rublev, *The Trinity*

> The LORD appeared to Abraham near the great trees of Mamre while he was sitting at the entrance to his tent in the heat of the day. Abraham looked up and saw three men standing nearby. When he saw them, he hurried from the entrance of his tent to meet them and bowed low to the ground. He said, "If I have found favor in your eyes, my lord, do not pass your servant by. Let a little water be brought, and then you may all wash your feet and rest under this tree. Let me get you something to eat, so you can be refreshed and then go on your way—now that you have come to your servant." "Very well," they answered, "do as you say." So Abraham hurried into the tent to Sarah. "Quick," he said, "get three seahs of the finest flour and knead it and bake some bread." Then he ran to the herd and selected a choice, tender calf and gave it to a servant, who hurried to prepare it. He then brought some curds and milk and the calf that had been prepared, and set these before them. While they ate, he stood near them under a tree.
>
> Genesis 18:1–8 (NIV)

Invitation

We are not told why Abraham stands nearby while his guests enjoy his hospitality, but according to the customs of his culture it was a sign of great respect and humility. Abraham sets the table and stands ready to serve, but he does not join the meal. That scene is the subject of Andrei Rublev's icon, in which he represents the persons of the Godhead through the portrayal of the three guests. Every feature of the image is intentional, including the open space at the table in the foreground. Rublev portrays the meal that Abraham prepared in a way that invites the reader to *join the fellowship of Father, Son, and Spirit*. The open space at the table invites us to imagine ourselves there. While Abraham did not join his guests, we are invited by Rublev's icon to do just that.

Holding the image and the scene in your mind, take a moment to be with the Lord. Maybe take a deep breath. Maybe three. Maybe relax your hands. These are, perhaps, not your normal activities at the start of a theology book, so it may take a moment to become present to where your heart and mind are currently, to then pause and offer this time to the Lord. When you are there, prayerfully remember the deepest truth of your life if you are a Christian reader: *You are already at home with God in Christ, and you are continually invited to live into that reality by the Spirit*. The spacious table of God's relational fellowship is set for you to enjoy. Thank God for this reality and what it could mean for you. Pray for the Holy Spirit's strength to follow that invitation and to remain open to what it could mean for your life with others.

If you don't normally pause when reading theology to consider how the Lord is inviting you to draw near to him, maybe lift that question to him: *Lord, has my study became a way to come near to you, or has it become a place to learn about you while my heart is far from you?*

Notes

CHAPTER ONE

Creedal Contours

For as the Father has life in himself, so he has granted the Son also to have life in himself.

John 5:26

Christian existence is the existence of people who have no option but to cling, yet also wish to cling, simply to what he is for them, to what they already are in him, to what they may continually become from him and through him and to him. They are the children of God who are allowed and commanded to call upon God as their Father.

Karl Barth[1]

THE DOCTRINE OF SANCTIFICATION, a locus of soteriology, is ordered first and foremost by God and his action to save. John Webster is certainly correct when he states, "Soteriology is a derivative doctrine, and no derivative doctrine may occupy the material place which is properly reserved for the Christian doctrine of God, from which alone all other doctrines derive."[2] To address sanctification *theologically*, in other words, our focus must remain fixed on God and his action; God in himself and

1. Barth, *The Christian Life*, 76.
2. Webster, "'It Was the Will of the Lord to Bruise Him,'" 16.

God for us orders and governs every feature of soteriology. This point must be particularly emphasized for sanctification, accounts of which quickly devolve into descriptions of human development. This is odd given that holiness is ultimately about *God in himself* and only secondarily attributed to creatures.[3] Taking this seriously requires that our attention rest first and patiently on God, the Holy One, before addressing the nature of creaturely participation in his self-giving.

If we do not establish the holiness of God as the foundation and fount of sanctification, at least two negative consequences follow: First, our focus migrates to humanity and human growth unmoored from God and God's self-giving. When this happens, sanctification is too easily reconceived as self-help, and natural virtue habituation establishes primacy over supernatural virtue formation. Second, just as often, when sanctification loses its grounding in God, it finds itself reoriented around the doctrine of justification. Christian teaching about sanctification should rest in the truth that Christ himself is our sanctification (1 Cor. 1:30), but too often sanctification finds its center of gravity in another benefit of Christ's salvific work—namely, justification. In both of these two shifts, the doctrine of sanctification struggles to hold its own doctrinal footing on the shifting sands of theological construction. In response to these problems, we hope to model how patient attention to the dogmatic shape of holiness serves to locate sanctification in a theological framing of life in the presence of God—*life at home with God in Christ.*

A Doxological Theology of Sanctification

Since this is a volume in a series on soteriology *and doxology*, our focus is not solely on material content, but more specifically on the theological task as a distinctively churchly, and therefore doxological, enterprise. Keeping our theological reflection on soteriology within the frame of our participation in the body of Christ and her worship helps guard against the unfortunate tendency to focus so heavily on semantic claims and doctrinal

3. I. Howard Marshall's comment is standard: "All of this material reinforces the non-controversial and familiar fact that 'holy' is a term which expresses the nature and status of God as God, and is applied by extension to the people, places, and things that are closely associated with him and are therefore sacrosanct, just as he is" ("Holiness in the Book of Acts," 116).

debates that the way sanctification *governs and guides Christian spirituality* is largely ignored. With Hans Urs von Balthasar, we lament both the spiritual subjectivism that has become unmoored from theology (i.e., the rise of the "spiritual but not religious") and the opposite theological error of trading Christianity's intellectual-experiential depths for a sterile objectivity.[4] Von Balthasar writes, decrying the separation between theology and spirituality, "The impoverishment brought about by the divorce between the two spheres is all too plain; it has sapped the vital force of the Church of today and the credibility of her preaching of eternal truth."[5] Churchly theology, of course, is not less intellectual or rigorous than academic theology, but it serves a different master. As such, a doxological theology of sanctification is always fixated on the God who has made himself known in Christ Jesus, the light that illumines our darkness and draws all things toward their restoration. No divide between Christian spirituality and theology can be tolerated in a churchly and doxological theology.

The divide between theology and spirituality can be felt in *every* feature of theological practice and training, but it is felt more acutely in certain doctrines. A theology of prayer, for instance, is trite when it comes from the mouth of a prayerless soul, just as a theology of preaching rings hollow when proclaimed by one who fails to be a true hearer of the Word. Again, von Balthasar names the issues that become apparent when theology drifts from its spiritual home: "As time went on, theology at prayer was superseded by theology at the desk, and this brought about the cleavage now under discussion. 'Scientific' theology became more and more divorced from prayer, and so lost the accent and tone with which one should speak of what is holy, while 'affective' theology, as it became increasingly empty, often degenerated into unctuous, platitudinous piety."[6] In the Protestant tradition, affective theology (or experiential theology) was the place that theology and spirituality thrived, refusing to accept the theoretical over the affective, and vice versa. But von Balthasar's warning remains significant. This is the Protestant spiritual imperative we need to recover.

4. Von Balthasar complains, thick with satire, "The saints in modern times are required to describe the way in which they experienced God, and the accent is always on experience rather than on God: for the nature of God is a subject for the theological specialist" (*Word and Redemption*, 64).

5. Von Balthasar, *Word and Redemption*, 65.

6. Von Balthasar, *Word and Redemption*, 85.

Affective theology embraces both the objective and the subjective—it is confronted by God from without and knows the God who descends within—such that that theological task is bound up with contemplation and prayer. This is a theology that erupts in praise, worshiping the God to whom the angels cry out, "Holy, holy, holy is the LORD of hosts; the whole earth is full of his glory!" (Isa. 6:3).

In the history of Protestant theology, the task of affective theology—a task of faith—was oriented by its perfection in the beatific vision. (See the sidebar "The Beatific Vision.") Our knowledge in this life is only partial and will fade away (1 Cor. 13:8–9). But in eternity we will see God face-to-face, and we will know as we have been known (1 Cor. 13:12). The theologian, in this age of faith, wrestles with holiness before the face of God. The theological task of faith is always, therefore, proclaiming the

The Beatific Vision

The beatific vision (Latin *beatificare*, "to make happy") is the sight of God revealed to God's people in eternity that brings happiness and perfection; it is the final end for which human persons were created (Ps. 17:15; Matt. 5:8; 1 Cor. 13:12; 2 Cor. 3:18; 4:6; 1 John 3:2; Rev. 21:3–4). Reflection on the beatific vision began early in the Christian tradition, with a focus on contemplation and union, which then developed into discussions concerning enjoyment in medieval theology through the enduring legacy of Augustine. Reformed theologians adopted the legacy of the medieval scholastics, engaging directly (and at times indirectly) with figures such as Thomas Aquinas, Bonaventure, and Duns Scotus, who provide detailed reflection on the nature of beatific enjoyment.

While the major emphasis of the doctrine in the Christian tradition gravitated toward anthropology (viz., which faculty of the human person was most directly actualized in the vision of God), we relocate the doctrine of the beatific vision within the specific register of God's presence. The beatific vision is about God presenting himself to his creatures, and therefore the focus of this doctrine is *God* and his self-giving and self-revealing love.[a]

a. See Strobel, "The Sight of God."

truth of God in the presence of God. The theologian should be able to say with Paul, "In the sight of God we speak in Christ" (2 Cor. 2:17). In this way, the theological task must move beyond a simple articulation of the holy and instead articulate a vision of human life before the face of God as people who stand in the presence of God. A doxological theology of sanctification will adhere to these contours.

The divorce of theology and spirituality is not the only issue plaguing a doxological theology of sanctification. Alongside this separation is the temptation to reason intellectually while losing sight of the long arc of Scripture. Our theological reasoning should be transparent to Scripture, illuminating rather than blurring or entirely obscuring the full scriptural witness. But such blurring or concealment is, we believe, exactly what has happened with the doctrine of sanctification in some forms of Protestant theology. At times the doctrine seems nonexistent, replaced by practical advice for Christian living. At other times it becomes a mere container for every topic left to exposit in soteriology beyond justification (e.g., mortification and vivification, the Christian life, Christian ethics). Sanctification, in this sense, loses its material content and becomes the doctrinal bucket in which we address practical considerations. The problem with this is that *Scripture doesn't reason this way*. A truly *Protestant* theology should always be a theology that allows Scripture to say what it says; doctrine should not cloud the biblical material but clarify it.

With these warnings and desires in mind, we introduce holiness and sanctification as a way of orienting all that follows. In brief, *holiness* names God's personal presence to give order to his own, such that he is the foundation, center, and end. *Sanctification* is God's act of making something holy, not by giving something called holiness but by giving his personal holy presence. As a doctrine, sanctification is that aspect of soteriology that articulates what it means for human persons to receive God in his self-giving personal presence and relationally reciprocate that presence by faith. Sanctification is never a mere placeholder for practical matters but is the doctrine that articulates practical and theoretical matters in light of how God makes himself the foundation, center, and end of the Christian within God's self-giving presence.

Our initial focus inoculates us against alienating sanctification in practical issues or simply deflating its importance in the broader scope of soteriology. Think of this early material as setting up a common space of reflection for the sake of deeper development as the book advances. Ultimately, the goal will be to consider the work of the Father for salvation in and through the Son and the Spirit for the sake of union and communion with him. Fellowship with God, and the patient contemplation of him and his work to redeem, is the context within which we want to consider sanctification. Developing such an account will require us to advance a biblical framework of holiness while attending to historical, doctrinal, and polemical realities to address the nature of this life in Christ. This account establishes the nature, task, and directives for spiritual formation, while also revealing how often contemporary accounts of spiritual practices are unmoored from the doctrine of sanctification. Sanctification is more than a place to address spiritual formation but is never less than that; it is the doctrine that governs and guides the Christian life in its fullness along the contours of holiness.

To focus our attention on God's self-giving in Son and Spirit, and following the history of doctrine, we will dwell in this chapter on creedal affirmations that guide the structure of theology and catechesis. (See the sidebar "The Apostles' Creed and the Nicene Creed.") The organization of these creeds around the three articles of Father, Son, and Spirit points to the proper focus of theology as a contemplation of God and his securing salvation in his Son (Eph. 2:18). Seen in this way, the doctrine of sanctification is not somehow sequestered in pneumatology, even as we confess that the Spirit is the sanctifier. Rather, the Spirit's presence and work is never unmoored from the presence and work of the *Holy* Father (John 17:11), who sends the Son to be our sanctification (1 Cor. 1:30).[7] The doctrine of sanctification found in these pages will be trinitarian from start to finish. Trinitarian theology, however, is not focused on divvying up God's economic work to find tasks for each person of the Trinity to perform; the external acts of God are in fact undivided. What we find revealed in the biblical material is that God enacts redemption to deliver a people from the world, flesh, and devil, *to and for himself*. This single

7. Michael Gorman notes a similar pattern in 1 Thessalonians—"God (the Father) calls in holiness (4:7), the Spirit effects holiness (4:8), and the Son ('the Lord') judges the unholy (4:6b)"—but also in Paul in general. He notes that, for Paul, "holiness is trinitarian in structure. . . . Holiness is the call and will of God the Father; it occurs in Christ, who defines holiness for the church; and it is effected by the Spirit, who is the *Holy* Spirit. . . . Human holiness is participation in divine holiness" ("'You Shall Be Cruciform for I Am Cruciform,'" 151, 153).

The Apostles' Creed and the Nicene Creed

The Apostles' Creed

I believe in God, the Father almighty, creator of heaven and earth.

I believe in Jesus Christ, his only Son, our Lord. He was conceived by the power of the Holy Spirit and born of the Virgin Mary. He suffered under Pontius Pilate, was crucified, died, and was buried. He descended to the dead. On the third day he rose again. He ascended into heaven, and is seated at the right hand of the Father. He will come again to judge the living and the dead.

I believe in the Holy Spirit, the holy catholic Church, the communion of saints, the forgiveness of sins, the resurrection of the body, and the life everlasting. Amen.[a]

The Nicene Creed

We believe in one God, the Father, the almighty, maker of heaven and earth, of all that is, seen and unseen.

We believe in one Lord, Jesus Christ, the only Son of God, eternally begotten of the Father, God from God, Light from Light, true God from true God, begotten, not made, of one being with the Father. Through him all things were made. For us men and for our salvation he came down from heaven; by the power of the Holy Spirit he became incarnate of the Virgin Mary, and was made man. For our sake he was crucified under Pontius Pilate; he suffered death and was buried. On the third day he rose again in accordance with the scriptures; he ascended into heaven and is seated at the right hand of the Father. He will come again in glory to judge the living and the dead, and his kingdom will have no end.

We believe in the Holy Spirit, the Lord, the giver of life, who proceeds from the Father and the Son. With the Father and the Son he is worshipped and glorified. He has spoken through the Prophets. We believe in one holy catholic and apostolic Church. We acknowledge one baptism for the forgiveness of sins. We look for the resurrection of the dead, and the life of the world to come. Amen.[b]

a. The Apostles' Creed, Anglican Communion, https://www.anglicancommunion.org/resource/apostles-creed/.

b. The Nicene Creed, Anglican Communion, https://www.anglicancommunion.org/resource/nicene-creed/.

act is given shape by the economic movement of the three persons of the Trinity, actions given their own contours by the eternal processions of God and *his infinite blessedness* (1 Tim. 1:11).

Issues in Defining Holiness and Sanctification

Before turning to the creedal shaping of sanctification, it will be helpful to name the issues confronting any definition of holiness or sanctification. For many, holiness and sanctification come preloaded as concepts without allowing Scripture to determine the shape of the sacred. When this happens, creaturely holiness is reduced to virtue or purity, and the doctrine of sanctification devolves into an exposition of human growth in virtue or a life of purity. Instead, we should attend to the biblical conception of sanctification through an analysis of holiness, thereby allowing the imagery of holiness within the story arc of Scripture to govern the doctrine of sanctification.[8] Said differently, we let the canonical portrayal of divine holiness set the terms for the doctrine of sanctification. When we do so, several things are illumined.

First, we find that the biblical material on holiness is varied and flexible, and any definition of holiness needs to mirror this reality. The temptation is to assert an aspect or a fruit of holiness as holiness itself, thereby limiting the biblical imagery and narrowing the doctrinal scope of sanctification. One result of this temptation is that we end up with various definitions of holiness that are unable to speak clearly of holiness as both a divine *and* creaturely attribute. Instead, we need first to address what it means for God to be holy so that we can fittingly address what it means for a creature (or an object) to be holy. Similarly, there is a misguided tendency to talk about holiness as meaning "set apart," based on its assumed etymology.[9] While it is no doubt true that something made holy is set apart, what defines

8. David Peterson's warning is well founded: "Writers have often been preoccupied with establishing the place of sanctification within the framework of a given theological system rather than letting the biblical evidence speak for itself. For many, sanctification has become such a broad concept that its particular New Testament meaning has been obscured" (*Possessed by God*, 16).

9. Philip Jenson is certainly correct when he claims, "The etymological derivation of *qdš* [root for "holy" in Hebrew] from a root meaning 'cut' or 'separate' is highly speculative, and the approach to its meaning through etymology has now largely been abandoned. What matters above all is how texts use words. And while essential, it is not clear that separation is

the holiness of an object or person is how it is set *into* God's presence and action *for* God's presence and action. It is the positive claim about being set within God's presence that defines holiness, not the negative claim of being set apart from other things.

Second, when viewed from within the entire arc of Scripture and from the standpoint of the incarnation, we see that holiness and sanctification are not *primarily* about Christian growth, even though they assume it. Rather, when the biblical emphases come to the fore, the ground shifts to reveal that sanctification is a much broader theological category that serves as the register within which to understand growth. Sanctification, therefore, should not be reduced to Christian maturity, transformation, or virtue formation, even though it will govern and guide these realities doctrinally. In what follows, we will read the nature of holiness and sanctification from the full canon of Scripture and relate these to a Christian understanding of transformation and growth.

Finally, and building on the prior point, we must consider how the doctrine of sanctification functions within a broader theological system. In the history of dogma, sanctification has done very little doctrinal work. Too often, sanctification simply reiterates soteriological decisions already made and does not advance new ground. Because of this, categories such as Christian ethics, the Christian life, and virtue have floated free from the doctrine of sanctification rather than finding their mooring there—whereas we will solidly anchor them all in sanctification as the proper doctrinal location to govern and guide all aspects of Christian faithfulness.

A Working Definition of Holiness

Here is a working definition of holiness that we will further explicate in our biblical and creedal emphases below. Holiness in creation specifies God's personal presence and action to make someone (or something) fit for the presence of God.[10] Holiness, as mentioned above, is not so much

---

the primary content of holiness. In particular, holiness is a positive attribute or status, not a negative one" ("Holiness in the Priestly Writings," 98–99).

10. Along these same lines, J. Scott Duvall and J. Daniel Hays argue, "Throughout Exodus, Leviticus, Numbers, and Deuteronomy the presence of God is always closely associated with holiness. That is, the presence of God here on earth in the midst of Israel is encircled with holiness, and God's presence emanates holiness outwardly" (*God's Relational Presence*, 42).

about being set *apart* as it is about being set *within*. God's *setting someone or something within his self-giving presence* is what makes them holy. God the Holy One *holies* that which he draws within his presence. (See the sidebar "To Holy.") This presence is the *personal presence of the triune God*, whose self-giving creates a relationship that calls for responsive postures and actions. God, as we will see, gives himself to his creation so it can be what he created it to be, which is never something independent but rather a creation ordered from, to, and within God and his providential and redemptive governing. In other words, when God specifies and gives himself to a place of his presence, that place is harmonized around God as its center and ordering reality. The tabernacle and temple, not to mention Israel itself throughout much of the Old Testament, are instances of this, as well as the vision of the new Jerusalem in Revelation 21.

It is important to speak about holiness within the creation, but we must first contemplate God's holiness within himself. We must perfect the notion of personal presence to discern what it means that God is holy. One problem with the assumption that holy means "set apart," besides its being without justification as a definition, is that it requires creation for God to be holy. Holiness becomes associated with a faulty understanding of transcendence.[11] God is seen as holy because he is set apart from creation, but our God is holy within himself regardless of any external relation. Our God self-defines, "I AM WHO I AM" (Exod. 3:14), and is not defined by another. Theologians address this self-funded reality of God in various ways, but terms such as *fullness* and *life* are used in Scripture to specify this reality.[12] It is the doctrine of aseity, or God's being "of himself," that holiness specifies most clearly, articulating the fullness of God's self-presence as God's life itself.[13] (See the sidebar "Aseity.") Said differently, the doctrine of God's aseity is a partial theological gloss on the scriptural

11. God's transcendence is best understood as a description of God's fundamental *otherness from created reality*, the *Godness* of God, but it is often understood to mean something like God's distance. Immanence is then taken to mean God's nearness as a contrast to the distance of his transcendence, but these are not good uses of the terms for a host of reasons. See Placher, *The Domestication of Transcendence*; see also the sidebar "Noncompetitive Agency," p. 50.

12. Puritan theologian Stephen Charnock claims that holiness is God's "very life" (*The Existence and Attributes of God*, 2:113).

13. As Herman Bavinck notes, "But as is evident from the word 'aseity,' God is exclusively from himself, not in the sense of being self-caused but being from eternity to eternity who he is, being not becoming" (*Reformed Dogmatics*, 2:152).

To Holy

The word *sanctification* means "to make holy." We get this from the Latin words *sanctus* (holy) and *facere* (to make), which render the Greek term *hagiazō* from the New Testament (e.g., "Sanctify them in the truth," John 17:17). To emphasize and remind the reader that sanctification is fundamentally an *action* that makes something, someplace, or someone holy, we sometimes use the words *holying* (sanctifying) or *holies* (sanctifies).

Aseity

An attribute of God, aseity names God's self-sufficiency or self-existence (from the Latin, *a se*, "of itself"). God has *life in and of himself*, unlike every created, living thing, whose existence is dependent on another for its origination and continuation. The fullness of God's life as Father, Son, and Spirit does not, however, entail or require God's isolation, as creation and the gospel demonstrate. From the plenitude of God's own life, he gives life.[a]

a. See Gen. 14:19, 22; Pss. 24; 50; Isa. 40:28; 41:4; 43:10–20; 44:6; 48:12; John 5:26; Acts 17:24–30; Rev. 1:8, 17–18; Barth, *Church Dogmatics* II/1:310; Bavinck, *The Doctrine of God*, 144; Horton, *The Christian Faith*, 230–35; Webster, *God Without Measure*, 1:14–28.

content of holiness. God is holy because God is the full act of personal presence within himself and of himself.[14] It is from this holiness that God gives himself freely for our sake without needing his creation to fulfill or advance his life. God's holiness names the fact that God has "life in himself" (John 5:26). Holiness can never be separated from life and is always held in conflict with its enemy—*death*. Thus, *holy* is the most scripturally transparent way of naming the fullness of God's self-presence (i.e., life).

14. Seventeenth-century Reformed theologian Edward Leigh writes, "God's holiness is that excellency of his nature, by which he gives himself (as I may say) unto himself, doing all for himself, and in all, and by all, and above all aiming at his own pleasure and Glory; or it is the absolute purity of his nature, and his abhorring of evil. . . . The transcendent excellency of his own being whereby he is advanced above all creatures, and distinguished from them" (*Systeme or Body of Divinity*, 231).

When applied to anything that is not God, holiness specifies both what is necessary to access God and what accrues as one shares in the presence of the Holy One.[15]

Sanctification in the Granular

Our working definition of holiness specifies that God's infinitely actual self-presence is made available to his creation by grace. In other words, to be holy, one must participate in God's holiness, or, to use more biblical language, we are to *be holy as God is holy* (1 Pet. 1:16). If this is true, we would expect that God must give us the holiness by which he himself is holy. That's exactly what happens when God sends the Spirit of his holiness to his people to sanctify them for life in the Son. God, as the one who is *of himself*, is eternal, infinite, and glorious presence and actuality itself.[16] As the fullness of being, presence, and life, God is the fountain of all, the foundation and the telos of all things.[17] That does not mean that God cannot be for his creature; rather, by reordering all things around him who is life itself, God establishes abundant living (John 10:10). As Paul declares in adoration, "For from him and through him and to him are all things. To him be glory forever. Amen" (Rom. 11:36).

The doctrine of sanctification—following the contours of the scriptural explication of holiness above—names the holy God's act of ushering objects and persons into his presence. God's presence orders the creation for flourishing in him and for him. God holies that which God draws into his presence. God is the proper end and center of human flourishing, and sanctification unveils what it means to have God as our center and end in Christ by the Spirit. God's life, replete and effulgent, reorders all to himself according to his holiness, and to reject that center is to live

15. Old Testament theologian L. Michael Morales notes this connection between holiness and life: "That 'fullness of life' is intrinsic to God can be seen in Israel's concept of holiness which was fundamentally linked to the distinction between life and death, God's fullness of life making him utterly holy" (*The Tabernacle Pre-Figured*, 105).

16. There is much precedent for this focus. Most recently, Bernie van de Walle writes, "God is the only one who owes his existence to no other. His holiness itself can be understood to be 'of itself,' to possess aseity" (*Rethinking Holiness*, 53).

17. The theme of fullness of life is often found among biblical scholars attending to the theme of holiness as well. For example, Morales argues, "Holiness, properly conceived, pertains to fullness of life" (*Who Shall Ascend the Mountain of the Lord?*, 31).

against the grain of true reality.[18] Like Moses called before the burning bush, the Christian theologian must recognize this presence and respond accordingly. The doctrine of sanctification calls us before the Lord, whose Pentecostal fire descends on us but does not consume us. Leviticus, perhaps most obviously, narrates the plan for God's people to live in the presence of a holy God at the center of the camp, whose economy is given shape around his self-giving presence. In Jesus, this sacred presence now radiates from within humanity, and the Spirit Jesus sends is *his* Spirit of holiness to reorient the entirety of our life around him.[19] In this Spirit, people are caught up into Christ in the presence of the Father (Eph. 2:18), standing face-to-face with the one who gives proper order to all things (2 Cor. 4:6). What Paul and many in the Christian tradition have rendered *seeing* can also be described with the metaphor of *home*. It is a fitting image that we will return to later in the book.

God's personal presence is given by grace for the sake of fellowship with God. Framing holiness this way clarifies why definitions of holiness and sanctification often center on growth, purity, and virtue. To be caught up in God's personal presence, as a person, is to share in God's life (2 Pet. 1:4, or negatively, Eph. 4:18). God does not simply arrive before the presence of others, as if he were one object of many in the world. God *reorders life* around and within his life and presence. God's presence has a kind of gravitational field in and by the Spirit around Christ—the lodestone of faith. To be caught up in his presence and action is to discover a new center for one's being and person (Gal. 2:20). To be sanctified is to be consecrated for God's personal presence—for fellowship, communion, and friendship with God—to partake of God's life and bear the fruit of

18. John Norton writes, "Holiness is God, *conformable to himself*, I Sam. 2.2, Hab. I.13. As created holiness (which some call moral goodness or perfection of manners) is the conformity of the reasonable creature to the Rule; so (God being his own Rule, and the Fountain of all created perfection) we may conceive of increated holiness, as of God's conformity unto himself" (*The Orthodox Evangelist*, 16).

19. Van de Walle writes, "The holiness of such things [i.e., temple buildings, etc.], things that Scripture declares to be holy, is not self-constituted. Rather, the holiness of such things is grounded in and flows from their relation to God. The holiness they possess is the result of being God's peculiar possession, of being set apart by him, of being used for his purposes, or of participating in his nature in some way. While it is proper to refer to such things as holy, it is essential to remember that their holiness is always a derived and alien holiness" (*Rethinking Holiness*, 63).

this life. Sanctification, therefore, is the act of making something holy (whether a utensil, a location, or a person) for the sake of harmonizing all things around God. A utensil is minor, but it still plays an important part in God's act to call his people to himself. A person made holy is someone consecrated for his presence. Therefore, virtue is not the primary end of holiness and sanctification but is implied in the fact that to be holy is to be caught up in God's presence and recharacterized by and for that presence. Virtue is the fruit of those who give themselves to God's personal presence and are increasingly formed by it.

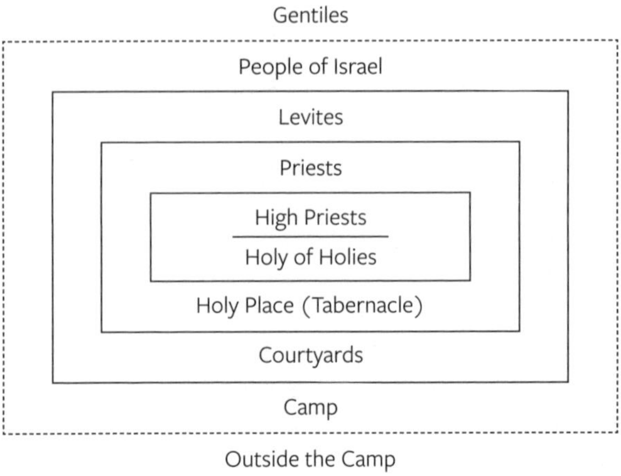

Figure 1.1. Degreed holiness (adapted from Walton, "Equilibrium and the Sacred Compass," 300)

While God is the pure act of holiness within himself, holiness in the creaturely sphere is always *degreed*. (See fig. 1.1.) This becomes clear when one considers the tabernacle and temple complexes and how the holy of holies differs in quality from other holy places.[20] It is not sufficient to determine simply whether something is or is not holy; one also has to

20. The Mishnah outlines ten degrees of holiness starting with the land of Israel as the broadest zone of holiness, narrowing to the holy of holies itself. Joseph Hellerman writes, "As can be seen in the citation from the Mishnah, permanent divisions between specific classes of persons (female/male, male/priest, priest/high-priest), and temporary distinctions that resulted from various kinds of impurity (menstruation, childbirth), delimited the 'territory' that a given person was permitted to frequent in and around the temple courts. The temple effectively functioned as 'a map for social relations'" (*Jesus and the People of God*, 170). Likewise,

determine to what degree something is holy. God calls people into his presence and fullness in ways that are meant to benefit them, but God's most potent presence is often dangerous. Isaiah's question is a legitimate one: "Who among us can dwell with the consuming fire?" (Isa. 33:14). In this sense, holiness is similar to a category such as goodness, which cuts across various registers and must be nuanced in light of which register it is qualifying. It is one thing to call a sandwich *good*, and another completely to talk about a good spouse or a good God; the word *goodness* is used in such varying ways that it is hard to specify what it could mean. In Scripture, similarly, we run into numerous holy realities, such as holy time (Sabbath), holy space, holy people, and holy utensils, so it is imperative that we specify how holy space, an unbeliever being made holy (as in 1 Cor. 7), and a believer being made holy differ. Our definition of holiness needs to be able to incorporate all of these things as well as the obvious fact that God is a *holy* God.[21]

Our focus on God's self-giving personal presence orders how the doctrine of sanctification functions within a theological system, because it refuses to shift the emphasis away from the Holy One to something like moral formation. This does not minimize virtue, obedience, or training in the Christian life, as if they were somehow irrelevant to holiness, but our approach relocates them *within God's presence and action*. The doctrine of God and his self-giving governs and guides every aspect of the formation of holiness. We will draw on several key figures from the tradition to show that this has been the overarching instinct in Western theological thought, even though it has not often been developed under the rubric of sanctification. Sanctification is life *in* the presence of God *for* the presence

---

John Walton notes, "This series of concentric circles of holiness has been referred to in recent literature as the 'sacred compass'" ("Equilibrium and the Sacred Compass," 299).

21. There are many books that point in a broadly similar direction, many of which focus less on holiness and more on God's personal presence as such. One example would be *God's Relational Presence* by Duvall and Hays. When they do focus on holiness, the parallels with our account are clear: "Whenever God's presence arrives, that space becomes holy and the demands on people for holiness and cleanness become important (and thus the need for Leviticus)." Furthermore, "the demarcations of holiness boundaries, the institution of numerous cleansings, and even the entire sacrificial system serve as a means of enablement so that God can indeed dwell in the midst of the people and they can truly worship him. . . . He comes in order to dwell in their midst so that he can fellowship with them and bless them. He gives them the law so that they can approach him in his holiness and his glory, and so that he can continue to live in their midst" (*God's Relational Presence*, 35).

of God. Mooring the Christian life and virtue to sanctification as sharing in God's life unveils a properly supernatural formation and unearths nascent pastoral implications.

The Creedal Contours of Holiness

Now that we have articulated our doxological approach and offered an initial portrayal of holiness and sanctification, we turn to the creedal shaping of the doctrine of holiness. This creedal focus allows us to attend to the God-centeredness of a doctrine of sanctification, continually reminding us that holiness is not foremost an aspect of creaturely realities but is grounded in the plenitude of God's blessed life (1 Tim. 6:15). Holiness names the fullness and infinite effulgence of God's life, signifying the *fullness* of God's personal presence *within himself*. The center of gravity of holiness is God in himself, not God in relation to something else. It is from his fullness and pure actuality that God moves to create, sustain, and redeem, calling his creatures into his life and making them holy as he is holy. To be holy as God is, for the creature, is to be centered in and on God, knowing God as the ground, center, and telos of life.

John Webster names this overarching theological instinct when he states concerning God's aseity: "The movement of God's triune life has its perfection in and of itself, and is utterly sufficient to itself; but this perfect movement is not self-enclosed or self-revolving. In its perfection, it is also a movement of self-gift in which the complete love of Father, Son and Spirit communicates itself *ad extra*, creating and sustaining a further object of love."[22] Applying Webster's insights to holiness both allows us to name the initial focus of holiness as God's life and refuses to either neglect or overemphasize the economic counterpart to this focus. God's holiness names the internal stability in the life of God, who relates out of his fullness and not out of need. God's relation to creation does not constitute his being or identity, but his engagement with creation flows from his fullness. The biblical articulation of holy space, which establishes God's availability and reign, along with holy rest (i.e., Sabbath), mirrors the eternal personal presence of God in himself and the self-repose of God's perfect life of blessedness.

22. Webster, *God Without Measure*, 1:24.

Centering our attention on the triune structure of the creeds trains us to contemplate holiness within the good news of God. Holiness specifies *the ground of all of God's movement*, including God's self-giving love. Remember, God moves in grace and love from and through his holiness; his movement to and for his creatures is entirely free and self-funded. His creatures cannot tether him to themselves, and even this is part of the good news. The tendency to try to manage and manipulate God, rather than embrace him by faith, is one of the constant temptations of God's people. But holiness is too often located on one side of God's action—his judgment, wrath, and righteousness—rather than also being recognized as what upholds his grace, mercy, and love. On many readings, God's holiness appears antithetical to his love, and accounts of atonement are put in place to make sense of how a holy God can be placated. Instead, it is in and through God's holiness that he offers himself to his creatures by grace.

A truly Christian theology of holiness, as with the creeds, centers on the incarnation. It serves as the interpretive key to Old Testament content and reveals the trinitarian shape of salvation. The Holy Father sends his Son, who sanctifies space in his life and presence *within humanity itself*, as Jesus of Nazareth. Jesus, upon his ascension, sends the Spirit of God's holiness to sanctify his people within the life of the Son, establishing persons to be holy as he is holy. The theological importance of this incarnational and trinitarian portrayal of holiness cannot be overstated. Believers are those with access to the Father within the Son and by the Spirit, as they are the new dwelling place for God (Eph. 2:18–19). The creeds establish the overarching context within which to consider the Spirit's application of Christ's work, recalling that all soteriological doctrines remain centered on God's action in Christ.

In centering on Christ, we find two poles to sanctified existence: Christ as our external sanctification, and Christ by the Spirit dwelling in our persons and establishing holy space in the soul (Eph. 3:16–19). The creeds teach us to remember that the movement into holiness, and holiness into regenerate humanity, is centered on Christ, who is our sanctification (1 Cor. 1:30). Christ holds together these two aspects within his person and presence by *his* Spirit. This focus on Christ as sanctification—and following this, on Christ as *our sanctification*—is unveiled by John Calvin when he writes,

> It is because he [Jesus] consecrated himself to the Father that his holiness might come to us; for as the blessing on the first-fruits is spread over the

John 17

[1]When Jesus had spoken these words, he lifted up his eyes to heaven,
and said, "Father, the hour has come; glorify your Son that the Son may
glorify you, [2]since you have given him authority over all flesh, to give
eternal life to all whom you have given him. [3]And this is eternal life, that
they know you, the only true God, and Jesus Christ whom you have sent.
[4]I glorified you on earth, having accomplished the work that you gave me
to do. [5]And now, Father, glorify me in your own presence with the glory
that I had with you before the world existed.

[6]"I have manifested your name to the people whom you gave me out
of the world. Yours they were, and you gave them to me, and they have
kept your word. [7]Now they know that everything that you have given me
is from you. [8]For I have given them the words that you gave me, and they
have received them and have come to know in truth that I came from you;
and they have believed that you sent me. [9]I am praying for them. I am not
praying for the world but for those whom you have given me, for they
are yours. [10]All mine are yours, and yours are mine, and I am glorified in
them. [11]And I am no longer in the world, but they are in the world, and I
am coming to you. Holy Father, keep them in your name, which you have
given me, that they may be one, even as we are one. [12]While I was with
them, I kept them in your name, which you have given me. I have guarded
them, and not one of them has been lost except the son of destruction,

> whole harvest, so the Spirit of God cleanses us by the holiness of Christ, and makes us partakers of it. Nor is this done by imputation only, for in that respect he is said to have been *made to us righteousness*; but he is likewise said to have been *made to us sanctification* (1 Cor. i. 30) because he has, so to speak, presented us to his Father in his own person, that we may be renewed to true holiness by his Spirit.[23]

Calvin is expositing John 17:19, where Jesus says, "For their sake I consecrate [or "sanctify"] myself, that they also may be sanctified in truth." (See the sidebar "John 17.") Reflecting on this passage, Augustine writes,

23. Calvin, *Commentary on John*, 181. Julie Canlis, reflecting on this aspect of Calvin's thought, notes that his emphasis on Christ sanctifying *himself* reveals "that our sanctification is not given abstractly to us but only as we participate in his person" (*Calvin's Ladder*, 100).

that the Scripture might be fulfilled. [13]But now I am coming to you, and these things I speak in the world, that they may have my joy fulfilled in themselves. [14]I have given them your word, and the world has hated them because they are not of the world, just as I am not of the world. [15]I do not ask that you take them out of the world, but that you keep them from the evil one. [16]They are not of the world, just as I am not of the world. [17]Sanctify them in the truth; your word is truth. [18]As you sent me into the world, so I have sent them into the world. [19]And for their sake I consecrate myself, that they also may be sanctified in truth.

[20]"I do not ask for these only, but also for those who will believe in me through their word, [21]that they may all be one, just as you, Father, are in me, and I in you, that they also may be in us, so that the world may believe that you have sent me. [22]The glory that you have given me I have given to them, that they may be one even as we are one, [23]I in them and you in me, that they may become perfectly one, so that the world may know that you sent me and loved them even as you loved me. [24]Father, I desire that they also, whom you have given me, may be with me where I am, to see my glory that you have given me because you loved me before the foundation of the world. [25]O righteous Father, even though the world does not know you, I know you, and these know that you have sent me. [26]I made known to them your name, and I will continue to make it known, that the love with which you have loved me may be in them, and I in them."

"For what does *And I sanctify myself for their sake* mean if not 'I sanctify them in myself, since they themselves are myself'? Because he says this about them, as I have said, they are his members, and Christ is one, head and body, as the Apostle teaches and says in regard to Abraham's offspring, *But if you are Christ's, then you are Abraham's offspring* (Gal. 3:29)."[24] Jesus, "conceived by the Holy Spirit," as the second article of the Apostles' Creed affirms, *sanctifies humanity to share in the life of God*. Augustine continues, noting how the truth is God's Word himself, born of Mary, such that becoming flesh was the Word sanctifying himself in himself, "because the Word and the man are one Christ, sanctifying the man in the Word."[25] Or, with Jonathan Edwards, "the Father sanctified him when he sent him into

24. Augustine, *Homilies on the Gospel of John 41–124*, 434.
25. Augustine, *Homilies on the Gospel of John 41–124*, 435.

the world, and sanctified him in sending him into the world; incarnated him by sanctification."[26]

In the Nicene Creed more specifically, we proclaim not only that he came down from heaven but that he came down *for our sake*. God is holy in the infinite actuality of his self-knowing and loving, and he has sanctified a space in humanity in the Son. He establishes his holiness in Christ Jesus—the one who is our sanctification—so we can be holy in him. To articulate the movement of the Son from his eternal generation through his incarnation, ministry, death, resurrection, and ascension is to articulate the movement of God's holy presence that establishes a way for us to draw near to himself. Only in Christ do we receive the Father, and only in seeing Christ do we see the Father (John 14:9). The reason we have access to the Father in Christ is that we are made holy in him, and by sharing in his holiness we are called to draw near in and with the one who has ascended beyond the veil (Heb. 6:19–20). Our access to the Father is secured by union with Christ in the Spirit, and we are holy by virtue of sharing in the holiness of the Holy One.

The manner in which the creeds center on Christ is particularly important in a doctrine of sanctification, which has a tendency to leave the ground of the second article to take up residence in the third—in pneumatology. But sanctification is first and foremost a second-article doctrine, as Calvin reminds us. Christ, the one who sanctifies himself for our sake, *is our sanctification*. In Christ we are already at home with God, sharing the divine, holying presence by virtue of our union with Christ. Put differently, in terms fleshed out more fully later in this volume, God does not give holiness per se, but God enlarges his life of holiness into union with humanity in the person of the Son, offering union with the Son and holiness in his person. The biblical and spiritual themes of ascent and ascension play a major role here, where the metaphor of ascent is understood in the register of communion. Julie Canlis, reflecting on Calvin, explains that "humanity's ascent is solely a participation in Jesus, whose bidirectional mission summarizes soteriology. . . . Calvin uses 'ascent' to denote the intended 'direction' or *telos*, of humanity. It is a word that summarizes the call to creatures to be in communion with God; as such, it encapsulates

26. Edwards, *The "Miscellanies," 501–832*, 334.

the Christian life."[27] Sanctification is established in Christ, as sanctification is first and foremost about the holiness of the Son that leads us to ascend within the relational presence of the triune God.[28]

The creeds point to a scriptural shaping of sanctification, where the biblical text reveals that God's economic movement is always fueled and ordered by God's life in himself. Eden, Sinai, the tabernacle, and the temple make sense as constructs of God's presence because of who God is as Father, Son, and Spirit. These constructs are mere shadows compared to that to which they point: the coming of Christ, who reveals the truth of God's personal presence and action within his own life (Heb. 8:5). In attending to this shaping of holiness and sanctification, we are again reminded of the methodological importance of starting with God as holy in himself and only then turning to how God's holiness establishes the proper ground by which a human person can be holy *as he is holy*. Our vision must remain fixed on God's presence in Christ Jesus as the ground for human formation through the Spirit. The ordering of our discussion is the fruit of a patient attending to the cadence of Scripture so that practical questions of Christian living do not replace holiness with an account of natural virtue. As we will see, while our definition of holiness might appear unique, it does not undermine instincts from the Christian tradition. Rather, our account seeks to draw together traditional instincts to reveal the emphasis on a truly supernatural formation in the Son and by the Spirit.

In this sense, salvation, which includes sanctification, is about a life reordered to God in full. To be made holy is to be recentered on God, the one who is the fullness of life, purity, and presence itself. But this objective reality, known in Christ by faith, is also a calling in the Spirit. Sanctification requires a life centered on God in Christ, such that every aspect of our persons is recharacterized in him and by him. The good news of salvation is that in Christ we are now his and he is now ours. Therefore, with sanctification, we must attend not only to the broad features of holiness in the action of God but also more specifically to the mission of God in Son and Spirit to redeem, reconcile, and save.

27. Canlis, *Calvin's Ladder*, 123–24.

28. This protects against the error of seeing sanctification as solely a feature of human obedience. Take, for instance, Barth's claim when he writes, "This is the reality of *sanctification*, or the problem of Christian *obedience*" (*The Holy Spirit and the Christian Life*, 32).

Holy as He Is Holy

Although holiness is an aspect of the triune life of God, and sanctification is grounded in the work of the Son to establish himself as the sanctified space available to humanity, the primary material exposition of sanctification is under the third article of the creeds, which specifies the work of the *Holy* Spirit to sanctify. Semantically, holiness appears to play an insignificant role in the Apostles' Creed, but the third article unveils a particular emphasis on the theme. The first three affirmations are governed by it, claiming a belief in the *Holy* Spirit, the *holy* catholic church, and the communion of *saints* (i.e., holy ones). Furthermore, the next three affirmations *presuppose* the redemption accomplished in Christ, offering the forgiveness of sins, the resurrection of the body, and the life everlasting. The resurrection of the body is not in reference to *any resurrection* but is resurrection to life itself, for the Spirit is the giver of life (John 6:63). This is the sense of Paul's claim, "God chose you as the firstfruits to be saved, through sanctification by the Spirit and belief in the truth" (2 Thess. 2:13). The Spirit is the guarantee of this life to come and is the proper sphere of the ongoing sanctification known in this age of faith (Eph. 1:14).

It is important to emphasize that the third article never stands apart from the second. To affirm one's belief in the Holy Spirit is to affirm that the Spirit is the Spirit of the Son (Gal. 4:6). It is the Spirit who works with power in one's inner being so that Christ dwells in the hearts of the redeemed (Eph. 3:16–17). We do not leave the ground of the Son when articulating the work of the Spirit. While this is generally affirmed, the theological tendency is to lose sight of this fact when addressing and framing sanctification. If sanctification begins with the Holy Father, known in the Son and offered in and by the Spirit, then it is important to refrain from reducing sanctification to one sphere of God's redeeming work, such as, on one extreme, the inner life or, on the other extreme, ecclesiology. Instead, tracing the contours of the life of God in the Son and the Spirit provides a framework of sanctification where every facet of life is within its purview, forging a doctrine of sanctification that includes both internal and communal dynamics of Christian faithfulness.

Holding the articles of the creeds together in a theology of sanctification makes sense of the biblical material that speaks of sanctification's past-tense nature. Christ truly is our sanctification, and thus sanctification is an accomplished reality *in him*. Nonetheless, there is a continuing dynamic to our sanctification as the Spirit works in the hearts of individuals and communities to harmonize persons around Christ. The undivided action of the Son and the Spirit tends to confound interpreters as it concerns sanctification, leading them to articulate either a completely accomplished reality or, more often, a reality needing to be generated. Scripture, as we will see, problematizes this dynamic, revealing a sanctification secured in the Son and a life of union and communion with the Son by the Spirit that leads to greater degrees of holiness. The theologian's task here is to employ language and categories that can shepherd a people into this truth without reduction and without losing sight of Christ as the center and sphere of sanctification. Metaphors such as home, fellowship, and friendship are especially appropriate, for they prompt our theological imagination to hold sanctification within the realm of relational proximity to the divine presence.

What becomes apparent as we attend to the ordering of the creeds around the persons of the triune God is that the *focus* of a doctrine of sanctification is never on something called "sanctification" but must always remain *fixed on the Son and the Spirit*. In other words, in our theological construction we are tempted to drift from God's action to the sphere of human self-construction, abiding in our ability to generate a life *rather than finding life in Christ*. But our theological work must remain here: Christ is the beginning and the end of the Christian life in and by the Spirit, a movement simply named *grace*. Grace is never simply a *beginning*, but an end also. Grace is the Christ-gift we receive that transforms us; grace is the divine gift that reforms a life in and by the Spirit. This creedal shaping of soteriology recollects the focus of soteriology as the movement of the Son and the Spirit, such that in the Son we discover life itself, and in the Spirit the giver of life. Holiness, as the personal presence of God, and sanctification, as God's act to consecrate us for his personal presence, are never less than access to God's *life*. God the Father, who has life in himself, grants the Son to have life in himself and sends the Spirit of life in the name of the Son (John 5:26; 14:26). Sanctification's essence is our relational access to *God's life*, holiness itself. The focus on life in the Gospel of John trades on these same contours because sanctification concerns sharing in the personal presence of God. Jesus is the way, the truth, and the life precisely because he is God of God and light of light, in whom we know righteousness, sanctification, and redemption.

Summary

A properly ordered doctrine of sanctification should be concerned primarily with God and his action to save. Human formation or other doctrines such as justification have often set the terms for sanctification, but its center of gravity is *God and God's self-giving*. Scripture provides this orientation, narrating across its long story arc how God's sanctifying activity (holy-making activity) is the *gift of his personal holy presence*. Thus, sanctification is that aspect of soteriology that portrays what it means for human persons to receive God in his self-giving personal presence and relationally reciprocate that presence by faith. In short: *Sanctification is life in the presence of God for the presence of God*. The three-article forms of the Apostles' and Nicene Creeds train us in our doctrine of sanctification to remain centered on the triune God throughout. God *in himself* is the gravitational center of holiness. To be holy as God is, for the creature, is to be *centered in and around the Holy One*.

DOXOLOGICAL INTERLUDE

Domenichino (Domenico Zampieri),
Landscape with Moses and the Burning Bush

> Now Moses was keeping the flock of his father-in-law, Jethro, the priest of Midian, and he led his flock to the west side of the wilderness and came to Horeb, the mountain of God. And the angel of the LORD appeared to him in a flame of fire out of the midst of a bush. He looked, and behold, the bush was burning, yet it was not consumed. And Moses said, "I will turn aside to see this great sight, why the bush is not burned." When the LORD saw that he turned aside to see, God called to him out of the bush, "Moses, Moses!" And he said, "Here I am." Then he said, "Do not come near; take your sandals off your feet, for the place on which you are standing is holy ground." And he said, "I am the God of your father, the God of Abraham, the God of Isaac, and the God of Jacob." And Moses hid his face, for he was afraid to look at God.
>
> Exodus 3:1–6

Invitation

Prayer is sometimes hard because God seems distant, and sometimes our loftiest ideas of God's greatness magnify the experience. Our ways of believing in the greatness of God lead us to pray to a distant, far-off deity. All such notions are *thoroughly dispelled* by this story.

God the Holy One becomes intensely present, but God's proximity doesn't displace the bush, or the ground, or Moses. Like Domenichino's *Landscape with Moses and the Burning Bush*, in which the environment is rendered with great detail, the story suggests no diminishment of the world when God arrives. Nor does the story suggest that God's presence requires any diminishment of God himself, as if the Holy One's greatness prevents him from being *really* among us. What we glimpse at the bush is only clarified by the incarnation: The Holy One's greatness does not require his distance but becomes the grounding for his radical *nearness*.

When praying in the presence of Christ we must discard any general notions of deity we hold in our minds. God is shockingly near because God is near *as God*, the Holy One whose presence among us doesn't diminish himself or displace our reality. "[God] need not diminish or confine or withdraw His own fiery Reality," Kate Sonderegger writes, "to descend from the realms of light to his darkened earth." She continues:

> We do not need to think away our world, cut away our thorns, transcend our landscape and pathways, and through such asceticism, discover the God who

> dwells in Light inaccessible. No! Divine Otherness is not won in such ways. God in Himself, the God glorious and free, the One Lord, beyond all and each: this very One is met in the waste places, the jackal dens, the temples, the mangers, the leper colonies, the prisons and the tombs, where the Lord God is pleased to dwell.[1]

Pause for a moment to prayerfully consider what this means for your life with God. Invite the Spirit to illuminate how it can shape your life with others.

Notes

1. Sonderegger, *Systematic Theology*, 1:84–85.

CHAPTER TWO

The Biblical Contours of Holiness

> I am in my Father, and you in me, and I in you.
>
> John 14:20

> God comes to the unsanctified world, dwelling among humans not in domestic tranquility, so to speak, but in the world's un-homed state. Christ's coming is the key step in God's mission of transforming the world—in sanctifying it—so it can be a genuine home of God.
>
> Miroslav Volf and Ryan McAnnally-Linz[1]

WITH THE INITIAL DEFINITION of holiness and the creedal emphasis in hand, we turn to Scripture to hold these things open to the biblical text. The goal is not to assert a view and then go looking for support but to attend to the biblical contours of the position already articulated. In Scripture, holiness is described in relation to time (i.e., Sabbath) and, more often, in relation to space (as the holy spaces of God's presence). By attending to these descriptions we find, first, a God who is holy in himself, in the

1. Volf and McAnnally-Linz, *The Home of God*, 8.

infinite actuality of God's self-repose and the fullness of his self-presence as life, love, and beauty. These emphases also reveal, second, something about what the creature is called *into*. To be holy is to embrace the call to lay down our works and rest in the work God has achieved (i.e., Sabbath). This is to receive the gift of God's life by grace. In receiving this grace, we are made holy to live within the space of God's presence and action to have our entire lives reordered by that presence and action.

Our goal is not to address all the varied themes of holiness and sanctification in Scripture in just one chapter. Rather, we want to sketch the biblical logic of holiness centered on the theme of God's intensive relational presence, which we believe is the core of the scriptural language, images, and symbols regarding holiness. In doing so, we seek to avoid an approach to holiness that simply collects biblical passages using the terms *holy* and *sanctification*, reducing the scriptural content to those passages alone. Thinking along the contours of Scripture requires more patient and far-reaching attention. Categories such as holiness rarely stay put in simple definitions, breaking out in various ways even when the words *holiness* or *sanctification* never appear.[2] What our analysis seeks, therefore, is a framework to understand Scripture's overarching instruction about a life of holiness.

From the outset is it important to recall that only God is holy in himself, and in Christ Jesus others are made holy in the presence of the Holy One. (See the sidebar "Holiness Is Not Innate.") The holiness that was limited to the tabernacle and temple systems breaks forth in the person of Jesus, who is the true manifestation to which the previous types (e.g., temple, altar, sacrifice, priest) pointed all along. To sketch the biblical contours of holiness, therefore, we begin with Jesus to offer a christologically intensive reading of the whole canon. Christ is the full manifestation of God's holiness in the world. By his Spirit he offers sanctification in and through union with himself. The invasive, proximate, and transformative presence of Jesus reveals the true character of God's holiness in action.

2. Michael Allen is certainly correct when he writes, "Too often, exegetical reasoning can be limited to offering literary and/or theological reflection upon those instances of Holy Scripture that speak directly to a particular theme or topic. Far too frequently, then, a doctrine of sanctification can be bound by those passages and portions of the Bible that employ the idioms of holiness and sanctification alone" (*Sanctification*, 28).

Holiness Is Not Innate

Holiness is not innate. The source of holiness is assigned to God alone. Holiness is the extension of God's nature; it is the agency of God's will. If certain things are termed holy—such as the land (Canaan), person (priest), place (sanctuary), or time (holy day)—they are so by virtue of divine dispensation. Moreover, this designation is always subject to recall. Israel is also commanded to distinguish between the holy and the common, as well as between the pure and the impure. The former antonymous set has a totally different rootage in Scripture. There is no holiness in creation except for the Sabbath. But this holiness rests in time, not in space. However, whenever Scripture designates space as holy—especially the sanctuary and its sanctums—this holiness does not inhere in creation but stems from divine revelation, God's unfathomable will and wisdom.[a]

a. Milgrom, *Leviticus: A Book of Ritual and Ethics*, 107.

Presence and Access

Throughout Scripture, holiness is first and foremost about God's presence and availability. At times these are set against each other, such that God's presence is in direct contrast to God's availability, but that is never the ultimate goal. Rather, the focus of Scripture is on how God shows up in history to make a way back into his presence for life with him. This is the main context for talking about creaturely holiness. In this sense the primary focus, contrary to many accounts, is not on the effects of holiness on the creature. Rather, the focus is on the presence of God and what is required for access, and *only then on how God's presence is transformative*. (See the sidebar "Intensive Presence," p. 36.)

There are two sides of God's presence and availability that must be kept in view as we traverse the canon of Scripture. On the one hand, God's holiness is precisely what seems to make his presence unavailable. On the other hand, his holiness orders a proper relation by which his people can draw near. For instance, Isaiah 57:15 declares, "For thus says the One who is high and lifted up, who inhabits eternity, whose name is Holy: 'I dwell in the high and holy place, and also with him who is of a contrite and lowly spirit, to revive the spirit of the lowly, and to revive the heart of the contrite.'"

Intensive Presence

When the nature of God's presence is considered across the whole range of Scripture, we find the following dynamic: While God is said to be *universally* present to all reality, the main emphasis of Scripture is that God is said to be *locally* present in particular places and to particular people. For instance, God is said to "fill heaven and the earth" (Jer. 23:24; see also Ps. 139), and God dwells *in* the tabernacle and temple (Exod. 25:8; 40:34–35), *in* those united to Christ (Rom. 8:9), *in* the church (1 Cor. 3:16), and ultimately *in* the new Jerusalem (Rev. 21). God is locally present in places established for his presence (e.g., bush, mountain, tabernacle, temple, the person united to Christ), but God's presence is not contained or limited by them. The dynamic is brought out in 1 Kings 8:27: "But will God really dwell on earth? The heavens, even the highest heaven, cannot contain you. How much less this temple I have built!" (NIV).

When addressing *God's relational presence to sanctify*, we derived the term "intensive presence" from J. Scott Duvall and J. Daniel Hays.[a] Intensive presence is our way of referring to God *drawing near*—even as God is universally present—to make covenant, bless, redeem, judge, speak, dwell within, make holy, and so on. God is everywhere present

God is the one who inhabits eternity, whose name is Holy. But it is not in spite of this holiness that he draws near to his creation; it is from *within his holiness*—the fullness of his life—that he creates spaces of presence for his people. It is in God's presence of power, fullness, and righteousness that he calls a people in their weakness (2 Cor. 12:9) and humility (James 4:6) and within the righteousness he offers in Christ (2 Cor. 5:21). Central to this reality are questions concerning righteousness, purity, and status, which is why purity laws and holiness regulations dominate books such as Leviticus, articulating what it means for the people of God to live with God and to draw near to him who is holy.[3] Only objects and persons

3. L. Michael Morales argues, "The primary theme and theology of Leviticus (and of the Pentateuch as a whole) is *YHWH's opening a way for humanity to dwell in the divine Presence*" (*Who Shall Ascend the Mountain of the Lord?*, 23 [emphasis original]).

as the Holy One, and God the Holy One is *intensively present* to holy those who share his life.

Moving from biblical studies to philosophy, *intensive presence* resonates with Eleonore Stump's term "significant personal presence." One's presence with another person can merely entail proximity, which she calls "minimal personal presence." But significant personal presence is being *present to* another in a way that entails *mutuality* and *shared attention*. Applying this insight to God, Stump writes, "It is one thing for God to be present always and everywhere with direct and unmediated causal and cognitive connection to everything but hidden from human view, and it is another thing entirely for God to be present to a human person in the stronger sense of presence represented by" *significant personal presence*. Being present to God in this sense requires us to know this "mutual awareness" and "joint attention" that Scripture calls faith.[b]

a. Duvall and Hays, *God's Relational Presence*, e.g., 27, 101, 148, 159. For comparison, G. W. Bromiley describes God's intensive presence as "the special realization of his presence" and J. Ryan Lister as God's "relational-redemptive presence" (Bromiley, "Presence, Divine," 873; Lister, *The Presence of God*, 50). See also Clements, *God and Temple*.

b. Stump, *Wandering in Darkness*, 113, 119. See also Dalferth, *Becoming Present*.

sanctified for God's presence may draw near to him. What are we to learn from these practices in light of the incarnation?

Fulfillment and the Pedagogy of Holiness

Books such as Exodus and Leviticus articulate what we might think of as a *pedagogy of divine presence* and what it means to live in the presence of the consuming fire (Isa. 33:14). (See the sidebar "Idioms and Modes of God's Presence," p. 38.) In Jesus, we find the deeper logic that these initial pedagogies point to. Just as the law is a guardian until Christ comes (Gal. 3:24), so the tabernacle and temple systems, with their priesthood, purifications, sacrifices, and spheres of holiness, are intermediary trainings until the arrival of the true High Priest. In Christ we discover a previously unfathomed access. The atoning work of Jesus, in this sense, is not only

Idioms and Modes of God's Presence

In Scripture we find a range of idioms for describing the intensive personal presence of God, most commonly *face* and *name*. When psalmists appeal for God's face to shine upon them (Ps. 80) or for God to not hide his face (Ps. 102), these are poetic idioms for the blessing, favor, and salvation that accompany God's intensive personal presence. Likewise, the scriptural idiom for describing the abiding personal presence of God with his covenant people is that God puts his "name" on them (e.g., Num. 6:24–27; Isa. 44; Rev. 22).

Glory and *Spirit* work linguistically in a slightly different way in Scripture. God is intensely present *as* glory or Spirit. Think of these as *modes* of God's presence, for they identify God's intensive presence when someone experiences it. God's *glory* fills the temple in Isaiah's vision (Isa. 6), and the *Spirit* rests on the apostles (Acts 2) and dwells within the Christian (Rom. 8).[a]

a. See Duvall and Hays, *God's Relational Presence*, 136–58, 191–92; Clements, *God and Temple*, 104–5, 118–19, 133, 137; Schuele, "The Spirit of YHWH and the Aura of Divine Presence"; Cocksworth and Ford, *Glorification and the Life of Faith*, 14–24.

about Jesus's death, but his life, death, resurrection, and ascension to the heavenly sanctuary. Christ's taking on flesh and faithfully fulfilling God's plan is what provides access to the Father in Christ's very person, as believers are now *one with him by faith*. In giving his Spirit and uniting them to his person, Christ purifies and sanctifies them for his presence by drawing them intimately into the sphere of the Holy One. Peter articulates these realities most clearly, introducing his letter to Christians who are chosen according to "the foreknowledge of God the Father, in the sanctification of the Spirit, by means of Jesus Christ's obedience and for sprinkling with his blood" (1 Pet. 1:2).[4] The Christian is purified by the blood of Jesus, blood

4. This translation by Darian Lockett differs from that of many who try to orient the term *obedience* to the Christian, so that it reads "for obedience to Jesus Christ," as in the ESV. But as Lockett notes, "Though grammatically possible, this understanding breaks the pattern of the previous two prepositional phrases, both of which cast the nouns (the Father and Spirit) as the *subject* of the verbal idea rather than the object" (Lockett, "Catholic Epistles," 316). Lockett's translation follows the insights of John Elliott, Joel Green, and Kelly Liebengood.

that purifies for the heavenly sanctuary, making God's presence available in and through Christ's high priestly ministry, sacrifice, and obedience.

In Hebrews 9 we are offered a lengthy description of how Jesus fulfills the tabernacle system, not somehow annihilating it but fulfilling it on earth so that he can enter its true archetype in heaven, God's "holy habitation" (2 Chron. 30:27).[5] It is in this context that Hebrews makes the incredible claim that as long as the outer courts of the tabernacle were still standing, the true way in to the holy place remained unopened. These outer courts represented the old age, which in Christ has now been brought to its proper end to inaugurate the new (Heb. 9:11–14). Through Christ's blood believers can draw near, but they can also draw near to have consciences purified, laying aside worldly schemes of self-help or self-soothing to discover hope in the only place it can be found—in and through the blood by which sins are forgiven.[6]

> Therefore, brothers and sisters, since we have confidence to enter the Most Holy Place by the blood of Jesus, by a new and living way opened for us through the curtain, that is, his body, and since we have a great priest over the house of God, let us draw near to God with a sincere heart and with the full assurance that faith brings, having our hearts sprinkled to cleanse us from a guilty conscience and having our bodies washed with pure water. (Heb. 10:19–22 NIV)

Christians are cleansed in Christ, and in him they can draw near with full assurance. Just as Moses sprinkled blood on the people to sanctify them to draw near to the Lord at Sinai, so in Christ Christians have been sprinkled by his blood and sanctified in his person, for he himself is our sanctification (1 Cor. 1:30).

5. There is an important scholarly discussion on what it means to say that the heavenly tabernacle is an archetype. See, e.g., Klawans, *Purity, Sacrifice, and the Temple*, chap. 4 ("Temple as Cosmos or Temple in the Cosmos"); Clements, *God and Temple*, esp. chap. 9; Koester, *The Dwelling of God*, esp. chaps. 4–7; Anderson, *That I May Dwell Among Them*, esp. chaps. 9–10. David Moffitt, engaging with Klawans and others, has a helpful discussion in *Rethinking the Atonement*, chap. 8 ("Serving in the Tabernacle in Heaven").

6. This drawing near is the creaturely correspondence to Jesus's high priestly action. Moffitt writes, meditating on Heb. 9:28 in light of 13:20–21, that "the blood of the covenant is the means by which God's people are being equipped to please God by doing his will. Jesus's ongoing high-priestly intercession is making God's people perfect—doing what the sacrifices and ministry of the priests in the old covenant aimed to do but ultimately could not do in such a way as to bring perfection (see 7:11, 19; 9:9; 10:1)" (*Rethinking the Atonement*, 154).

The author of Hebrews picks up on the themes of atonement, sacrifice, and access to his presence—all glossed by the notion of drawing near—and shows how the greater is now available in Jesus. In Jesus, there is a deeper and more profound drawing near. In Paul's articulation of redemption, access to the Father is in the person of the Son by the Spirit of God (Eph. 2:18), which he describes using a temple metaphor, writing, "You are fellow citizens with the saints and members of the household of God, built on the foundation of the apostles and prophets, Christ Jesus himself being the cornerstone, in whom the whole structure, being joined together, grows into a holy temple in the Lord. In him you also are being built together into a dwelling place for God by the Spirit" (Eph. 2:19–22). In Christ we are a *holy temple*. In Christ we are being built up together as a dwelling place for the Spirit of God.

Perhaps the clearest discussion of this fellowship with God and access to the Father in the Son is found in John 14–17. There, we find Jesus explaining his followers' relationship to him on the basis of his own relationship to the Father:

> I am in my Father, and you in me, and I in you. (John 14:20)

> As the Father has loved me, so have I loved you. Abide in my love. (John 15:9)

> But when the Helper comes, whom I will send to you from the Father, the Spirit of truth, who proceeds from the Father, he will bear witness about me. And you also will bear witness, because you have been with me from the beginning. (John 15:26–27)

> Holy Father, keep them in your name, which you have given me, that they may be one, even as we are one. (John 17:11)

> I do not ask for these only, but also for those who will believe in me through their word, that they may all be one, just as you, Father, are in me, and I in you, that they also may be in us, so that the world may believe that you have sent me. The glory that you have given me I have given to them, that they may be one even as we are one, I in them and you in me, that they may become perfectly one, so that the world may know that you sent me and loved them even as you loved me. (John 17:20–23)

> I made known to them your name, and I will continue to make it known, that the love with which you have loved me may be in them, and I in them. (John 17:26)

In this final verse, Jesus makes an important claim about the kind of fellowship he offers in himself. He does not pray, "Father, love them," but instead prays that the Father would give them "the love with which you have loved me," so that Jesus himself would be in us. In Jesus, the Father-Son relation is made available by the Spirit, such that the salvation made available in Christ is one of receiving God's life in Christ by the Spirit. This is why union with Christ is central to any Christian soteriology.

As we mentioned above, it is possible to ignore these passages when talking about sanctification because the term itself is not used. This unfortunate (and all too common) hermeneutical mistake skews one's understanding of holiness. John 14–17 focuses on how Jesus's relation to his people is predicated on his relation to the Father. The Father sends the Son, and Jesus will send his people. The Father sent Jesus, and Jesus comes back to him, which establishes the *from* and *for* movement at the heart of John's Gospel (e.g., John 16:28). Jesus is the one who is not *of* the world but is sent from *above*, which is another significant theme throughout John (e.g., 3:31; 8:23, 42; 9:39; 10:36; 16:28–30). So now, in Christ, believers are hated by the world because they are not of the world, just as Christ is not of the world (17:14). In light of this, Jesus prays, "Sanctify them in the truth; your word is truth. As you sent me into the world, so I have sent them into the world. And for their sake I consecrate myself, that they also may be sanctified in truth" (17:17–19).

In John 17:17–19, Jesus is locating sanctification within a wider discussion of his being sent by God and returning to God. In going back to the Father, Jesus sends the Spirit so that Christians are no longer *of* the world but are born from above (John 3:3). As such, they are those now sent by the Son into the world, just as the Father sent the Son into the world. Jesus has consecrated himself, such that *being in him is knowing the holiness by which God himself is holy*. God's consecration of Christ is his sending him into the flesh to establish a new space for sanctification (John 10:36), no longer spatially oriented as with the tabernacle, temple, and land but available in the person of Christ *through union with Christ*.

Christians are sanctified *in Christ's sanctification*, as Augustine, Calvin, and Edwards emphasized (as noted in the last chapter).

From Mountain to Mountain

It is important to begin with Jesus's fulfillment of prior forms, but we shouldn't move too quickly off the Old Testament witness to provide the primal framing of holiness. Too often accounts of sanctification presuppose well-worn doctrinal frameworks without noticing that they have become untethered from the biblical account. To avoid this we want to pause and consider, in particular, the Old Testament presentation of holiness. The manner in which the Old Testament presents holiness helps make sense of what Jesus fulfills and how Jesus secures holiness within his person for us. In short, what was spatial in the Old Testament narratives always assumes the relational dynamics of presence, availability, and presenting oneself to God, who had given himself to his people. All these realities are taken up in Jesus, where *the spatial becomes the personal in the person of the Son*.

In Exodus 3 (burning bush) and Exodus 19 (Sinai), there is a kind of *inclusio* that frames the whole of the exodus. As in Eden, we discover that holiness is spatially located, and like Eden, it is established on a mountain.[7] The first mountain, named "the mountain of the Lord," is Horeb, where Moses discovers the burning bush.[8] When Moses turns aside to see this

7. John Walton argues that

> it is fair to say that sacred space has not been a central plank in the theological platform of Christianity. There is, of course, good reason for this. A generation before the temple was destroyed by the Romans in 70 CE, a remarkable event took place. At the moment when Jesus died, the Gospels report that the veil was torn in two (Matt. 27:51; Mark 15:38; Luke 23:45). We do not often enough recognize the significance of this because we have so little understanding of sacred space. The tearing of the veil indicated the end of restricted access to God. Heb. 10:20 clarifies the new situation further because it uses the imagery of Christ's flesh as the veil that gives us access. Through the blood of Christ we are able to enter the Holy Place. Paul works out some of the ramifications of this in Eph 2:11–22 as he explains that the Gentiles were excluded from God's presence (that is, outside the camp) but are now brought near. ("Equilibrium and the Sacred Compass," 297)

8. Jon Levenson notes how Mount Sinai was archetypal but became absorbed by Mount Zion, as is evident in Ps. 97 (*Sinai and Zion*, 91). Throughout Scripture, the mountain theme remains central, but the actual mountain shifts. This is true with Jerusalem as well; see Gal. 4:21–26.

odd sight, the Lord calls out to him: "'Do not come near; take your sandals off your feet, for the place on which you are standing is holy ground.' And he said, 'I am the God of your father, the God of Abraham, the God of Isaac, and the God of Jacob.' And Moses hid his face, for he was afraid to look at God" (Exod. 3:5–6).

In what follows, three features of this passage will be important: First, it is on the mountain that Moses discovers holy ground. Second, this space is holy not because the mountain is holy in itself but because God has chosen to be intensely present to this place. Last, because of this unique presence of God, there is a proper response, seen here as Moses's fear and removal of his sandals.[9] Each of these features will continue throughout Scripture, helping establish the logic of holiness. But this initial encounter will be fleshed out in broader strokes at Sinai.

After Moses leads the Israelites through the sea (the waters of death) and into the wilderness, the Lord guides them to Mount Sinai (Exod. 19:1–6).[10] In preparation for the third day, when the Lord would descend upon the mountain, God calls Moses to consecrate the people and have them wash their garments (Exod. 19:10). We are told that the Lord would come down in the sight of all the people, and the people were warned that anyone, human or animal, who touched the mountain would be put to death (Exod. 19:11–13). After Moses is called up the mountain to meet with the Lord, the Lord commands Moses to consecrate the priests so they can draw near (Exod. 19:21–22). It is in this context that we find the initial presentation of the Ten Commandments. But rather than break through to look at the Lord, the people instead stand far off, asking Moses to speak to them instead of God (Exod. 20:19).

9. Jo Bailey Wells connects the three theophanies of Sinai as a framework for considering the whole narrative (*God's Holy People*, 31–32). For the sanctuary as a place of vision, see Levenson, *Sinai and Zion*, 94–95.

10. Morales notes that there is a pattern throughout God's action in redemption history that goes through the waters, to the mountain, for life in God's presence/house. This pattern helps highlight the spiritual pedagogy of God's action: "Of prime significance here is what this divinely orchestrated providence is meant to convey about the nature of re-entering God's Presence. Israel's groaning under bondage and Pharaoh's ever-hardening heart combine for a highly particular theological drama: humanity must be redeemed from bondage—from death itself—before it can be brought into life with God. This theology would be rehearsed daily through the tabernacle (and later temple) cult inasmuch as any approach to the divine Presence demanded the shedding of blood" (*Who Shall Ascend the Mountain of the Lord?*, 76–77).

The same three features of the passage about the burning bush are present here. First, the mountain is holy ground, so much so that only certain people, at certain times, are allowed to ascend the mountain of the Lord.[11] There is an ordered system for drawing near to God, with leaders who draw near for the sake of the people. Second, what makes the mountain both holy and dangerous is that the holy God is uniquely present to this place. God descends once again with fire, but this fire is much more menacing than the burning bush. This fire, lightning, and smoke are meant to test the people so that the "fear of him may be before you" (Exod. 20:20). Third, like Moses, who was afraid to look at God, the people of Israel are afraid even to hear from him. Furthermore, the law given at Sinai reveals that God's holy presence demands an ethic, just as God's holy presence to Moses required him to remove his sandals.[12] But now God's presence orders a whole society around himself. Rather than merely sanctifying a space for his presence, now we see God calling a people *into his holiness itself*. God is looking to make *a people* holy for his holy presence, and at Sinai we discover how he plans to do so.

God's presence on the mountain serves a pedagogical purpose. The theme of the holy mountain—the mountain of the Lord—is fundamental to the biblical narrative, starting in Eden, reestablished in the life of Moses, and carried on through the prophets until Jesus recapitulates and fulfills the mountain typology in his own life (the Gospel of Matthew, for instance, is given shape by seven mountain scenes).[13] What we might call the *pedagogy of the mountain* is actually the pedagogy of *holiness*, where God is training his people to revere him, to draw near to him, and to recognize that full participation in his personal presence is available only for those made holy.[14] In the narrative we discover that there are holy places, with restricted access, and yet with mediations that allow one to enter into the

11. See, for instance, Wells, *God's Holy People*, 30.

12. Wells, addressing the phrase "the mountain of God," argues, "It is no coincidence that the same language is used elsewhere of Mount Zion; the similarities are both typological and 'genetic.' As [Walter] Moberly points out, 'Sinai is portrayed as the archetypal sanctuary, the holy place at which access is restricted and controlled'" (Wells, *God's Holy People*, 29).

13. I believe it was Michael Wilkins who first pointed this out to me (Kyle).

14. The pedagogy of purity is that human persons are like the sacrifices they offer. They need to offer a perfect sacrifice, which orients this pedagogy ultimately to Christ and the necessity of a divine act of atonement. Purity laws helped them see their own imperfections

presence of God, to be with him, and to in some sense receive his presence (as either a kind of seeing or a kind of hearing). This pedagogy trains the people to know that abundant life comes from having God among them and to embrace the only path that allows for access to him.[15]

Importantly, as we will see, the New Testament witness does not ignore these themes but establishes them in Christ through faith. The training of the Old Testament is caught up in Christ and advanced to deeper intimacy with him. Through Sabbath we are taught to lay down our works to rest in the God who sanctifies. Through the tabernacle and temple, we learn that God establishes his presence and makes a way for access to him through his priests, purity, and sacrifices. Through sacrifice, coming from a verb meaning "to bring near,"[16] we learn that we are not bringing an animal near but are supposed to draw near ourselves in and through the sacrifice to ascend the mountain that is now the altar ("Sinai is now in the sanctuary," Ps. 68:17). This is why the imperative of Hebrews is to draw near and why, when Paul turns to spiritual practices, his call is to "present your bodies as a living sacrifice" (Rom. 12:1). What holiness reveals is the call to draw near through laying down our works, embracing the God who sanctifies, and being conformed to his life in our midst. Holiness is always a state and a calling because it is about life in the presence of God.

God's Presence as a Way of Life

What these various features of holiness and the pedagogy of holiness reveal is that God establishes systems and structures of availability and mediation *to call his own people into his life to share in that life*. The problem with systems and structures is that it is easy to see them as modes of manipulating God and his presence for our own ends. The temptation, in other words, is to see God's presence as static—to assume that God is *their* God and they are *his* people—in a way that undermines creaturely obedience or God's

and impurities, even those that were not moral (e.g., skin disease), which is all a part of the broader pedagogy of drawing near.

15. As noted above, Morales discerns a pattern in Scripture of passing through waters, to the mountain of God, for the sake of worship: "that is, for the abundant life of the divine presence." This is exactly right and helps provide the overall liturgical and personal features of sanctification. See Morales, *The Tabernacle Pre-Figured*, 1.

16. Milgrom, *Leviticus: A Book of Ritual and Ethics*, 17. Milgrom explains, "Thus a sacrifice is that kind of an offering that enables us to approach God."

freedom.[17] But what we find throughout Scripture is that God's presence establishes a way of life ordered around his presence, a way governed by notions of purity, holiness, and fearing the Lord. But this obedience is not set against the rest that God has promised. God offers his people his rest, practiced through Sabbath, which serves as the framework for the feasts of the Lord eaten in the presence of the Lord.[18] Likewise, when we hear about human sin creating a separation between God and his people such that he hides his face from them (Isa. 59:2), the answer is that God's own arm will bring salvation and righteousness (59:16).

At Sinai, God teaches Israel of their utter neediness before his presence, unveiling the truth to show them who he is and who he is calling them to be.[19] God is ordering his people to the truth while, at the same time, *revealing the truth of their hearts* (Deut. 8:2), showing them how their hearts turn away from him and turn back to Egypt (Acts 7:39). Moses, the priesthood, Sabbath, and the tabernacle are the answers given to their dilemma. As stated in Exodus 29:43–46 concerning the tabernacle, "There I will meet with the people of Israel, and it shall be sanctified by my glory.

17. Ever tempted by ways to manipulate and control, God's people often tried to use God's gracious means of drawing near to manage him and seek to instrumentalize his presence. This was the word of the Lord that came to Jeremiah: "Thus says the LORD of hosts, the God of Israel: Amend your ways and your deeds, and I will let you dwell in this place. Do not trust in these deceptive words: 'This is the temple of the LORD, the temple of the LORD, the temple of the LORD'" (Jer. 7:3–4). God's people always attempt to tether God's holiness to objects, sanctifying them beyond possible defilement, and in doing so seek to wield them for their own ends. But God's message is clear: He has no problem rejecting his sanctified temple when his people try to use it for their own ends.

18. Notice that after the introduction of the Feast of Unleavened Bread, there is a short recollection about Sabbath (recalling the significant earlier teaching about Sabbath) before introducing the other two feast's all males were required to attend: the Feast of Weeks and the Feast of Ingathering. See Exod. 34:18–24.

19. Morales (*Who Shall Ascend the Mountain of the Lord?*, 87) writes,

> The dominant attribute of Mount Sinai is its holiness, brought out in a variety of ways by the narrative—chiefly by the fear-inspiring descriptions of the theophany associated with it. Mount Sinai is utterly holy because the unapproachable glory, the thunderous and fiery Presence of God, has descended upon its summit. That holiness is also brought out by the many warnings against approaching or even touching the mount ([Exod.] 19:12–13, 21, 23–24; 24:2); by the tripartite division of the mount into bands of holiness (top, 19:20; 24:12, 16–18; midsection, 19:24; 24:1–1, 9–15; base, 19:12, 17); and the need to maintain these boundaries; by the need for consecration (19:10–11, 14–15, 22); and, in addition to all these precautions, by the need for a mediator (19:3; etc.).

I will consecrate the tent of meeting and the altar. Aaron also and his sons I will consecrate to serve me as priests. I will dwell among the people of Israel and will be their God. And they shall know that I am the LORD their God, who brought them out of the land of Egypt that I might dwell among them. I am the LORD their God." Whereas Moses can meet face-to-face with God in the tent of meeting as a friend, Exodus ends with what appears to be a problem: "Then the cloud covered the tent of meeting, and the glory of the LORD filled the tabernacle. And Moses was not able to enter the tent of meeting because the cloud settled on it, and the glory of the LORD filled the tabernacle" (Exod. 40:34–35).

Leviticus, according to L. Michael Morales, is an answer to the problem at the end of Exodus.[20] The tabernacle is the construct that addresses the fundamental issue confronting God's people after Eden. The main threat to the existence of God's people is not foreign nations who want them destroyed, however existentially difficult that reality may have been. Rather, the fundamental problem that confronts God's people concerns the truth that the God of Sinai, the God of fire and fury, of pure and infinite holiness, is the God in their midst. Before *this God* they are confronted with contrasting calls—to be *with* and therefore near this God while also knowing that his presence is profoundly dangerous. The tabernacle is what allows these realities to come together, providing a path of drawing near while simultaneously serving as a construct of separation that instructs the people about the complete and perfect life of God (his holiness).

Attending to the long arc of Scripture up to this point, we can see that the fall away from the Edenic mountain and the attempt to create a "mountain" to ascend to God (i.e., Babel) led God to bring his people to *his* mountain to reveal to them whom they should fear.[21] Furthermore, Jacob Milgrom explains, "The tabernacle, in effect, becomes a portable Sinai, an assurance of the permanent presence of the Deity in Israel's midst."[22]

20. Morales, *Who Shall Ascend the Mountain of the Lord?*, 107. Furthermore, chap. 4 of Morales's work depicts how the tabernacle answers this problem.

21. Michael Allen rightly notes, "The climax of the curse matches the climax of nature in the creation account: the presence of God. Whether in the Sabbath gift of the seventh day or the final curse of Genesis 3, we see that human beings are made for life with God. And by implication, we might say that God is intent upon sharing the triune life with us. For this reason, the creation accounts make use of temple imagery to depict their purpose in helping us understand human life as meant for the very presence of God" (*Sanctification*, 95).

22. Milgrom, *Leviticus: A Book of Ritual and Ethics*, 89.

The pedagogy of God's presence oriented Israel around the notion that to ascend to God is to draw near to the one you must revere above all else with your whole self, and through the cleansing waters and purifying blood to offer yourself to him. The sacrificial system is the pedagogical structure given to train God's people in the ways of drawing near.[23] For Israel during the era leading up to God's incarnation, the presence of God and access to it by various means was the gravitational field that held their life together.[24] Frank Gorman explains how holiness functions spatially through the tabernacle:

> Holiness radiates out, by degrees, from the holy of holies. Thus, the outer room of the tent proper is less holy than the holy of holies but more holy than the area outside the tent. The area around the outer altar, in the courtyard, is more holy than the area outside of the large tabernacle structure but less holy than the holy area within the inner tent. The camp outside the large tabernacle structure is less holy than the areas within but more holy than areas outside the camp.[25]

Holiness was more potent, as it were, in the holy of holies, and with each sphere there was a way of drawing near to God to know his presence and have his life order the camp, itself ordered around the tabernacle at its center.[26]

If we can summarize the movements of holiness just sketched, it becomes clear that the calling of holiness is ultimately about God, about

23. Duvall and Hays argue that "the entire sacrificial system is designed by God so that sinful Israel, both as individuals and as a nation, can approach, worship, and fellowship with him as he dwells right among them in the sanctuary" (*God's Relational Presence*, 41).

24. Duvall and Hays argue, "Once God comes to reside in the tabernacle, his holiness projects outward in gradations of holiness—the most holy place, the holy place, the courtyard of the tabernacle, and then the camp of Israel surrounding the tabernacle." Furthermore, "on the Day of Atonement the high priest is allowed to enter right into the most holy place, the deepest allowable penetration through the multiple gradations of holiness, right into the very presence of God in the most holy place" (*God's Relational Presence*, 42, 43).

25. Frank Gorman, *Divine Presence and Community*, 14.

26. The spatial, while primary for much of the Old Testament, is not the only way to measure holiness. Philip Peter Jenson notes four dimensions of holiness: spatial, personal, ritual, and temporal modes. "Holiness, or rather the holiness word group," Jenson avers, "is employed in all four dimensions, and reflects a graded conception of the world. In various contexts, it is possible to detect levels of holiness ranging from extreme sanctity to extreme uncleanness" (*Graded Holiness*, 35). Furthermore, as we have noted, holiness is not an end in itself, but it establishes the way one can draw near.

how he has made a way for us into his presence, and about what it means to dwell with the God who is the purifying fire. "Deeper fellowship with God," Morales writes, "was the goal of holiness, and the clean/unclean laws were set within the context of pursuing holiness." Furthermore, the gradations in holiness in the tabernacle and temple do not signify static divisions, but "the gradations rather created a graduated path of holiness, leading into the divine Presence."[27] Holiness is about a path to God based on God's action. Sabbath, establishing the primal logic of holiness, reveals that we must lay down our works to know the truth that God is the one who sanctifies (Ezek. 20:12). The heart of the gospel is embedded in the Old Testament refractions of holiness, where we are taught that life with God is made available *through God's action to save*. But it will take faith to know that drawing near to *this God*—the God of fire and fury—is where true life is found.

Drawing Near to the God Who Is Everywhere

In seeing these features of Israel's story as constructs of holiness, there is a temptation to focus on the tabernacle or temple as such while missing their overall purpose.[28] The role these constructs played in the history of Israel was to train God's people for access to God's presence and teach them about life with God. These institutions were established for a people deemed *holy* (a "holy nation," Exod. 19:6),[29] and they aided the people in embracing their holiness—being with God and drawing near to him as his own. These constructs taught that holiness always requires *reception* and *reciprocation*, even for an object used in worship. A bowl sanctified for temple use reciprocates that holiness by playing its role in God's action

27. Morales, *Who Shall Ascend the Mountain of the Lord?*, 165.

28. "What matters for the people of God is not the city of Jerusalem per se; what matters is God's presence with them, wherever that may be. 'Jerusalem,' as the place where God dwells, is to be understood spiritually and metaphorically, not simply geographically and literally" (Wells, *God's Holy People*, 180). This becomes especially clear in Galatians, when Paul links the Jerusalem of his day to slavery and points instead to the "Jerusalem above" (Gal. 4:21–31).

29. Wells argues that Israel's title "holy nation" "describes an identity which is to become both a reality when the covenant is made, and a priority, according to which Israel is required to live. This rather ambivalent state, whereby Israel is *declared* holy yet equally called *to be* holy, I describe as 'the call to holiness.' 'Holy' describes a status and a standard and a function" (*God's Holy People*, 56).

Noncompetitive Agency

In Christian theology there is no place more intensely focused on the commerce and communion between God and his creatures than sanctification. We must, therefore, be self-conscious and intentional about our presuppositions and habits of thought concerning divine and human agency. If sanctification is life in the presence of God for the presence of God—as we portray—then what is the nature of God's holying causation *as it relates to* the agency of the one being made holy? When God's agency meets a person for their holiness, what does it entail for their desiring, willing, and acting?

We presuppose throughout this book that the agencies of those involved in sanctification—God and the person—are irreducibly *noncompetitive*, because they are not agencies of the same ontological sort. "[God is not] a rival to human freedom along the lines of the biggest being in the universe throwing the same metaphysical weight around by overpowering all other sources of action," Brian Shanley explains. This is so because "God is not a being like any other being, sharing the same metaphysical space as a potential rival. . . . We are free because God creates and sustains us in freedom, not despite God. . . . We are talking about the action of Creative Spirit upon spirit which finds its

and presence. This will function differently with persons, but the overall contours remain the same.

Sanctification is the doctrine we use to make sense of persons made holy for the purpose of drawing near to God, accepting God's call to be a people of his presence, and reciprocating this call by *embracing him*. (See the sidebar "Noncompetitive Agency.") To be the people of God is to be holy as he is holy; God's people are named holy and reciprocate that reality by living according to its truth. God's relational presence, however, is far from simple, and throughout the biblical history (and certainly human history) people seek to avoid, manipulate, and manage that presence, to use God and the things of God for their own ends.[30]

30. It could be that the mobility of the tabernacle was meant, in part, to highlight this reality. John Gammie claims, "The tabernacle does not represent the fixed presence of God

consummation in the peculiar kind of causality originating in the love between two persons in grace."[a]

It is not in any way necessary for God to push aside or negate some aspect of a person in making them holy. *Their agencies are not rivals*. God is God, the Living God, wholly and truly Godself—and God acts in created reality *as such*. God holies a person without needing to diminish any aspect of their being in the world as a creature.

The logic of this is long-standing in Christian theology, derived in some quarters from Hebraic habits of thought (as in Paul the apostle), or from conceptualities of causation (as in Thomistic theology's appropriation of Aristotle), or more recently from the doctrines of God (e.g., John Webster) or Christology (e.g., Rowan Williams). This issue seems to have made its way into theology first through the Pelagian controversy, where orthodox Christianity prevailed with an emphasis on Philippians 2:12–13.

a. Shanley, "Beyond Libertarianism and Compatibilism," 89. See also Barron, *The Priority of Christ*, chaps. 11–14; Eilers, *Faithful to Save*, chap. 1; Placher, *The Domestication of Transcendence*; Riches, *Ecce Homo*; Tanner, *God and Creation in Christian Theology*, chap. 2; Webster, *God Without Measure*, vol. 1, chaps. 8–9; Rowan Williams, *Christ the Heart of Creation*, 1–35, 169–218.

God's people are *called* holy while also receiving the call *to be* holy. We have just seen how that reality is woven throughout the Old Testament. "The notion of holiness," Jo Bailey Wells claims, "determines, firstly, the nature of Israel's relation to God (not to mention the nature of God himself); secondly, the lifestyle of its individuals; and thirdly, its relationship to outsiders."[31] This threefold orientation to holiness in Scripture focuses first on the nature of holiness as derivative and therefore oriented primarily to God. Second, Wells's emphases refuse to divorce ethics from presence, because the triune God's presence calls for reciprocation. God orients his people around himself, but he also transforms the heart of persons who

in a given spot or locale; rather, precisely because it was collapsible, portable, and capable of being erected in different locations, the tabernacle constituted a powerful symbol of the mobility of the divine presence and holiness" (*Holiness in Israel*, 17).

31. Wells, *God's Holy People*, 71.

stand with him, establishing both social and individual callings in holiness. Admittedly, Wells's addition of outsiders may not seem obvious at first glance, but think of it this way: Holiness includes a state of being within God's special presence and action in such a way that one shares in God's life and mission for the sake of the world.[32] To be holy is to be caught up in God's special presence and action of being holy *to* God and holy *for* him.[33] There is no place this is more tangibly revealed than in the incarnation of the Son of God. Jesus calls people into proximity and then missionally sends them.

Thus, across the long arc of Scripture we find what John Webster asserts about doctrines of salvation: They are focused on God and his action and must be protected against the temptation to gravitate toward the creature. But—and this is important—it would be easy to make the opposite error, focusing so exclusively on God that the turn is never made to address the calling of the Christian in the presence of God. The main tension in Scripture concerning holiness and sanctification is that persons are both *called holy* and *called to be holy*; something can be deemed holy while still being commanded to be holy.[34] At times in Scripture we find that God's people are called to make something holy that already is: God's name (Matt. 6:9); the Sabbath (Lev. 23:3);[35] the tent of meeting (Exod.

32. Wells, attending to the language of Exod. 19:6, notes that "the attribute of holiness is directional. The description relates to the particular relationship between Israel and their God." Furthermore, argues Wells, it is not merely that God's people are holy as such but that they are holy "to me" (i.e., to *God*; see *God's Holy People*, 65).

33. For Jesus, "'holiness' does not provide the grounds for defending or protecting a special status," Wells argues. "To the contrary, it is a dynamic, transforming power which is the result of ongoing encounter with the living God. Therefore it is not so much something to be maintained defensively as lived openly, and thus expressed as much through acts of mercy to those excluded from 'Israel' as through faithful obedience to the Torah" (Wells, *God's Holy People*, 234).

34. In his discussion of holiness in Isaiah, Gammie turns to the language of paradox, dialectic, and dialogue to try to make sense of how holiness functions. But his exposition does not seem helpful. Much of what appears in this section is far from paradox but would more accurately be described as simply unexpected. For instance, Gammie seems flummoxed by the notion that Zion is where God manifests himself in glory and holiness, while at the same time the whole earth is filled with God's glory. There may be ways to understand this dialectically or paradoxically, but that seems far from necessary. See Gammie, *Holiness in Israel*, 92–95.

35. "The sabbath is thus not in and of itself," Gammie argues, "a 'surety of Israel's sanctity' but rather the keeping of it serves as a declaration, a sign of Israel's knowledge of the source of her holiness; the keeping of sabbath is a symbol of Israel's awareness of it" (*Holiness in Israel*, 21). Likewise, Daniel Timmer writes, "The single explicit purpose of the sabbath as

29:43; Lev. 8:10–11); and God's people themselves, whom God makes holy (Lev. 22:32) and yet calls to actualize that holiness (Lev. 19:2; 20:7).[36] Holiness includes God "manifesting the divine life in the world" while also specifying what it means to live along the contours of that holiness.[37] God's self-giving establishes what it means to walk with God and to image him to the world.

You Have Been Sanctified

Throughout our compressed overview of Old Testament Scripture, we have discerned that sanctification has a decisively God-centered and God-initiated focus, and the same is true in the New Testament. As we have seen, in 1 Corinthians 1:30 Paul claims that *by the Father's doing* Christ is our sanctification, and similarly, the practice of Sabbath was to teach that God is the one who sanctifies to call us into his rest (Ezek. 20:12; Heb. 4:1–11). Building on the Old Testament framework, the New Testament focuses almost exclusively on the completed reality of sanctification. For instance, Paul claims, "But you were washed, you were sanctified, you were justified in the name of the Lord Jesus Christ and by the Spirit of our God" (1 Cor. 6:11). Here we find washing and sanctification along with justification as an action of God in Christ Jesus by the Spirit. These realities are past tense—they are *already accomplished*—and the focus is on the Son and the Spirit. Perhaps the most emphatic passage is Hebrews 10:10: "We have been sanctified through the offering of the body of Jesus Christ once for all." In this cross section of key texts, we see what we pointed out in our consideration of the creeds: God has sanctified a place for human

---

instituted at Sinai is to renew in Israel the awareness that Yahweh is her sanctifier (Exod 31:13)" (*Creation, Tabernacle, and Sabbath*, 61).

36. See Frank Gorman, *Divine Presence and Community*, 14, for his discussion of what he calls a "shared construct."

37. Frank Gorman, *Divine Presence and Community*, 14. Gorman explains this by turning to imitation: "The call to holiness is a call to imitate Yahweh," and while there is something clearly right about this, it falls short of how Scripture addresses, in our minds, the nature of holiness (14). Later, expanding on this notion, Gorman argues, "The divine life and holiness must be reflected in the life of the community. The self-identification formula—'I am Yahweh who sanctifies (*meqaddishkem*) you' (v. 8) [Lev. 20]—introduces a call to obedience. Yahweh and the people share in the construction of a holy community: 'I am the one who sanctifies you; sanctify yourselves!'" (*Divine Presence and Community*, 118).

persons to know God's holiness and presence, and that place is the person of Christ Jesus, a place available in and through the Spirit of God.[38]

Later in this volume we will consider how doctrinal formulations do or do not relate to the material we've covered, but here we attend to the completed reality of sanctification and how it relates to any ongoing sanctification. Importantly, in light of our biblical considerations, it is helpful to recall that holiness is a degreed or graded category. Something could be more or less holy based on how it stood in relation to God. The holy of holies had a greater degree of holiness than the holy place or than the average citizen of Israel as a member of God's holy people. The tabernacle and the temple reveal this logic. It is not enough to say something either is holy or is not; there are grades of holiness presupposed in something's being made holy. First, we must inquire whether something is holy, but then, second, we have to consider the nature of that holiness as a graded reality.[39] This means that those in Christ Jesus, who are indwelled by the Spirit of God's holiness, are holy, and at the same time their holiness may be internalized and deepened. God's holiness forms a soul as a feature of the graded dynamic of holiness. We will go into more detail on this in later chapters, but here it is important to attend to key texts that highlight that dynamic.

The primary way the New Testament talks about sanctification is to say that the triune God acts to make his people holy and that in Christ believers are now "saints," the "holy ones" of God.[40] Even to the church at Corinth, a church whose fractures and disobedience are legendary, Paul begins his first missive by saying, "To the church of God that is in Corinth, to those sanctified in Christ Jesus, called to be saints" (1 Cor. 1:2). The Christians at Corinth are saints, called to live by virtue of their union

38. David G. Peterson writes, "Holiness cannot simply be acquired by human effort. It is a status or condition which God imparts to those whom he chooses to bring into a special relationship with himself through covenant and redemption. But it is a status that carries with it particular responsibilities" (*Possessed by God*, 23). Roy E. Ciampa and Brian S. Rosner claim, "Sanctification in the New Testament generally does not refer primarily to growth in holiness but to God's taking possession of believers" (*The First Letter to the Corinthians*, 55–56). While this is true in one sense, it is a reductive approach to reading these texts and to understanding what *holiness* entails.

39. Key here is Jenson, *Graded Holiness*.

40. See Rom. 1:7; 1 Cor. 1:2; 2 Cor. 1:1; Eph. 1:1; Phil. 1:1; Col. 1:2; 1 Pet. 1:1–2. Don Payne has a helpful discussion of these; see *Already Sanctified*, 58–62.

with Christ, the one who has sanctified himself for their sake. Thus Paul's use of adoption language: You are really part of the divine fellowship in Christ, even as you continue to exist in the temporal and spatial reality of God's creation as a finite creature. But the location of your person—your most fundamental *where*—has changed such that you are *in Christ* and therefore hidden with Christ in God (Col. 3:3). Or, from a different angle, as those who have Christ, they are now displaced from the center of their life and re-grounded in Christ, who is in them, as Paul says in Galatians 2:20: "I have been crucified with Christ. It is no longer I who live, but Christ who lives in me."

God has made his people holy in himself, the Holy One, as they are united to Christ by the Spirit in faith. In 1 Peter 2:9, God's people are described as a "holy nation" and a people for his possession, once again highlighting that creaturely holiness centers on God's life and presence. That much is clear, but in speaking about sanctification two errors can easily arise: First, we can focus on its completed nature and override its continuing and developmental realities; and second, we can articulate solely its progressive dimension as a way to address practical matters or virtue formation. We seek to avoid both of these errors by keeping our attention on the nature of holiness as *God's presence and action to unite his people to his life to reorder all of his creation around himself*. This is the true center of a properly ordered doctrine of sanctification that follows the scriptural logic of holiness.

When we consider the portions of Scripture that point beyond the completed realities of sanctification, we see imagery of a deepening or intensifying of the holiness offered in Christ by the Spirit. In Ephesians 4, Paul instructs the church to put off the "old man" before telling them to put on the "new man." The old man is Adam, and the new man is Christ (something lost in translations that use the language of "old self" and "new self"). As Christians, they have already put on Christ, but now they are encouraged to put off indwelling corruption and embrace the life offered in Christ. This is not a mere mental exercise but parallels the call to "present yourselves" to God (Rom. 6:13). In short, Paul is encouraging Christians he calls "saints," as those who have been made holy, to put on holiness *by continuing to abide in Christ*. Sanctification is enacted by God's presence *for* God's presence, as is seen with priests, space, and objects being made holy by God's presence for the sake of drawing near to God's presence. Christians are sanctified by union with Christ so that they can put on holiness by putting on Christ (Eph. 4:24). They stand before him as those who know the "light of the knowledge of the glory of God in the face of Jesus Christ" (2 Cor. 4:6) to have their life oriented to and in him. In this way Paul presents the relational and irreducibly reciprocal nature of sharing the presence of God.

A contemporary example of this completed and developmental reality is the difference between a legal conception of marriage and how marriage is discussed colloquially. Legally, you either are or are not married. This is not a degreed category. In this sense there is no difference between day 1 of marriage and day 1,000. But colloquially, people can ask, "How is your marriage?" When they do so, they are not asking, "Are you still married?" They are probing about the growth, intimacy, and responsiveness of one partner to another. There is a recognition, colloquially, that marriage is both a state *and* a developmental maturation of intimacy and union as one partner discerns the other and responds in love and attention.

The Bible talks about holiness in a similar way. Consider, for instance, Romans 6:19: "For just as you once presented your members as slaves to impurity and to lawlessness leading to [εἰς, *eis*] more lawlessness, so now present your members as slaves to righteousness leading to sanctification [ἁγιασμόν, *hagiasmon*]."[41] One way of reading this is to think that sanctification is something we are trying to achieve now that we are justified. This would miss the theme that we are already sanctified. Translation can often obscure what is going in on Paul's train of thought in Romans 6, as we will attend to momentarily.

Don Payne, perhaps the writer most convinced of the view that sanctification is entirely completed, ends up downplaying the way the New Testament also presents sanctification developmentally. He writes,

> The New Testament clearly and unapologetically calls believers toward the pursuit and outworking of sanctified lives. Numerous texts indicate that responding to the call is a process that involves intentionality, seeking God's

41. Payne writes, "In keeping with the trajectory and ethos of sanctification established thus far, sanctification here focuses on submitting to and serving God rather than on the process of developing or accruing greater levels of personal character" (*Already Sanctified*, 90). In one sense we can affirm this, but we wouldn't want to see these as mutually exclusive. Submitting to and serving God are precisely what form the character of the Christian.

> cleansing from sin, submission to God, and abandonment of competing allegiances. That process leads to increased, and ultimately to full, experiential realization of a cleansed and forgiven heart, awareness of and responsiveness to God's presence, and empowered participation in God's purposes. In this qualified sense, the pursuit and the realization of sanctification are "progressive," though sanctification itself is not progressive.[42]

Payne rightly worries that the terms *sanctification* and *holiness* are often reduced to descriptions of growth in Christian character, such that the good news that "you have been sanctified" is lost in an imperative that pushes one into a moralistic register.[43] We share this worry.[44] He is exactly right when he states, "I wish to underscore that the biblical terminology in both testaments refers to being prepared for God's *presence* as well as God's purposes," going on to add that "proximity to the Divine presence seems to be often overlooked in treatments of consecration/sanctification, resulting in constricted—perhaps even anemic—applications of sanctification terminology."[45] All this is right.

We affirm that God is the one who holies us in Christ by the Spirit, such that being in Christ means being holy. Nonetheless, it is important to recall

42. Payne, *Already Sanctified*, 105.

43. There is much nuance to how Payne develops this, but it seems clear that he is driven by this specific worry, which may lead him to divorce sanctification and transformation too cleanly. This concern comes to the fore when he writes, commenting on Heb. 12:14 and the question of whether we should *pursue* holiness, "This warning, ironically, has often disturbed if not crippled the assurance of those who are most intent on the pursuit of holiness." He continues, "If this holiness refers primarily to purity of heart or personal character relative to God's holy nature, then the equation is set up for perpetual failure and frustration" (Payne, *Already Sanctified*, 96, 97). Payne's worry about existential frustration seems to drive a lot of his view.

44. Payne's primary worry seems to be that too often people collapse transformation and sanctification together such that they become virtual synonyms. "Healthy pursuit and experience of transformation depends on accomplished sanctification and on understanding how they are related. The assumption that they are synonymous, or that transformation is synonymous with one aspect of sanctification ('progressive'), seems to create as many problems as it attempts to solve" (*Already Sanctified*, 107). Importantly, Payne does not want to lose transformation: "Across the biblical canon, God's presence can be seen, both implicitly and explicitly, as the reality that changes or transforms people" (Payne, "Response to Steve L. Porter," 300). Payne admits that "the type of distinction I suggest is rather subtle and I acknowledge having possibly overstated that distinction in an effort to differentiate concepts that various Protestant theological traditions have often (and problematically) fused so as to be virtually indistinguishable" (301).

45. Payne, "Response to Steve L. Porter," 300.

that holiness, with its graded nature, also includes a person's transformation or recharacterization. Returning to the marriage metaphor, sanctification is both a state and something that should deepen and expand through reciprocally responsive relationship. As with marriage, this deepening is a part of sanctification itself. There are moral imperatives that are grounded in being with God and sharing in his life, and there are transformative effects to living within the dynamics of a responsively reciprocal relationship with the Holy One. Theological emphases in the tradition for addressing this include communion with God and the internal work of the Spirit in the soul (Eph. 3:14–19).

Therefore, returning to Romans 6:19, in light of how Scripture uses holiness language broadly, is it adequate to interpret this passage as calling us to "present our members as slaves to righteousness *leading to* [*eis*] sanctification" (*hagiasmon*)? (See the sidebar "Romans 6:1–14.") The King James Version does a better job attending to *eis* by rendering it as "righteousness *unto* holiness." Keeping in mind that holiness includes deeper communion with God following from the union with Christ known by faith, we don't have to force this passage into an either/or between definitive and progressive sanctification.[46] In context, this passage falls under Paul's two overarching questions: "What shall we say then? Are we to continue in sin that grace may abound?" (Rom. 6:1); and "What then? Are we to sin because we are not under law but under grace?" (6:15). Under the first question, Paul's imperative is to "present yourselves to God" (6:13). This self-presentation is to the one who has already brought us from death to life. There is an accomplished reality assumed here as well as a call to present oneself to God in the truth that these things are the case. Similarly, just prior, after telling them that they have died with Christ, Paul writes, "So you also must consider yourselves dead to sin and alive to God in Christ Jesus" (6:11). The movement from *being* dead to *considering themselves* as dead is a movement of living according to the truth. They have been

46. In Rom. 6:23, Paul juxtaposes the "wages of sin" being death with "the . . . gift of God" being eternal life. Calvin, in expositing this section, notes that Paul "knew that it is through God's gift we obtain it, and not through our own merits; and that it is not one or a single gift; for being clothed with the righteousness of the Son, we are reconciled to God, and we are by the power of the Spirit renewed unto holiness. And he adds, *in Christ Jesus*, and for this reason, that he might call us away from every conceit respecting our own worthiness" (Calvin, *Commentaries on Romans*, 243).

Romans 6:1–14

[1]What shall we say then? Are we to continue in sin that grace may abound? [2]By no means! How can we who died to sin still live in it? [3]Do you not know that all of us who have been baptized into Christ Jesus were baptized into his death? [4]We were buried therefore with him by baptism into death, in order that, just as Christ was raised from the dead by the glory of the Father, we too might walk in newness of life.

[5]For if we have been united with him in a death like his, we shall certainly be united with him in a resurrection like his. [6]We know that our old self was crucified with him in order that the body of sin might be brought to nothing, so that we would no longer be enslaved to sin. [7]For one who has died has been set free from sin. [8]Now if we have died with Christ, we believe that we will also live with him. [9]We know that Christ, being raised from the dead, will never die again; death no longer has dominion over him. [10]For the death he died he died to sin, once for all, but the life he lives he lives to God. [11]So you also must consider yourselves dead to sin and alive to God in Christ Jesus.

[12]Let not sin therefore reign in your mortal body, to make you obey its passions. [13]Do not present your members to sin as instruments for unrighteousness, but present yourselves to God as those who have been brought from death to life, and your members to God as instruments for righteousness. [14]For sin will have no dominion over you, since you are not under law but under grace.

brought from death to life, which is precisely why they can live this way. So Paul implores, "Do not present your members to sin as instruments for unrighteousness, but present yourselves to God as those who have been brought from death to life, and your members to God as instruments for righteousness" (6:13).

In Romans 6:19, then, the focus is on presenting oneself to righteousness, which is synonymous with presenting oneself to Christ. To present one's "members" as slaves of righteousness "unto" (translating *eis*) sanctification is to offer up one's life to God in Christ. The end of one's servitude to sin is death, Paul argues in 6:21, whereas continually giving oneself over to Christ is for "sanctification and its end, eternal life. For the wages of sin is death, but the free gift of God is eternal life in Christ Jesus our Lord" (Rom. 6:22–23). Rather than death, the believer receives life. This life—eternal life—is not merely a promised place in eternity but is a particular kind of life offered *in Christ*. The believer who presents themselves to God is presenting themselves to the truth of who they are, not generically as a person but as one whose life is found in God. When Paul claims that the believer's life is "hidden with Christ in God" (Col. 3:3), he goes on to assert, "When Christ who is your life appears, then you also will appear with him in glory" (Col. 3:4). Christ is the life of those united to him because Christ is life itself (John 11:25).

The movement of these passages, as well as the long arc of Scripture, links the objective reality of sanctification—how God has sanctified his own to be a "holy nation" (Exod. 19:6; 1 Pet. 2:9)—to the subjective dimension of how sanctification is appropriated. It may be conceptually helpful to distinguish these, but biblically they are deeply wedded. God's people are never *merely* called into his life; they are called to *share in his life*, to be *shaped* by it, and to be *conformed* to his mission for the world. Payne is right that we don't want to let the imperative ("put to death," Col. 3:5) undermine the indicative ("you have died," Col. 3:3), and he is right that we need to articulate the difference. But just as in marriage, there is a state *and* a calling that are woven together. In sanctification, the states of a person—death or life, sinful or righteous, "lawlessness unto more lawlessness" or righteousness "unto sanctification"—all include within them *a state* and *a way*. None of these, even death, are seen as mere states of existence, but all name a way of life.

New Testament language repeatedly appropriates tabernacle/temple terminology to talk about the Christian life and action because it portrays this "state and way" dynamic. Amid other metaphors, this can be seen in the language of drawing near to God. Picking up on the emphasis of being made holy for the sake of drawing near, the New Testament links this drawing near in Christ by the Spirit to a developmental process of Christian maturation. For instance, in Romans 12:1, Paul implores, "Present your bodies as a living sacrifice, holy and acceptable to God, which is your spiritual worship." Here, *holy* is an adjective describing the Christian who is presenting *themselves* to God.[47] Holiness is what allows the believer to draw near (i.e., to present themselves), and in presenting themselves they

47. Payne, *Already Sanctified*, 91.

are being transformed, which is why Paul adds: "Do not be conformed to this world, but be transformed by the renewal of your mind" (Rom. 12:2). This is the fulfillment of the sacrificial and purity forms, which have been fulfilled in and by Jesus, our great high priest who has gone beyond the veil, has sprinkled our hearts clean, and has washed our bodies with pure water (Heb. 6:19–20; 10:19–22). It is in and through the presence of God by virtue of union with Christ that the Christian is purified, is sanctified, and by drawing near to him is "transformed by the renewal" of their mind (Rom. 12:2). This movement to God, to make someone holy for his presence, to share in his life and be ordered by him, reveals the logic of holiness throughout Scripture. Sanctification, as a doctrine, exposits the nature of God's presence, but it should also name the transformation and restoration that occurs in his presence.

The Unity of Sanctification in Christ

As we saw earlier in the burning-bush passage and with Sinai, God establishes places of holiness for life in his presence, to set our eyes on him in fearful awe, so we can present ourselves to him. This self-presentation uses the sacrificial language of "bringing near" to offer oneself to God, making God the telos of properly Christian action (a key feature of supernatural holiness). According to the pedagogy of holiness, one first receives the self-giving of God in his holiness, which makes us holy, and then responds with self-giving. The relational dynamic is reception and reciprocity, which establishes communion and fellowship. This framework weds purity, sight, presence, and intimacy with the internal dynamics of a renewed nature by the Spirit for life in Christ's kingdom. The Spirit is at work in one's inner being, Paul declares, "so that Christ may dwell in your hearts through faith" (Eph. 3:17). Sanctification names the definitive and *responsively progressive* dynamics of holiness because holiness is ultimately about the work of the Son and the Spirit to offer the life of God to his people. This means that sanctification holds together what has often been called the definitive and progressive but also the individual and communal. To be sanctified in Christ Jesus by the Spirit is to be a son or daughter of God and therefore, necessarily, siblings of one another.

The New Testament makes clear that purity and holiness are bound together to address an *entire life*—including both the internal psychological functioning of an individual and what Wesleyans call "social holiness." This is why discussions of holiness and ethical teaching are so often woven together. For instance, in 1 Thessalonians 4, Paul writes,

> For this is the will of God, your sanctification: that you abstain from sexual immorality; that each one of you know how to control his own body in holiness and honor, not in the passion of lust like the Gentiles who do not know God; that no one transgress and wrong his brother in this matter, because the Lord is an avenger in all these things, as we told you beforehand and solemnly warned you. For God has not called us for impurity, but in holiness. Therefore whoever disregards this, disregards not man but God, who gives his Holy Spirit to you. (1 Thess. 4:3–8)

God has called his people "in holiness," Paul tells us in this passage, *for sanctification*. This is not setting a state and a way of life in opposition but instead highlights holiness bestowed by God in virtue of union with Christ as a reality that embraces a way established by him. God's life, by the necessity of who he is, reorders everything else around himself. Or, to render the reality in the idiom of Genesis 1, God's Spirit hovers over the chaos to bring order to it. This is not generic ordering but is bringing into harmony with the Father, in the Son, through the Spirit.

Holiness names things that have been put in a specific state in reference to God's presence and action for the sake of being ordered to that presence and action. This is what it means to be holy in conduct, as Peter claims: "As obedient children, do not be conformed to the passions of your former ignorance, but as he who called you is holy, you also be holy in all your conduct, since it is written, 'You shall be holy, for I am holy'" (1 Pet. 1:14–16). Being holy is never *merely* a state, because it is being called into a reciprocally responsive relation to God. At Sinai, being holy involved ordering the entire camp around the presence of the God who was with them, shaping their lives away from their "former passions" (the idolatry and immorality of Egypt) to the God who is holy. The movement Peter articulates is important, starting with the foreknowledge of the Father, moving to the sanctification of the Spirit, and grounding these realities in Christ's obedience and sprinkling with his blood (1 Pet. 1:2). What we normally categorize as ethics is the intensification or deepening of the holiness we have in Christ through the presence and availability of his life and action. The centrality of God's work does *not undermine human activity* but embeds it in a reciprocally responsive relationship.

The Biblical Logic of Holiness

From devotional and liturgical acts to the state of our holiness in Christ, we discern a cohesive biblical logic of holiness. It is unsurprising, therefore, that Peter turns to temple imagery as his argument unfolds: "As you come to him, a living stone rejected by men but in the sight of God chosen and precious, you yourselves like living stones are being built up as a spiritual house, to be a holy priesthood, to offer spiritual sacrifices acceptable to God through Jesus Christ" (1 Pet. 2:4–5). Notice how the temple imagery in Scripture holds together the tensions we have been exploring. Jesus is the true temple, and in him believers make up the new temple, which holds together the individual and the corporate, the centrality of God in Christ by the Spirit, and the call to conformity and purity found in the passages we have explored. In the words of Ephesians 2, believers are "built on the foundation of the apostles and prophets, Christ Jesus himself being the cornerstone, in whom the whole structure, being joined together, grows into a holy temple in the Lord. In him you also are being built together into a dwelling place for God by the Spirit" (Eph. 2:20–22).

The temple imagery consistently undermines whatever temptation we have to reduce sanctification to either a state *or* a way. To be conformed to Christ, the cornerstone, and grow into a *holy temple* is to be shaped corporately and individually by Christ as those called into his presence. It is, as Paul goes on to say in Ephesians 4:15, to "grow up in every way into him who is the head, into Christ." To share his presence is not to be ushered into his geographical space but to be restoratively drawn into his life made available through the incarnation and indwelling of the Spirit. Knowing the presence of the Father, in the Son, and by the Spirit is to be formed by and from within that presence, such that "the whole body, joined and held together by every joint with which it is equipped, when each part is working properly, makes the body grow so that it builds itself up in love" (Eph. 4:16).

What may appear as a tension in Scripture between definitive and progressive sanctification is unified in Christ, and a doctrine of sanctification must unveil the logic of this unity. Sanctification is life in the presence of God for the presence of God. Believers *have been* sanctified by Christ because they have been caught up into his life by faith, and God's action is something done not merely *upon* the believer but *within and through the believer*. One's union with Christ in the Spirit is their sanctification, which entails a reciprocally responsive participation in God's life. The order matters: One *is being sanctified* because one *has been sanctified*. Payne is certainly right to worry that the second we insert an imperative unmoored from the indicative, moralism becomes an issue. The solution is often to jettison the framework of holiness for something else, but Scripture paints a beautifully integrated reality from within the holiness frame. The remaining chapters of this book will exposit how that reality works through our development of the doctrine of sanctification.

Before moving on, however, there is a final text that proves helpful to consider. It is significant that the vision John receives concerning the heavenly Jerusalem is about a city entirely harmonized by God's presence. The new Jerusalem descends from heaven—not generated or constructed by humankind, nor as the culmination of creaturely virtue—but as *a gift* (Rev. 21:1–2). The declaration that accompanies this city is that God's dwelling place is now with his people. As John considers this in his vision he declares, "I saw no temple in the city, for its temple is the Lord God the Almighty and the Lamb. And the city has no need of sun or moon to shine on it, for the glory of God gives it light, and its lamp is the Lamb" (Rev. 21:22–23). It is in the presence of God that his creatures will finally see, and they will be like him because they will see him as he is (1 John 3:2). This sight does not somehow take their eyes off everything else; rather, in God's light his creatures can finally see truly, just as in God's love they can finally love completely.

The various features of holiness we recognized in the burning bush and at Sinai find their fulfillment in this vision. Here we discover holy *space* as a fellowship ordered by God in his self-giving love, a vision and light that enables people to see God, to know him, and to allow his fullness to radiate through them. We see holy *time* where the Alpha and Omega reigns over all (Rev. 21:5–6) and where true Sabbath rest is known. In this scene we see the biblical themes of mountain, temple, and city of God all coalesce into one unified vision of all creation at home with God. Jon Levenson considers the psalmists' longing for the temple of the Lord—the desire to dwell in the temple (Ps. 23:6), to see God in the temple (Ps. 27:4), and to commune with God in his own house (Ps. 84:2–5)—and reflects on how Psalm 84 depicts the ascent up the mountain of the Lord toward Jerusalem. His depiction is worth quoting in full:

> The second stanza (Ps 84:6–8) is a vignette of pilgrims as they make their way up the mountains towards Jerusalem and then (in line with the imperatives of Ps 48:13–14) take a tour of the fortification of Zion itself. The Hebrew of Ps 84:7 is quite garbled; one can only guess at its meaning. If I render it accurately as "They pass through the Valley of Tears," it implies a kind of natural/spiritual transformation: *natural* in that a valley becomes a mountain, Zion, and *spiritual* in that the ascent somehow enables the worshippers to make the water of tears into springs, changing a symbol of grief into one of fertility. In other words, the road up to the Temple is the objective correlative of an inner spiritual development which is crowned by a vision of God in his palace on Mount Zion. The physical ascent is also a spiritual ascent. Its motive force is the magnetic attraction exerted upon a person by the object of his love, in this case God manifest in his palace. The centripetal force of that love, which propels the psalmist toward God and Zion, is a thousand times stronger than the centrifugal forces that pull him toward other concerns (v 11).[48]

As Christians set their eyes on the promises of the Lord, looking to walk through the Valley of Tears, their hope is broadcast in Revelation 21: "He will wipe away every tear from their eyes, and death shall be no more, neither shall there be mourning, nor crying, nor pain anymore, for the former things have passed away" (v. 4). The pedagogy of holiness finds its culmination in a vision of a community ordered in and around love as they are ordered in and around God.

Summary

The biblical logic of holiness centers on God's intensive personal presence. A christological reading of Scripture interprets the Old Testament material of tabernacle, mountain, and temple as pedagogies of divine presence that point toward Jesus and the holiness he secures for us in his person. Old Testament narratives present holiness in consistently spatial ways (bush,

48. Levenson, *Sinai and Zion*, 177–78.

mountain, tabernacle, temple) that assume the relational dynamics of presence, availability, and presenting oneself to God, who gives himself and provides access to himself. These spatially oriented portrayals of divine and creaturely holiness are taken up in Jesus, where *the spatial becomes the personal* in the person of the Son. The heart of the gospel is embedded in Old Testament refractions of holiness, through which we are taught that life with God is made available through *God's action* to save. Christians are saints and holy ones because they are ushered into the holy presence of the Father by union with Christ through his Spirit and thus sanctified for a *relationally responsive life* in God's presence. Sanctification is thus a state and a way.

DOXOLOGICAL INTERLUDE

William Dyce, *The Woman of Samaria*

> [Jesus] came to a town of Samaria called Sychar, near the field that Jacob had given to his son Joseph. Jacob's well was there; so Jesus, wearied as he was from his journey, was sitting beside the well. . . . A woman from Samaria came to draw water. Jesus said to her, "Give me a drink." . . . The Samaritan woman said to him, "How is it that you, a Jew, ask for a drink from me, a woman of Samaria?" (For Jews have no dealings with Samaritans.) . . . Just then his disciples came back. They marveled that he was talking with a woman, but no one said, "What do you seek?" or, "Why are you talking with her?" So the woman left her water jar and went away into town and said to the people, "Come, see a man who told me all that I ever did. Can this be the Christ?" . . . So when the Samaritans came to him, they asked him to stay with them, and he stayed there two days. And many more believed because of his word. They said to the woman, "It is no longer because of what you said that we believe, for we have heard for ourselves, and we know that this is indeed the Savior of the world."
>
> John 4:5–7, 9, 27–29, 40–42

Invitation

When Jesus is present with the Samaritan woman and her community, we encounter his strange hospitality. *Strange* may seem an odd way to describe anything about Jesus, but it's appropriate if you (perhaps unthinkingly) imagine that Jesus only relates *at you*: giving, offering, delivering, teaching, hosting, and so forth. If that's your sense of Jesus sharing life with others, then your sense of his hospitality is at odds with the Gospels. Jesus teaches *and* listens; he approaches *and* is approached; he gives *and* receives; he hosts *and* guests. His hospitality is mutual: Jesus gifts what comes from himself and receives what comes from others.

Jesus is already resting at Jacob's well when the Samaritan woman approaches (v. 6), but many artists focus so heavily on their later interactions, often rendering Jesus dynamically teaching, that any mutuality is lost from our imagination. But the portrayal of William Dyce in *The Woman of Samaria* invites us into their interactions at the moment *just before* they begin: Jesus rests as she approaches. Given her gender and ethnicity, it's strange they would interact at all, but Jesus first receives her presence, then her water, and only then teaches her. Likewise, when her community invites Jesus to stay, he first becomes their guest and only then, in the space of their communion, "many more believed because of his word" (v. 41). He dwells where he isn't expected to dwell, sharing meals, sharing conversation, guesting and hosting.

Holding the story in mind, prayerfully consider the mutuality of God's hospitality. Even as God requires nothing from us, God loves *and* receives our love, glorifies *and* is glorified, serves *and* receives our service. Perhaps you immediately perceive what the mutuality of life with God means for you, or maybe God's Jesus-shaped hospitality isn't something you've considered.

You might engage the scene in John 4 with your imagination. If you were the one approaching Jesus, what would happen? The following questions may be helpful:

Lord Jesus, as I come to you at the well, what perceptions do I carry about you? Do I expect you to be eager, patient, and welcoming, or indifferent, impatient, hostile, disappointed, bored, or . . . ? Do I expect what you demonstrate—that your extravagant welcome is unconditionally loving and engaged? Help me see you truly as you did the Samaritan woman and her community, and help me perceive what your welcome means for my life with others.

Lord Jesus, as I come to you at the well, what perceptions do I carry about who I am and what I bring? Are my self-perceptions true, formed by what you say about me? Or are they false and distorted, coming from someone or someplace else, harming me and others? Please help me see myself truly, as you did the Samaritan woman.

Lord Jesus, as I come to you at the well, I have questions about all sorts of things. Maybe my questions are insightful or wrongheaded or naive. I don't know, but they are mine and they are real, so here they are. Please receive them as you did those of the Samaritan woman.

Notes

CHAPTER THREE

Comparative Soteriology

And because of him you are in Christ Jesus, who became to us wisdom from God, righteousness and sanctification and redemption.

1 Corinthians 1:30

[God] is wholly present in all [the world] in such wise as to be wholly in heaven alone and wholly in the earth alone, and wholly in heaven and earth together; not confined in any place, but wholly in Himself everywhere.

Augustine[1]

WE HAVE TRACED sanctification's creedal contours and followed its scriptural portrayal to discern its shape. God is the Holy One who sanctifies, and sanctification is both a state and a way; it is ultimately about God and living with God as one's center. In this theological study on sanctification, we must now turn to questions about the function of sanctification as a doctrine. Before doing so, we turn to three key figures from the tradition. Our purpose here is to consider various emphases in prior accounts of soteriology so that we can situate our view in light of what has come before. Even though our language and categories may shift, it

1. Augustine, "Letter 187, To Dardanus (On the Presence of God)," 231.

will become clear that what we have suggested in previous chapters is well situated within Protestant and broadly Western accounts of life with God.

We have seen several temptations in defining *holiness*, and those temptations do not cease when we turn more specifically to the doctrine of sanctification. As a doctrine, it is important to continue to locate the question of holiness—and the holiness of the creature specifically—in relation to God and his self-giving. Two key temptations concerning the doctrine of sanctification immediately rise to the surface. First, there is a temptation to allow sanctification to shift away from its primary location in Christology and pneumatology, refocusing sanctification's content on other doctrines. This misorders the doctrine away from Christ and the Spirit to something else. Second, there is a temptation to move too rapidly into practical considerations such that one's practical theology is divorced from the gains advanced by focusing on the Son and the Spirit. When sanctification floats free of its proper location, Christian formation morphs into self-help or Aristotelian moral formation, and practical guidance thereby loses its distinctively supernatural vision.

In advancing the previous biblical considerations and in anticipating the doctrinal material in the next chapter, here we pause to consider three figures and how they developed accounts of sanctification and related themes. We will attend to the doctrinal instincts of John Calvin, Thomas Aquinas, and John Wesley, seeking to name various theological structures emerging in their doctrines of sanctification. The goal is not to identify necessary and sufficient conditions for a Protestant doctrine of sanctification, even though we are articulating a Protestant doctrine, but to highlight how various instincts from the tradition apply pressure—rightly or wrongly—to how sanctification has been understood. We are not looking for an expansive treatment of sanctification from these figures but are seeking to discern a central feature of their thought that has significance for how we proceed. Rather than working through these figures chronologically, we will proceed in a more doctrine-focused way, first attending to how Calvin situates sanctification within his soteriology.

John Calvin: Christ as Salvation

Calvin's soteriology is centered on the unity of Christ and, from within this, the reception of a unified salvation in the reception of Christ himself.

John Calvin

John Calvin (1509–64) was born and raised in France and trained as a lawyer, but he was unexpectedly caught up in the reform movements of the sixteenth century. Calvin encountered the teaching of Martin Luther sometime when he was in his mid-twenties and converted to Protestantism. Once he identified himself as a Protestant, he was not altogether safe in France, so he moved to Switzerland and helped establish the Reformation there. Within a year he was officially installed as a pastor and subsequently helped shape the city's religious and civic life. Unlike Luther, who vividly recounts his spiritual development, Calvin rarely spoke of it and never at length. "God by a sudden conversion subdued and brought to a teachable frame my mind," he writes, "which was more hardened in such matters than might have been expected from one at my early period of life."[a] Like Thomas Aquinas before him, Calvin was a systematic thinker with a knack for seeing across the range of Christian belief, and his work *Institutes of the Christian Religion* (1536) offers an account of its breadth and depth. A talented exegete of Scripture with a heart for the church as well, Calvin produced scores of biblical commentaries and preached thousands of sermons.[b]

a. Calvin, *Commentary on Psalms*. Translated by James Anderson. Christian Classics Ethereal Library, https://ccel.org/ccel/calvin/calcom08/calcom08.vi.html.

b. Lightly revised from "John Calvin (1509–1564)," in Eilers et al., *The Grammar of Grace*, 253.

The first word of salvation is Christ, Calvin stresses time and again, because in Christ salvation is accomplished. Thus Calvin writes that Christ is "offered not only for righteousness, forgiveness of sins, and peace, but also for sanctification [cf. 1 Cor. 1:30] and the fountain of the water of life [John 7:38; cf. 4:14]," emphasizing that "without a doubt, no one can duly know him without at the same time apprehending the sanctification of the Spirit."[2] The Son is unified in himself, and therefore we have a unified salvation. Likewise, the Son and the Spirit share an undivided

2. Calvin, *Institutes* III.ii.8 (1:552).

work in the economy, such that salvation is always by Word and Spirit. Therefore, one cannot know salvation in the Son without the sanctification of the Spirit.

Calvin's famous *duplex gratia* (double grace) is the theological construct he employs to keep Christ at the center of his account of salvation, and this dictum must remain at the forefront when he orders Christ's benefits in relation to one another. Calvin shows this emphasis when he sums up his doctrine: "Christ was given to us by God's generosity, to be grasped and possessed by us in faith. By partaking of him, we principally receive a double grace: namely, that being reconciled to God through Christ's blamelessness, we may have in heaven instead of a Judge a gracious Father; and secondly, that sanctified by Christ's spirit we may cultivate blamelessness and purity of life."[3] *Christ was given to us*, asserts Calvin, a point that underlies his soteriology.[4] Faith, on this understanding of salvation, is the proper response to grace and the instrument by which one *receives Christ* and in him receives his benefits. Faith, importantly, is the instrument by which we receive Christ, and not primarily justification.[5] It is in receiving Christ that we are justified, and in receiving Christ that we are sanctified.

We might say that the proper way to articulate Calvin on double grace is to say that there is a *single* double grace, protecting against the impulse to rend this grace apart. Or we could say with Cornelis Venema that there is a twofold grace and not two graces.[6] In this Calvin follows Luther, claiming

3. Calvin, *Institutes* III.xi.1 (1:725).

4. Calvin, expositing 1 Cor. 6:11, writes, "Christ himself with all his blessings, is communicated to us by the Spirit. For we receive Christ by faith, and it is by faith that his benefits are applied to us. The author of faith is the Spirit" (*Commentary on the Epistles to the Corinthians*, 212).

5. Calvin opines on Eph. 3:17,

> What a remarkable commendation is here bestowed on *faith*, that, by means of it, the Son of God becomes our own, and "makes his abode with us"! (John xiv. 23.) By faith we not only acknowledge that Christ suffered and rose from the dead on our account, but, accepting the offers which he makes of himself, we possess and enjoy him as our Savior. This deserves our careful attention. Most people consider fellowship with Christ, and believing in Christ, to be the same thing; but the fellowship which we have with Christ is the consequence of faith. In a word, faith is not a distant view, but a warm embrace, of Christ, by which he dwells in us, and we are filled with the Divine Spirit. (*Commentaries on Galatians and Ephesians*, 262)

6. See Venema, *Accepted and Renewed in Christ*. This emphasis on the *singularity* of the double grace is at the heart of Venema's project, and he is right to emphasize it. Reflecting on

that to preach justification without sanctification would be to "tear Christ in pieces."[7] The image of Christ torn in two helps name three errors in soteriology: first, ordering soteriology around a benefit rather than around Christ (whether implicitly or explicitly); second, collapsing justification and sanctification into a singular reality; or third, so separating justification and sanctification that sanctification appears optional (or, perhaps, only for an elite few). Whereas Protestant polemicists would invoke the second error in debates against Roman Catholics, their Roman Catholic counterparts would wield the third error against Protestants. But Calvin is adamant that this criticism isn't possible on his view:

> Justification and Sanctification, are constantly conjoined and cohere; but from this it is erroneously inferred that they are one and the same. For example:—The light of the sun, though never unaccompanied with heat, is not to be considered heat. Where is the man so undiscerning as not to distinguish one from the other? We acknowledge, then, that as soon as any one is justified, renewal also necessarily follows: and there is no dispute as to whether or not Christ sanctifies all whom he justifies. It were to rend the gospel, and divide Christ himself, to attempt to separate the righteousness which we obtain by faith from repentance.[8]

It is evident how closely connected Calvin's *duplex gratia* is to his understanding of salvation accomplished in Christ and unified in his person, and how that accomplished salvation is applied in and by the Spirit. (See the sidebar "Appropriation," p. 76.) Calvin labors this point in the *Institutes* but also the commentaries, writing on 1 Corinthians 6:11: "Christ, then, is the source of all blessings to us: from him we obtain all things; but Christ himself, with all his blessings, is communicated to us by the Spirit. For it is by faith that we receive Christ, and have his graces applied to us."[9] Or,

---

the singularity of Calvin's account in Christ, he writes, "Indeed, it is not incidental to Calvin's view that he chooses to use the language of a 'twofold grace' and not the language of 'two graces,' when he describes the double benefit of redemption in Christ" (269).

7. Calvin, *Commentary on the Epistles to the Corinthians*, 1 Cor. 1:30 (p. 93). Furthermore, commenting on Rom. 6:1, Calvin writes, "Throughout this chapter the Apostle proves, that they who imagine that gratuitous righteousness is given us by him, apart from newness of life, shamefully rend Christ asunder" (*Commentary on Romans*, Rom. 6:1 [p. 217]).

8. Calvin, *Acts of the Council of Trent*, 116.

9. Calvin, *Commentary on the Epistles to the Corinthians*, 1 Cor. 6:11 (p. 212).

Appropriation

In theology, *appropriation* is the designation of a divine attribute or action specifically to one person of the Trinity while maintaining, at the same time, that God's essence *is one* and that Father, Son, and Spirit act in concert *as one*. For instance, attending to the witness of Scripture, one may rightly say that God the Son is the author of our redemption, or that the Spirit illumines our hearts, or that the Father receives our prayers. Behind such statements and implicit in them is the theological affirmation that God's essence and action are *ever one*.[a]

a. See Sanders, *The Triune God*, esp. 121–53; Sanders, "The Triune God"; Webster, *God Without Measure*, 1:6–8, 83–113, 127–41.

with more economy, "We see that our whole salvation and all its parts are comprehended in Christ."[10] Salvation is what we know in Christ, and Christ's benefits must never be separated from his person.[11] This is the overarching theological instinct that gives rise to Calvin's famous claim, "We must understand that as long as Christ remains outside of us, and we are separated from him, all that he has suffered and done for the salvation of the human race remains useless and of no value for us. Therefore, to share with us what he has received from the Father, he had to become ours and to dwell within us."[12]

The double grace offered in Christ can be glossed as justification and sanctification/regeneration.[13] Unlike other accounts that might relate but more clearly delineate sanctification and regeneration, *Calvin explicitly links the two*: "He sanctifies by renewing our depraved nature by his Spirit.

10. Calvin, *Institutes* II.xvi.19 (1:527).

11. This is why Calvin claims, "We have said that perfect salvation is found in the person of Christ" (*Institutes* III.i.4 [1:542]).

12. Calvin, *Institutes* III.i.1 (1:537).

13. Venema notes, "In the history of theology, the customary terminology has been that of 'justification' and 'sanctification.' Though referring to the same subject and issue, Calvin ordinarily uses the terminology of 'justification' and 'regeneration' or 'repentance.' Only infrequently does he speak of 'sanctification,' though it is clearly for him a synonym for either regeneration or repentance" (*Accepted and Renewed in Christ*, 9n1).

Thus sanctification is connected with regeneration."[14] This instinct continues on in the Reformed tradition, such that sanctification is often equated with regeneration, differentiated only temporally. In regeneration, "we become new creatures [cf. 2 Cor. 5:17]; and he consecrates us, purged of worldly uncleanness, as temples holy to God."[15] The *beginning* is regeneration; its *advancement* is sanctification.

In focusing soteriology, and therefore spiritual formation, on receiving Christ and the Spirit, Calvin sharply distinguishes the moral formation we can achieve by nature from the supernatural formation of grace, moored specifically to holiness. Apart from Christ and his body there is "nothing but pollution," Calvin argues, which is why the Scriptures focus on our being a new creature in Christ who is sanctified in Christ.[16] Grounding sanctification in the calling and election of God, Calvin emphasizes that "it is not through our own efforts that we are holy, but by the call of God, because He alone sanctifies those who were by nature unclean."[17] Just as God is the one who, by his own goodness and mercy and through the work of Christ, declares the ungodly righteous in justification, so too in

14. Calvin, *Commentary on the Epistles to the Corinthians*, 1 Cor. 6:11 (p. 212). Venema explains, "Just as Calvin ordinarily uses 'regeneration' and 'repentance' as synonyms, so also he ordinarily uses 'sanctification' as synonymous with either of these terms. As was true of his conception of repentance, sanctification is the process of consecrating ourselves and all our devotion to the will of God. Peculiar to the idea of sanctification is our being set apart for God's service by his Spirit. We are sanctified in order that our whole existence might belong to God and be put to a sacred, rather than a common, use" (*Accepted and Renewed in Christ*, 121). In the Reformed tradition, sanctification is often seen as an extension of, or even as synonymous with, regeneration in various ways. John Brown of Haddington argues that sanctification includes "gracious habits implanted, Christian tempers acquired, and holy exercises performed." Furthermore, he adds, "In this view, [sanctification of life] includes regeneration, which properly means God's implantation of gracious or holy principles in our heart . . . and sanctification, strictly taken, which means the continuance, strengthening, and increasing those gracious principles, and exercising them in holy and virtuous actions" (*Systematic Theology*, 405).

15. Calvin, *Institutes* III.i.4 (1:542).

16. Calvin, *Commentary on the Epistles to the Corinthians*, 1 Cor. 1:2 (p. 52).

17. Calvin, *Commentary on the Epistles to the Corinthians*, 1 Cor. 1:2 (p. 53). In an interesting pastoral aside, Calvin writes, "It will, however, be objected, that there were not many such among the Corinthians. I answer, that the weak are not excluded from this number; for here God only begins his work in us, and by little and little carries it forward gradually and by successive steps. I answer farther, that Paul designedly looks rather to the grace of God in them than to their own defects, that he may put them to shame for their negligence, if they do not act a suitable part" (53).

sanctification does God declare unclean sinners holy. Reflecting on Jesus's statement that he sanctifies himself for his people's sake, Calvin emphasizes that Christ is our holiness and we are called to partake in the holiness by which Christ himself is holy.[18] The only way to be united to Christ and thus share in his benefits is *through the Spirit by faith*, because one never has Christ without the Spirit. This is Calvin's doctrine of sanctification by Word and Spirit. Sanctification is always accomplished by God in such a way that Christ becomes the location of our salvation and the telos of life.

As already noted, just as we cannot rend Christ asunder by separating justification and sanctification, so too we must not emphasize Christology to the neglect of pneumatology. Concerning the work of the Spirit, Calvin writes that "he has been given to us for sanctification in order that he may bring us, purged of uncleanness and defilement, into obedience to God's righteousness. . . . Second, we are purged by his sanctification in such a way that we are besieged by many vices and much weakness so long as we are encumbered with our body."[19] Calvin continually emphasizes the work of the Son and the Spirit—what the Son achieves for us is applied by the Spirit—such that God's benefits are offered in Christ by the Spirit.[20] The objective work of Christ is made available through the application of the Spirit, such that sanctification is given in the instant of the double grace that is known in Christ and received in the Spirit. Said another way, for Calvin sanctification is *in* Christ but does not remain *outside* of the believer; the Spirit's work in the inner person brings holiness and establishes Christ's life in the soul. Calvin is emphatic on this point: "Whoever is moderately versed in Scripture will understand by himself, without the admonition of another, that when we have to deal with God nothing is achieved unless we begin from the inner disposition of the heart."[21] "Infused" with the holiness of God, the believer is now able to follow Christ where he calls.[22]

18. Calvin, *Commentary on John*, John 17:19 (pp. 180–81).

19. Calvin, *Institutes* III.iii.14 (1:607).

20. In his "Reply to Sadolet," Calvin writes, "For if he who has obtained justification possesses Christ, and at the same time Christ never is where his Spirit is not, it is obvious that gratuitous righteousness is necessarily connected with regeneration. . . . Wherever, therefore, that righteousness of faith which we maintain to be gratuitous is, there too Christ is; and where Christ is, there too is the Spirit of holiness who regenerates the soul to newness of life" (236).

21. Calvin, *Institutes* III.iii.16 (1:609–10).

22. Calvin, *Institutes* III.vi.2 (1:686).

Thomas Aquinas: Infused Virtue

With Calvin's soteriology of Son and Spirit as our point of departure, it is helpful to turn now to Thomas Aquinas, who articulates a broadly Western approach to supernatural virtue formation. (See the sidebar "Thomas Aquinas," p. 80.) Many mistakenly understand Aquinas to provide a mere Aristotelian account of human formation. While Thomas certainly followed Aristotle in much of his moral theology, as did Protestants in the era to come,[23] reducing Thomas to a *mere* Aristotelian account fails to read him on his own terms. On a more popular level, it is sometimes assumed that Roman Catholics believe one can generate virtue through simple habit formation. However, Thomas's view emphasizes grace and the work of the Spirit in the cultivation of virtue. Starting with the first question of the second part of his *Summa Theologiae*, Thomas considers the purpose of humankind, presenting a vision of human flourishing and obedience.[24] In this section Thomas discusses the inner workings of human psychology, commenting on specific ways sin warps the soul. In what follows we attend closely to his notion of infused virtue, showing how his instincts about virtue are given shape by his reception of Augustine and reading of Scripture.

The first seventy questions of the *prima secundae* are Thomas's articulation of human happiness, moving from natural happiness and virtue to supernatural happiness and virtue.[25] If we fail to read these questions as a whole within the overall movement of the *secunda pars*, we might think that Thomas is articulating a vision of human formation based on natural habituation (not unlike Aristotle). But when the whole work is held in view, such a reading becomes impossible. Rather, we find Thomas presenting a theological vision of happiness that assumes true happiness is

23. See Svensson, *The Aristotelian Tradition in Early Modern Protestantism*; Sytsma, "John Calvin and Virtue Ethics."

24. In Aquinas's preface to the *prima pars* he explains his outline of *sacra doctrina* as "by treating, first, of God, secondly, of the journey to God of reasoning creatures, thirdly, of Christ, who, as man is our road to God" (ten Klooster, *Thomas Aquinas on the Beatitudes*, 143).

25. Ten Klooster writes, "In our reading, the treatise on grace rounds off the discussion of human happiness that he began in the first five questions, and it connects the two books of the secunda pars. Rather than to consider the first five questions as the prelude to an extended treatise on happiness, we could consider them as laying out the structure for the entire prima secundae" (*Thomas Aquinas on the Beatitudes*, 150).

Thomas Aquinas

Thomas Aquinas (1225–74) was born to a noble family but shunned the family castle, choosing against his family's wishes to enter the newly founded Dominican Order at nineteen. Educated initially at the Benedictine monastery of Monte Cassino, he later studied in Paris and eventually under the supervision of Albert the Great in Cologne. Seeing Thomas's brilliance, Albert nominated him for advanced degrees in theology at the University of Paris, where he received his doctorate and was immediately employed as the Dominican chair of theology. His academic development involved deep immersion in a wide variety of authors, especially Augustine and the Latin transmission of Pseudo-Dionysius, Plato, Aristotle, and the scriptural commentaries of the fathers, both East and West, all of which led to Thomas's creative synthesis of philosophy and theology. He is best known for his *Summa Contra Gentiles* (which rescued Aristotle for Christians) and his theological magnus opus, *Summa Theologiae*, which he ceased writing late in life after a mystical experience of God. As a Dominican, preaching was also a regular feature of his ministry, and he wrote biblical commentaries on Job, the Psalms, the Song of Songs, Isaiah, Jeremiah, and the Gospels of Matthew and John.[a]

a. Lightly revised from "Thomas Aquinas (1225–1274)," in Eilers et al., *The Grammar of Grace*, 215.

grounded in a vision of God.[26] Thomas's discussion, in other words, begins with happiness—and the necessity for *supernatural* happiness—ultimately revealing the limitations of natural habituation in his account of infused habits (i.e., habits that are received from God and not generated through repeated activity).[27] True virtue comes from without, on Thomas's con-

26. Aquinas, *Summa Theologiae* I-II, q. 3, a. 8.

27. Aquinas argues,

> It is impossible for any created good to constitute man's happiness. . . . Now the object of the will, i.e., of man's appetite, is the universal good; just as the object of the intellect is the universal true. Hence it is evident that naught can lull man's will, save the universal good. This is to be found, not in any creature, but in God alone; because every creature has goodness by participation. Wherefore God alone can satisfy the will

ception, as God infuses virtuous habits in the soul. Following Aristotle's notion that "happiness is a certain sort of activity of the soul in accord with virtue," Aquinas argues that the Holy Spirit brings the infused virtues to their proper end in delight.[28] In other words, there is no *true supernatural virtue* without the work of the Spirit and God's gracious action in a person.

To understand Thomas rightly we must distinguish between acquired and infused virtue, which becomes relatively standard language in the history of Western moral theology (developed by Protestants, typically, as "infused grace"). When Thomas writes about habits and acquired virtue, he begins with a broadly Aristotelian account of habituating the good. But as he develops his account of acquired habituation, he inquires "whether any habits are infused in man by God." At this point, Thomas claims that there are some habits that dispose a person to an end that "exceeds the proportion of human nature," and he reminds the reader of his prior discussion of the beatific vision. The habits that correspond to this true end *cannot be habituated* (i.e., they cannot be acquired, as with natural virtues). Instead, they can only be *received* through an infusion by God.[29] This is Thomas's turn from natural formation to supernatural formation, and it is critically important to grasp when reading Thomas.

Up until this point in the *Summa Theologiae*, one may think that infused virtue is perhaps an anomaly within Thomas's view, an idiosyncratic tic that does not get to the heart of his discussion. But in addressing the essence of virtue, he actually affirms that *true* virtue is infused virtue. Considering the nature of human personhood, Thomas addresses the formation of a person. An unbeliever can develop habits as much as a believer can, and so Thomas addresses habituation in general before turning to the nature of true virtue. In doing so he employs the distinction between

---

of man, according to the words of Ps. cii. 5: *Who satisfieth thy desire with good things*. Therefore God alone constitutes man's happiness. (*Summa Theologiae* I-II, q. 2, a. 8)

28. Aristotle, *Nicomachean Ethics* 1.9.7. We are following ten Klooster's articulation of the movement of the *secunda pars*, building on the articulations of Pinckaers (*The Sources of Christian Ethics*) and Mattison ("Beatitude and the Beatitudes in the *Summa Theologiae*"). Ten Klooster helpfully integrates questions 68–70 into the whole (*Thomas Aquinas on the Beatitudes*, 149–54). In question 11 of the *prima secundae*, Thomas writes, "In delight there are two things: perception of what is becoming; and this belongs to the apprehensive power; and complacency in that which is offered as becoming: and this belongs to the appetitive power, in which power delight is formally completed" (*Summa Theologiae* I-II, q. 11, art. 1, reply to obj. 3).

29. Aquinas, *Summa Theologiae* I-II, q. 52, a. 4.

acquired and infused virtue to address how it is that we can talk about "pagan" virtue, a problem at the forefront of Christian ethics since at least Augustine. Recognizing that there is moral difference among unbelievers, Thomas addresses this difference while simultaneously establishing a distinctively *super*natural virtue. In other words, we need to be able to talk about how an unbeliever can be in some sense good, while also affirming that "none is righteous, no, not one" (Rom. 3:10).

When Thomas defines virtue, he makes what appears to be a surprising claim: "*Virtue is a good quality of the mind, by which we live righteously, of which no one can make bad use, which God works in us, without us.*" Reflecting on this definition, Thomas claims, "This definition comprises perfectly the whole essential notion of virtue."[30] Furthermore, he avers, "God is the efficient cause of infused virtue, to which this definition applies; and this is expressed in the words *which God works in us, without us*. If we omit this phrase, the remainder of the definition will apply to all virtues in general, whether acquired or infused."[31] Thomas's definition of virtue is a definition of infused virtue. Likewise, the notion that God works in us without us should not be taken to mean that God's action is somehow against us. This is not a unilateral act that God does violently or against the person, because Thomas assumes a noncompetitive relationship between divine and human agency. Reflecting on Paul's comment in Philippians 2:13 that "it is God who works in you, both to will and to work for his good pleasure," Thomas adds, "Infused virtue is caused in us by God without any action on our part, but not without our consent. This is the sense of the words *which God works in us, without us*."[32] The virtue that defines the Christian life, in other words, is by grace.[33]

30. Aquinas, *Summa Theologiae* I-II, q. 55, a. 4, obj. 1 (emphasis original). Robert Miner argues, "The elements of the Augustinian definition correspond to the four causes in a particular order: formal, material, final, efficient. That Thomas adopts this very order in the sequencing of questions 55–63 can be seen in his decision to begin with the formal cause—that is, the essence of virtue, the topic of question 55. Likewise, question 63—the end of the sequence of questions on virtue itself, before the turn to its 'properties'—plainly concerns the efficient cause" ("Infused Virtue as Virtue Simply," 414–15).

31. Aquinas, *Summa Theologiae* I-II, q. 55, a. 4.

32. Aquinas, *Summa Theologiae* I-II, q. 55, a. 4, reply to obj. 6.

33. Thomas argues that "virtue which directs man to good as defined by the Divine Law, and not by human reason, cannot be caused to human acts . . . but is produced in us by the Divine operation alone" (*Summa Theologiae* I-II, q. 63, a. 2). Furthermore, on grace: "The principal cause [of an efficient cause] works by the power of its form, to which form the effect

The biblical material is close to the surface throughout Thomas's exposition, and his reading of Scripture leads him to an account of virtue that orders human action from *within God's prior action in the soul.* Meditating on Psalm 84:11, "The Lord will give grace and glory," Thomas notes that grace and glory are above human persons, and therefore, "if anything need to be done that is above nature, it is done by God immediately; such as raising the dead to life, restoring sight to the blind, and such like."[34] Furthermore, when Peter asserts in 2 Peter 1:4 that Christians are made "partakers of the divine nature," Thomas believes such participation as this necessitates that persons "receive from God some additional principles" to direct them to "supernatural happiness."[35]

Central to Thomas's exposition is the notion that certain habits and virtues are *proper* to human perfection according to its nature, whereas other habits and virtues are *above* human nature.[36] A relation exists between how nature works and how *super*nature works, and Thomas clarifies his view by relating these two features. Characteristically, Thomas orders the supernatural according to the natural, showing how grace perfects nature: "The theological virtues direct man to supernatural happiness in the same way as by the natural inclination man is directed to his connatural end."[37] The natural inclination of a person is directed to its end by the universal principles embedded in their intellect. These are the seeds of intellectual knowing, and they are mirrored by the same in the will.[38] "But these fall

is likened; just as fire by its own heat makes something hot. In this way none but God can cause grace: since grace is nothing else than a participated likeness of the Divine Nature, according to 2 Pet i.4: *He hath given us most great and precious promises; that we may be* (Vulg.,—*you may be made*) *partakers of the Divine Nature*" (III, q. 62, a. 1).

34. Aquinas, *Summa Theologiae* I-II, q. 5, a. 6.

35. Aquinas, *Summa Theologiae* I-II, q. 62, a. 1.

36. Andrew Pinsent warns against using metaphors like our use of *above* here. He claims, "If an infused virtue is a 'higher' version of an acquired virtue, where 'higher' indicates some relationship of proportional equivalence, then the 'higher' virtue can be thought of as a proportionally greater version of its 'lower' equivalent. Since the 'lower' virtue is Aristotelian, then the infused virtue can also be understood, albeit indirectly, in Aristotelian terms" (*The Second-Person Perspective in Aquinas's Ethics*, 12). Pinsent is one of several scholars who are worried that the Aristotelian shape of Aquinas's ethics becomes the primary form by which his ethical thought is understood. When this happens, acquired virtue becomes seen as virtue as such, and infusion is seen as a specific type of that virtue—in the example considered here, a "higher" version.

37. Aquinas, *Summa Theologiae* I-II, q. 62, a. 3.

38. Thomas explains that "certain seeds or principles of acquired virtue pre-exist in us by nature" (*Summa Theologiae* I-II, q. 63, a. 2, reply to obj. 3). These seeds or principles are what

short of the order of supernatural happiness," Thomas avers.[39] Along similar lines, and through more biblical meditation, this time on 1 Corinthians 2:9, Thomas asserts that persons need additional supernatural principles of faith, hope, and love to orient them properly to God.

Thomas is clear about the origin of theological virtues: *The theological virtues are infused by God*. As such, these virtues are entirely from without and not at all in us by nature.[40] By infusing faith, hope, and love into the Christian, God has given supernatural principles that correspond to the natural principles. "The theological virtues," he notes, "direct us sufficiently to our supernatural end, inchoatively: i.e., to God himself immediately. But the soul needs further to be perfected in infused virtues in regard to other things, yet in relation to God."[41] It is only after this development that Thomas asserts what has, up until this point, been left implicit: "It is therefore clear from what has been said that only the infused virtues are perfect, and deserve to be called virtues simply: since they direct man well to the ultimate end. But the other virtues, those, namely, that are acquired, are virtues in a restricted sense."[42]

As Aquinas navigates all these issues related to virtue and their reception, a number of biblical passages are clearly in his view. With infused virtue in particular, two seem especially important. First, regarding faith, is Romans 14:23, which claims that "whatever does not proceed from faith is sin." This is why "pagan virtue," while still a kind of virtue according to natural human ends, is nothing before God. Without faith, these things

---

allow for further development. We can habituate only what we already have in seminal form. This is why it would not be possible to habituate supernatural virtue. Following Augustine's definition, it is entirely "from without." Angela McKay Knobel writes,

> God gives natural creatures principles that incline them to the types of acts appropriate to their nature, so that "the movements by which they are moved by God become connatural to those creatures and easy for them—this according to Wisdom 8:1 ('. . . and [wisdom] orders all things agreeable' (*suaviter*))." In the same way, then, when God grants human beings participation in the divine life, he infuses into them "certain forms, i.e., qualities, by which they might be moved agreeably and promptly by Him toward attaining that eternal good." Thus, along with grace, which makes us participants in the divine life, Aquinas holds that God also gives us virtues, which order us to participation in that nature. (*Aquinas and the Infused Moral Virtues*, 50)

39. Aquinas, *Summa Theologiae* I-II, q. 62, a. 3.
40. Aquinas, *Summa Theologiae* I-II, q. 63, a. 1.
41. Aquinas, *Summa Theologiae* I-II, q. 63, a. 3, reply to obj. 2.
42. Aquinas, *Summa Theologiae* I-II, q. 65, a. 2.

are merely "beautiful vices," or, to use language that would be used more frequently later in the Protestant tradition, they are the filthy rags that are meaningless in the presence of God. This is a point Thomas continues to advance through his use of Hebrews 11:6, "Without faith it is impossible to please [God]," as well as 1 Corinthians 13, which claims that without love, virtues are *not* truly virtuous. This is also one of the key texts concerning the theological virtues, ordering them eschatologically to their end in God and emphasizing that we will be like him only when we see him as he is (1 Cor. 13:12; 1 John 3:2).

When we step back from close consideration of Thomas's argument, it becomes clear that Thomas reads Scripture to pull its whole multivalent message into a vision of Christian formation. But his account also offers something easily missed: He seeks to explain how Christians *experience* growth in virtue.[43] In one instance he addresses our struggle to act according to infused virtue. Unlike acquired virtue, which we develop through repeated acts over time to habituate virtuous action, infused virtue comes from *without*. It is by grace. Because of this, some previously developed dispositions in the soul are contrary to the grace of God, and they must be reformed in and by love.[44] This way of rendering the Spirit's work in the soul—one we return to later in our own constructive development of the doctrine—can help make sense of the ongoing struggle with sin in

43. In *Summa Theologiae* I-II, q. 68, a. 2, Thomas talks about how the supernatural virtues are greater than the natural virtues, but we possess the natural virtues in more perfect ways. So infused virtue is possessed imperfectly. From here he talks about how the ease of working out a virtue is based on how perfectly it is possessed, and he goes on to use the image of the sun illumining versus the moon, and a doctor versus his student.

44. This is the focus of Jared Brandt's dissertation, "Growth in Infused Virtue in the Work of Thomas Aquinas," but is also discussed by ten Klooster, who articulates the three degrees of charity, claiming:

> Charity has three degrees: that of the beginners (*incipientes*), those making progress (*proficientes*), and the perfect (*perfectos*). These stages of spiritual growth "can be marked according as growth in charity leads a man to fix his main attention on different things." The first of these is to withdraw from sin, and to resist concupiscences which move the subject away from charity. In the second stage, the primary object is to advance in doing good. The perfect, finally, are firmly directed toward adhering to God and enjoying Him (*eo fruatur*). The progression we can see on the way of the beatitudes is the external reflection of the interior increase of charity. As it grows stronger, the subject turns away from evil and eventually seeks nothing but to know and love God. The end is peace, taken here as the *fruitio* of God, and resting in Him. (*Thomas Aquinas on the Beatitudes*, 192–93)

a believer's life and the phenomenology of their sanctification. We who are in Christ have something by grace that is not yet habituated into our character, precisely because infusion works in the opposite direction from our acquired virtues. Ours is an admittedly confusing state, and much has been written in the Christian tradition about our unique experience of supernatural formation.

Any account of spiritual formation seeking to be grounded in grace has to articulate how God works in the soul by the Spirit. This leads to questions concerning virtue formation and how our action and God's action relate, bringing to the fore passages that depict the Spirit's working by power in the soul (as in Eph. 3:16) and pouring forth love into the soul (Rom. 5:5). Once Aquinas establishes his account of virtue (intellectual and moral, acquired and infused, cardinal and theological), one might think his ethical vision is complete. One might expect that all that remains to be done is a detailed exposition of each virtue before turning to their opposing vices. Instead, Aquinas discusses "the gifts of the Holy Ghost" (question 68), "the beatitudes" (question 69), and "the fruits of the Holy Ghost" (question 70). These considerations are driven by Thomas's exposition of Scripture, where he seeks to understand the full breadth of biblical language concerning God's action to form his people. In particular, Thomas is attentive to how Scripture speaks of these three categories differently from virtues.

The movement from the infusion of the theological and moral virtues to the gifts of the Spirit, Beatitudes, and the fruit of the Spirit is, for Thomas, *necessary for the perfection of the creature*. Since perfection is the perfection of happiness (i.e., beatitude), it takes more than the habituation of certain activities but requires an infusion of supernatural habits by grace, which are perfected *through the work and gift of the Spirit* to bear the fruit of delight in accord with the supernaturally virtuous Christian life. All this derives from the Spirit, who is the "first gift in whom all gifts are given."[45] The culmination of this movement of the moral life is in the Beatitudes and the fruits. They represent the perfection and delight that come upon internalizing the life of God in one's person.[46]

45. Ten Klooster, *Thomas Aquinas on the Beatitudes*, 199.

46. Ten Klooster explains that the fruits "are a sort of navigation system for the moral life," are the goods "to be pursued," and help explain "what evils are to be avoided" (*Thomas Aquinas on the Beatitudes*, 175).

John Wesley: Grace Increasing to Perfection

Our discussion of Calvin emphasized that salvation is a singular, twofold reality of justification and sanctification in Christ, and we ended that section with his articulation of how believers need an infusion of holiness. Aquinas provided language to describe the Spirit's work to infuse holiness in the soul and how this might look, something we will address in a later chapter. We now turn to John Wesley, well aware that we could just as well attend to nearly any figure among the Reformed High Orthodox to articulate a vision of sanctification that resonates with Calvin and Aquinas. Aquinas, along with other key sources such as Bernard and Scotus, advanced accounts of infusion and supernatural virtue formation that were broadly followed, although idiosyncratically, by Reformed theologians after Calvin. Reformed accounts vary significantly, and none follow Aquinas's account wholesale, but nonetheless they advanced a similar vision of supernatural virtue formation for the same reasons that Thomas articulates.[47] As one of the great founts of evangelical thought and practice, however, Wesley proves particularly interesting as one of the only theologians whose most well-recognized doctrine concerns sanctification.

Nearly every commentator on Wesley notes that Wesley's task differed significantly from that of someone like Aquinas or even Calvin.[48] (See the sidebar "John Wesley," p. 88.) Wesley's science was Christian experience more than scholastic distinction. Wesley sought to articulate a vision of holiness whose theological heft was justified by how it showed up practically in the lives of those called Methodists. This emphasis and approach appear most obviously in his account of Christian perfection, but our focus rests instead on the nature of sanctification in his theological system as it is ordered *in and by love*. Wesley's vision is one of holy love, not unlike his contemporary Jonathan Edwards; they both grounded this vision in the Spirit of love cast abroad into the hearts of people to regenerate and sanctify.[49]

47. This is the purpose of the book *Virtue Ethics, Grace, and a Protestant Doctrine of Infusion*, edited by Lucy Peppiatt and Kyle Strobel (forthcoming).

48. Nonetheless, there has been recent interest in comparing Wesley with Aquinas specifically. See Colón-Emeric, *Wesley, Aquinas, and Christian Perfection*; Long, *John Wesley's Moral Theology*; and Loyer, *God's Love Through the Spirit*.

49. See my (Kyle's) chapter on Jonathan Edwards in Peppiatt and Strobel, *Virtue Ethics, Grace, and a Protestant Doctrine of Infusion*.

John Wesley

John Wesley (1703–91) was instrumental in the formation of the evangelical revival movement known as Methodism that was spreading within the Church of England in the eighteenth century. The fifteenth of nineteen children, John was raised in a deeply religious family and attended the prestigious Charthouse boarding school before completing undergraduate and graduate degrees at Oxford University. While at Oxford, he led a group that was committed to strict spiritual disciplines, accountability, and Bible study, mockingly called "The Holy Club," from which the name "Methodist" first emerged. The focus of that group on the rigorous application of one's Christian commitment to everyday life reflects Wesley's overall theological orientation. His theology—which he called "practical divinity"—revolved around his understanding of God's grace and the importance of the active pursuit of holiness in the day-to-day. Wesley's theology was not worked out in the philosophical or systematic registers of Aquinas's *Summa* or Calvin's *Institutes* but instead through thousands of sermons, commentaries, liturgies, prayers, journals, and letters.[a]

a. Lightly revised from "John Wesley (1703–1791)," in Eilers et al., *The Grammar of Grace*, 323–24.

For Wesley, as for Calvin, salvation entails a double grace. Wesley accepts even as he adapts the Westminster Shorter Confession, which asks, "What are the benefits which in this life do accompany or flow from justification, adoption, and sanctification?" Wesley cuts adoption to set forth a more streamlined twofold work of salvation as *justification* and *sanctification*.[50] This twofold work is based on God being a just judge and a holy God, who, respectively, cannot clear the guilty and cannot associate with the impure. As Wesley understands it, this twofold problem is addressed by the twofold salvation God offers—justification and sanctification. In justification, the righteousness of Christ is *imputed*, and in sanctification, the holiness of Christ is *imparted*; or, put differently,

50. MacDonald, *Wesley's Revision of the Shorter Catechism*, 62.

justification is Christ's work *for us*, and sanctification is Christ's work *in us*.[51]

Both Calvin and Wesley present soteriologies that emphasize the work of both the Son and the Spirit, just as they both seek accounts of salvation that hold together justification and sanctification. In Calvin, however, justification serves as a foundation on which one can embrace the call of sanctification. Justification is the "till death do us part" that allows life to flourish in the stability of the covenantal union of marriage. Wesley, on the other hand, advances an account of justification that refuses to rest in itself but is *tilted toward sanctification as its proper end*.[52] Wesley and Calvin are equally focused on Christ's work and grace as the necessary conditions for sanctification, but the emphases change in Wesley. Whereas we might say, with some potential reduction, that Calvin seeks to order sanctification in Christ, with its anchor in justification, *Wesley seeks to order sanctification in the work of the Spirit as the proper end of justification*.[53] In this sense, justification is anchored in its perfection in sanctification for Wesley, rather than serving as the fountain for sanctification as in Calvin.

This comparison is admittedly too clean, but it is still helpful to identify some of Wesley's distinctives. Calvin is captivated by the completeness of salvation in Christ and the response of gratitude in the believer by faith. Wesley, on the other hand, is captivated by the incompleteness of salvation in being saved by grace through faith, focusing on the ongoing—and necessary—perfection of the believer in sanctification. While his views on entire sanctification or Christian perfection varied throughout his life, his focus remained fixed on the completion of the work of sanctification prior to death. Sanctification, for Wesley, ends

51. MacDonald, *Wesley's Revision of the Shorter Catechism*, 63. Wesley asks, "What is justification?" and responds, "It is evident from what has been already observed that it is not the being made actually just and righteous. This is *sanctification*; which is indeed in some degree the immediate *fruit* of justification, but nevertheless is a distinct gift of God, and of a totally different nature. The one implies what God *does for us* through his Son; the other what he *works in us* by his Spirit" (Wesley, "Justification by Faith," 187).

52. Wesley emphasizes that this means God is the ultimate end of the creature: "Have no end, no ultimate end, but God" ("The Circumcision of the Heart," 28).

53. Harald Lindström argues, "The real purpose of the imputation of the righteousness of Christ is thus declared to be the sanctification of man" (*Wesley and Sanctification*, 101).

up being more than just one aspect of salvation; it is *the metanarrative of salvation itself.*[54]

Wesley is in the tradition that follows Calvin in using a double grace to structure soteriology, and yet there is a further "double" feature to the second grace in Wesley's construction.[55] The double grace of justification and sanctification establishes another double grace in sanctification itself. This is the twofold giving and receiving of the Spirit. The first giving of the Spirit is regeneration and is the beginning of sanctification, but the second is for proper sanctification and maturation into perfection.[56] In this sense, in sanctification we are entering *a new realm of soteriology* that will inevitably require not only both subjectivity and development but also an increasing emphasis on human action.[57]

54. An example of this concerns the term *theosis*. Theosis, in the Christian tradition, is not simply one aspect of salvation but is the ordering dynamics of an entire soteriology. This gets confused today when people assume theosis is a type of justification or sanctification. Significantly, however, Wesley saw sanctification in a similar vein, suggesting that his view of sanctification is more akin to how theosis functions in historic soteriologies. Along these lines, Colón-Emeric writes, "In fact, in preparing the edition of Macarius' sermons for inclusion in the Christian Library, Wesley replaced all references to the term *theosis* with 'sanctification,' a change that arguably underlies not just a difference of vocabulary but of actual theological understandings" (*Wesley, Aquinas, and Christian Perfection*, 2). We are less convinced that Wesley, at least, believed the difference to be apparent. Rather, it was his understanding of sanctification as the overarching reality of salvation that brought about this change. Similarly, Steve McCormick writes, "It is just such an understanding of *theosis* which Wesley seems to employ as the organizing principle of his *ordo salutis*. And, as Wesley wrote his *ordo salutis* to the tune of *theosis*, it is probably better to understand it as a *via salutis*: that is to say, we are *becoming* 'like' God by the energy of love (coinciding with our freedom) as He was *becoming* what we are in condescending love" ("Theosis in Chrysostom and Wesley," 39). McCormick's focus on theosis as an organizing principle and Wesley's particular focus on love as God's energy of transformation seems correct. McCormick, however, is incorrect in his assumption that this paradigm is *Eastern*, rather than simply the Christian tradition as a whole. Important in this discussion is Mark Gorman's "John and Charles Wesley on Deification."

55. It would be more accurate to start with the double feature of salvation as the Son and the Spirit, "the two grand heads of doctrine," as Wesley articulates it. Building on these two heads, however, Wesley advances the double grace of justification and sanctification as "those two grand branches." He claims specifically, "By justification we are saved from the guilt of sin, and restored to the favour of God: by sanctification we are saved from the power and root of sin, and restored to the image of God" ("On Working Out Our Own Salvation," 200, 204).

56. For a helpful discussion, see both Lindström, *Wesley and Sanctification*, 83–84, and MacDonald, *Wesley's Revision of the Shorter Catechism*, 64–65.

57. See Lindström, *Wesley and Sanctification*, 92. Colón-Emeric builds on this, advancing an account of the "objective-juridical" dynamics of sin and justification, comparing it with

Sanctification functions for Wesley primarily in a moral register, but this is not the only connotation. For instance, Wesley writes that holiness entails that God is "infinitely distant from every touch of evil. He 'is light; and in him is no darkness at all.' He is a God of unblemished justice and truth; but above all is his mercy."[58] This establishes a point of tension. Is God's mercy an act to make what is impure pure and therefore receivable, or is it an act to receive the impure to himself, sanctifying them in and by his presence? Wesley chooses the former. The holiness of God establishes a work that God *must do* for the sinner to have access to him and his presence. In the words of Edgardo A. Colón-Emeric, "The whole purpose of the way of salvation is to turn a sinner into a saint to enjoy communion with the Triune God."[59]

In the first chapter we traced the contours of the three articles of the creeds, showing that each article could be specified with unique appropriations concerning salvation as a whole and sanctification in particular. The tensions in accounts of sanctification concern how one situates the work of the Son and the Spirit and the nature and end of holiness in the creature. Typically, this leads to a focus on the third article, on the Spirit, and Wesley is no different:

> I believe the infinite and eternal Spirit of God, equal with the Father and the Son, to be not only perfectly holy in himself, but the immediate cause of all holiness in us; enlightening our understandings, rectifying our wills and affections, renewing our natures, uniting our persons to Christ, assuring us

---

the "subjective-therapeutic" dynamic of sanctification as a real change in the person (*Wesley, Aquinas, and Christian Perfection*, 45).

58. Wesley, "The Unity of the Divine Being," §7. Mark Gorman was kind enough to point out this reference. It seems significant that Wesley's definition leads him into an account of God's *distance* from sin. Similarly, expounding the holiness of the law, Wesley writes,

> It is, indeed, in the highest degree, pure, chaste, clean, holy. Otherwise it could not be the immediate offspring, and much less the express resemblance, of God, who is essential holiness. It is pure from all sin, clean and unspotted from any touch of evil. It is a chaste virgin, incapable of any defilement, of any mixture with that which is unclean or unholy. It has no fellowship with sin of any kind: For "what communion hath light with darkness"? As sin is, in its very nature, enmity to God, so his law is enmity to sin. ("The Original, Nature, Property, and Use of the Law" III.3)

In describing both God and the law as holy, Wesley must invoke impurity and evil, grounding holiness not in perfection as such but in contrast to the impure and imperfect.

59. Colón-Emeric, *Wesley, Aquinas, and Christian Perfection*, 11.

> of the adoption as sons, leading us in our actions, purifying and sanctifying our souls and bodies to a full and eternal enjoyment of God.[60]

In his *Christian Perfection*, Wesley argues that the "circumcision of heart" specified in Scripture is "that habitual disposition of soul, which in the sacred writings is termed holiness, and which directly implies the being cleansed from sin, from all filthiness both of flesh and spirit, and by consequence, the being endued with those virtues which were in Christ Jesus; the being so *renewed in the image of our mind* as to be *perfect as our Father in heaven is perfect*."[61] This habitual disposition of the soul, however, is not fully circumscribed by the term *holiness* but is known in and through *love*.

For Wesley, as for Calvin and Aquinas before him, *only God can give holiness*, and he does so by infusing the soul with an entirely new disposition that will transform and recharacterize it. Yet, even as God grants holiness in this manner, our response to God's gracious initiatives is also entailed by our sanctification. For Wesley, therefore, sanctification is a doctrine that must articulate what it means for regenerate people to give their "heart wholly to God."[62] This includes a focus on the character of Christians as those governed by love. Importantly, Wesley corrects those who are tempted to move from Christ to their own resources for this formation and claims, "Accordingly, when it is said, *You shall love the Lord your God with all your heart, and with all your soul, and with all your mind* (Matt. 22:37); it is not only a direction of what I shall do, but a promise of what God will do in me."[63] Building on regeneration, which serves as the ground of God's work in the soul, Wesley explains, "And Christianity, considered as an inward principle, is the completion of all those promises. It is holiness and happiness, the image of God impressed on a created spirit; a fountain of peace and love springing up into everlasting life."[64]

60. Wesley, "A Letter to a Roman Catholic," quoted in Loyer, *God's Love Through the Spirit*, 32.

61. Wesley, *John and Charles Wesley*, 300.

62. Wesley, *John and Charles Wesley*, 162.

63. Wesley, *John and Charles Wesley*, 126.

64. Wesley, *John and Charles Wesley*, 129. D. Stephen Long writes, "Wesley clearly follows the tradition of moral theology in that all human action takes place under a common telos: the desire for happiness. This is the good. He sides with Aquinas against Aristotle in finding that common telos to be our participation in God. Holiness and happiness go together. In spite

Even as Wesley emphasizes the Spirit, though, Christ remains central to his theology of sanctification. For instance, Wesley argues vehemently against antinomianism, seeking to undermine any such tendency in the Christian,[65] while also denying the value of our "filthy rags" before the eyes of God. Wesley writes, "I renounce all confidence therein, and acknowledge that I am of myself a hopeless, helpless, undone creature, without righteousness or strength."[66] His attempt to undermine confidence in ourselves, as well as his defense against antinomianism, consistently turns him to consider the work of the Son *and* the Spirit for us and in us, calling the Christian to a life shaped by God's action. For the former, he writes to the Father, "And since you have appointed the Lord Jesus Christ the only means of coming unto you I do here upon the bended knees of my soul accept of him as the only new and living way, by which Sinners may have access to you; and do solemnly join myself in a marriage-covenant to him."[67] Even as Wesley emphasizes pneumatology, he never leaves Christ aside or suggests that the believer move beyond needing Christ.[68]

---

of efforts to make John Wesley an *agape* deontologist, he was without a doubt a teleological thinker" (*John Wesley's Moral Theology*, 48).

65. Lindström explains how Wesley's polemic against antinomianism uniquely shaped his theology:

> Wesley's rejection of the idea of a fulfilment of the law by proxy is an outcome of his struggle against antinomianism. He finds its very essence to lie in the idea that Christ has met the claims of the law on man's behalf and that therefore he is not called upon to fulfil the moral law. Accordingly he disassociates the fulfilment of the law from atonement and justification and attaches it instead to sanctification. This explains why sanctification in the sense of fulfilment of the law occupies such an important place in his theology. (*Wesley and Sanctification*, 75)

66. Lindström, *Wesley and Sanctification*, 143. "If we were not utterly impotent, our good works would be our own property; whereas now they belong wholly to God, because they proceed from him and his grace; while raising our works, and making them all divine, he honors himself in us through them" (371–72).

67. Lindström, *Wesley and Sanctification*, 143–44.

68. Accentuating Christ, Wesley writes,

> In every state we need Christ in the following respects: (1) whatever grace we receive, it is a free gift from him; (2) we receive it as his purchase, merely in consideration of the price he paid; (3) we have this grace not only *from* Christ, but *in* him. For our perfection is not like that of a tree, which flourishes by the sap derived from its own root, but, as was said before, like that of a branch, which united to the vine, bears fruit; but severed from it, *is dried up and withered*; (4) all our blessings, temporal, spiritual, and eternal, depend on his intercession for us, which is one branch of his priestly office, whereof therefore we have always equal

Wesley's conception of Christian perfection therefore does not shift away from grace or faith to somehow establish a Pelagian perfection. Rather, Christian perfection is the work of God in the soul to love the Christian into a virtuous life.[69] If we were to use Aquinas's terminology for this idea, we could say that God has infused faith, hope, and love into the soul in regeneration such that the believer has been given the internal dispositions necessary, and the relation to the Son and the Spirit necessary, to walk into perfection in and through the action and calling of God.[70] Wesley undermines antinomianism by demanding a life of striving, but he also undermines Pelagianism by claiming perfection is an instantaneous work of God, the progress of which always requires God's action along with our own.[71] In ways that resonate with Aquinas, Wesley

---

> need; (5) the best of men still need Christ, in his priestly office, to atone for their omissions, their short-comings (as some not improperly speak), their mistakes in judgment and practice, and their defects of various kinds. (*John and Charles Wesley*, 328–29, emphasis original)

69. Wesley writes, "The loving God with all our heart, mind, soul, and strength. This implies that no wrong temper, none contrary to love, remains in the soul; and that all the thoughts, words, and actions are governed by pure love" (*John and Charles Wesley*, 327–28).

70. Colón-Emeric makes a similar claim. Expounding Wesley's view, he writes, "Only an infusion of God's own love can restore our loves to their proper order." Likewise, making the connection with Thomas clear, "By centering his mature moral psychology on tempers Wesley comes very close to Aquinas' 'virtue ethic.' The late Wesley regarded the holy tempers as seeds of God's sanctifying grace. These seeds are implanted in human nature for the purpose of grounding holy actions on holy affections. For this reason, [Randy] Maddox refers to this moral psychology as 'habituated holistic affections'" (*Wesley, Aquinas, and Christian Perfection*, 37). Also interested in a comparison with Thomas, Loyer explains, "For Wesley, tempers are the stable, enduring dispositions of a person—'that fixed posture of [the] soul.' As such, tempers are more than simply passive feelings, and more than even motivating dispositions" (Loyer, *God's Love Through the Spirit*, 183). Likewise, Loyer asserts, "Seen in this way, love, joy, peace, and the rest of the virtues associated with life in the Spirit are the divinely infused affections that stimulate ongoing growth in holiness" (185).

71. In his own fourfold summary, he writes, "(1) that Christian Perfection is that love of God and our neighbor which implies deliverance from all sin; (2) that this is received merely by faith; (3) that it is given instantaneously, in one moment; (4) that we are to expect it (not at death, but) every moment: that now is the accepted time, now is the day of this salvation" (Wesley, *John and Charles Wesley*, 326). Likewise, Wesley writes that "the work of God is undoubtedly instantaneous with regard to sanctification as well as justification, and it is no objection at all that the work is gradual also" (Wesley, "Letter to George Gibbon [1785]," quoted in Collins, *The Scripture Way of Salvation*, 97).

portrays God's infusion into the believer's soul not as God giving over something to the creature abstracted from himself, as if God's continuing action were unnecessary.[72] Rather, with his Reformed counterparts, Wesley argues that God's activity to infuse grace into the soul does not replace his ongoing action. Wesley writes,

> The holiest of men still need Christ, as their prophet, as *the light of the world*. For he does not give them light, but from moment to moment: the instant he withdraws, all is darkness. They still need Christ as their king. For God does not give them a stock of holiness. But unless they receive a supply every moment, nothing but unholiness would remain. They still need Christ as their priest, to make atonement for their holy things. Even perfect holiness is acceptable to God only through Jesus Christ.[73]

Beyond Wesley's account of Christian perfection, it is perhaps the manner in which he intimately links holiness and love that most marks his doctrine. The connection Wesley holds between holiness and love is so profound that interpreters are tempted to *reduce one into the other*. Against any such impulse, Kenneth M. Loyer writes: "Rather than a direct equation between the two, there is a 'conjunction,' and even some tension, in holiness and love as Wesley described them, with holiness entailing what [Kenneth] Collins calls 'a movement of separation for the sake of purity' and love, for its part, involving 'a movement of revelation, engagement, and, at its highest levels, communion.'"[74] The broader movement of sanctification, we would say, is the *perfection of love*, with holiness specifying

72. Wesley explains,

> From what has been said we may learn, secondly, what the life of God in the soul of a believer is, wherein it properly consists, and what is immediately and necessarily implied therein. It immediately and necessarily implies the continual inspiration of God's Holy Spirit: God's breathing into the soul, and the soul's breathing back what it first receives from God; a continual action of God upon the soul, the re-action of the soul upon God; an unceasing presence of God, the loving, pardoning God, manifested to the heart, and perceived by faith; and an unceasing return of love, praise, and prayer, offering up all the thoughts of our hearts, . . . to be an holy sacrifice, acceptable unto God in Christ Jesus. ("The Great Privilege of Those That Are Born of God," 442)

73. Wesley, *John and Charles Wesley*, 350.
74. Loyer, *God's Love Through the Spirit*, 20.

the necessary framework for that perfection to occur.[75] Wesley's own summary is helpful:

> But we must love God before we can be holy at all; this being the root of all holiness. Now we cannot love God till we know he loves us: "We love him, because he first loved us." And we cannot know his pardoning love to us till his Spirit witnesses it to our spirit. Since therefore this "testimony of his Spirit" must precede the love of God and all holiness, of consequence it must precede our inward consciousness thereof, or the "testimony of our spirit" concerning them.[76]

In Wesley's doctrine, the beginning and end of holiness is love, revealing that holiness is not for its own sake but for sharing God's life. As such, Wesley's doctrine pushes beyond the inward dynamics of holiness to address the social realities necessary for a complete doctrine of sanctification. Social holiness is not minor or secondary in his view but is a necessary outworking of his entire doctrine. Importantly, his advancement of social holiness was never in conflict or tension with the inward realities of sanctification.[77] Instead, the seeds of new life are planted in the soul, bringing order, purity, and simplicity to the person as they grow and develop in holiness and love. Furthermore, the field of growth for both personal and social dynamics is first and foremost ecclesial; the church is the proper location for Christian formation, and the impact of that formation has societal and political imperatives and ramifications.

To summarize Wesley's view: In salvation, the creature is caught up in the life of God, justified and given new dispositions in the soul that are ordered to the perfection of love. There is an instantaneous dynamic to regeneration and sanctification, where the Lord reorders the soul in

75. Wesley writes, "This then is real, genuine, solid virtue. Not truth alone, nor conformity to truth. This is a property of real virtue, not the essence of it. Not love alone, though this comes nearer the mark; for 'love' in our sense 'is the fulfilling of the law.' No: truth and love united together are the essence of virtue or holiness. God indispensably requires 'truth in the inward parts,' influencing all our words and actions. Yet truth itself, separate from love, is nothing in his sight" ("An Israelite Indeed," 289).

76. Wesley, "The Witness of the Spirit, I," 274–75.

77. Collins writes, "The contrast to social religion, then, is not personal religion, as is sometimes mistakenly supposed, but solitary religion" (*The Scripture Way of Salvation*, 159).

"inward holiness," establishing the supernatural life in seed form.[78] But the gradual dynamics of salvation—in reliance on God's work—is wrought as holiness and love recharacterize the person from the internal into the external dynamics of their life and relationships.[79] "According to Wesley," Loyer explains, "it is by sharing in God's own life that our affections are renewed, and the holy tempers that orient those affections properly are freely given to us by God for the corresponding shaping of our thoughts, words, and actions. They are the very tempers in which vital Christianity consists."[80]

Reflection and Advance

The three theologians canvassed here demonstrate, we believe, a threefold instinct in the Western tradition. First, a doctrine of sanctification must focus on the shared work of the Son and the Spirit that secures salvation and works in the creature to make them holy in order to grow in holiness. None of the thinkers addressed here advocate for *something* being given to the soul that the Christian must now cultivate apart from God's presence and action. All of them articulate a robust account of the Spirit's continued work in the soul and Christ's continued action and ministry.

Second, sanctification entails a uniquely supernatural formation that differs from any natural counterpart in a person. One might develop as a person in any number of ways (i.e., growth in virtue or character formation), but sanctification requires the supernatural, gracious activity of God.

Third, God works in the regenerate to make them holy, but not in a way that a new and separate capacity is given to the person that enables

78. Wesley articulates a view of regeneration that uses the language of "seed"; e.g., "The divine seed of loving, conquering faith remains in him that is 'born of God'" ("The Great Privilege of Those That Are Born of God," 440).

79. Wesley writes, "Inward holiness is mostly instantaneous . . . but outward holiness is mostly gradual" (Wesley, "Letter to Mary Bosanquet [1775]," quoted in Collins, *The Scripture Way of Salvation*, 115). Collins notes there is a kind of category distinction necessary between the growth of sanctification as such and "entire sanctification," revealing that Wesley will often use images of maturation to describe the growth of sanctification but will shift into metaphors of death to talk about entire sanctification. "The first image, then, entails the beginning of sanctification, being born to God; the second image, reflective of the passage of time, entails an end to the carnal nature, a death to sin" (Collins, *The Scripture Way of Salvation*, 178).

80. Loyer, *God's Love Through the Spirit*, 184.

them to establish themselves *apart from* life in and with God. Rather, the Christian life—as we find it portrayed in the works of Calvin, Aquinas, and Wesley—is the life of sanctification in which one shares in the divine nature (2 Pet. 1:4) and bears the fruit of God's life in and through one's own.

In each of these figures, three very different kinds of theologians, we discover that the developmental maturation of the Christian (a life increasing to perfection) is never excised from salvation. Grace is not inert in the believer. The Spirit is at work. While not emphasized equally in this chapter, all three articulate a vision of love as essential to the growth of the Christian. Likewise, for each it is for a life *with God*, with him as our end, that the Christian life is cultivated and fulfilled. This is the vision of holiness that we are seeking to reinvest into a doctrine of sanctification. Furthermore, as we saw in the prior two chapters, this gets to the core of the scriptural vision of holiness. Holiness is never understood apart from God's presence and action, and in each of these thinkers we see the unique features of supernatural formation based on the presence and activity of God.

Summary

Christian doctrines are put to various kinds of work, and attending to the Christian tradition is essential for us to discern a doctrine's proper function. Through considering how John Calvin, Thomas Aquinas, and John Wesley portray sanctification, we attend to their instincts and emphases in order to discern aspects of how sanctification functions within their thought. Calvin's "double grace" teaching (*duplex gratia*) stresses the importance of holding together what Scripture presents as the unified work of salvation in the Son. Salvation is a singular, twofold reality. Aquinas's account of virtue formation emphasizes that the soul's perfection is grounded not in natural virtue habituation but in God's *super*natural work that perfects nature. The infusion of virtue and the work of the Spirit is the grace that transforms. Wesley's practical divinity links creaturely holiness with the perfection of love; Christian holiness is not for its own sake but rather for sharing God's life, which ever pours out toward others. Each of these elements from Calvin, Aquinas, and Wesley is accentuated in our account of sanctification as *life in the presence of God for the presence of God.*

DOXOLOGICAL INTERLUDE

Anonymous, *Meal at the House of Zacchaeus, the Tax-Collector (Luke 19:1–10)*

> Jesus entered Jericho and was passing through. A man was there named Zacchaeus, who was a chief tax collector and wealthy. He wanted to see who Jesus was, but because he was short he could not see over the crowd. So he ran ahead and climbed a sycamore-fig tree to see him, since Jesus was coming that way. When Jesus came to the tree, he looked up and said to him, "Zacchaeus, come down immediately. I must stay at your home today." So he came down at once and welcomed him gladly into his home. All the people saw this and began to mutter, "He has entered the home of a sinner to stay." But Zacchaeus stood up and said to the Lord, "Look, Lord! I give half of my possessions to the poor, and if I have cheated anybody out of anything, I will restore it fourfold." Jesus said to him, "Today salvation has come to this home, because he is also a son of Abraham. For the Son of Man came to seek and to save the lost."
>
> Luke 19:1–10 (authors' translation)[1]

Invitation

This fifteenth-century Bible illustration shifts our focus from the climbing of the tree to the *hospitality* of Zacchaeus. The scene at the tree is indeed dramatic, but the real drama happens in Zacchaeus's home (see note on translation below). The cultural norm for his hospitality was table fellowship, and we understandably long for details about their interaction—what did Jesus say and do? But instead, the story simply invites us to contemplate the setting. A home. A table. Conversation. Give-and-take. The presence of God amid all the mundane things of Zacchaeus's home, perhaps even the money ledgers that made him despised by his neighbors (that "sinner").

1. Some English translations give the impression that Jesus's entire interaction with Zacchaeus was at the base of the tree, and we are thus led to imagine his surprising and dramatic declaration happening on the spot. However, several textual features of the story strongly suggest a different picture. We bring these out with our translation. (1) Zacchaeus "received" Jesus into his home (v. 6), and (2) the crowd grumbled that Jesus "entered" (v. 6). Luke uses the same word for "enter" in verse 1 to indicate Jesus coming into Jericho. It's a subtle touch linking the two events, the first into the city and the second into Zacchaeus's home. (3) Zacchaeus "stood" (v. 7), which makes little sense apart from a shared meal that was the cultural expectation for his hospitality. (4) "Home" (*oikos*) is the object of Jesus's sweeping declaration of salvation in verse 9, and the same word appears in verse 7 and verse 8. The reference to home makes no sense if the interaction occurs entirely at the foot of the tree. Thus, the conjunction of verse 8 (*de*) should not be read as an indication of a sudden turnaround by Zacchaeus but as a cue that highlights the contrast between the crowd's estimation of Zacchaeus in the previous verse ("sinner") and his declaration in the present verse, which Jesus affirms in the following verse ("he is also a son of Abraham").

In Jesus's religious culture, "sinner" is the way you name those who don't conform to the standards of uprightness—not gentiles *but your fellow Jews*. Sex workers are sinners. Alcoholics are sinners. Adulterous women are sinners. Tax collectors like Zacchaeus are sinners, and the social norms are *clear* about associating with them. You don't darken the doors of their home, much less share a meal. And yet Jesus doesn't merely accept an invitation but *invites himself* to Zacchaeus's home. No misperceptions are allowed about his intentions: This is where Jesus wants to be. Whatever prompted Zacchaeus's dramatic course correction (the story can be read several ways), Luke's Gospel holds our attention on the intimate, relational setting in which it occurred. A home. A table. The give-and-take that Jesus initiates.

Prayerfully hold the story in mind and consider how the presence of Jesus has ignited course corrections in your life. A new priority? A new direction? A new perception? A new posture toward others? Allow the realities of your life to show up in your prayer, and open your heart to the Lord to present yourself to him in the truth.[2] Did God use a person? An experience? An inner awakening? A fresh reading of Scripture? God can use them all *and more* to invite reversals from death *to life*, darkness *to light*, distance from God *to life in God's holying presence*. Invite the Spirit to illumine how God is *even now* graciously igniting reversals. What could these mean for your life with God and others?

Notes

2. We are loosely following a form of prayer known as examination. This form of prayer takes the realities of one's life and considers them with God in the presence of God. For more on this, see Strobel and Coe, *Where Prayer Becomes Real*, 141–54.

CHAPTER FOUR

Doctrinal Construction

Therefore, my beloved, as you have always obeyed, so now, not only as in my presence but much more in my absence, work out your own salvation with fear and trembling, for it is God who works in you, both to will and to work for his good pleasure.

Philippians 2:12–13

The circle of God's repleteness, the whole and integrated fellowship that he is as Father, Son and Spirit, is not a closed circle. In its very completeness, it is a life-giving movement, bestowing, guarding, healing, restoring and perfecting the life of what is not God, as its lordly creator and preserver.

John Webster[1]

OUR WORK THUS FAR—focusing on the creed, attending to biblical material, and comparing select soteriologies—reveals a central impulse of sanctification. Christian teaching about life with God should first and foremost attend to God's act to give himself to his creatures, calling us into his life to reorder our lives around himself.[2] Salvation is most fundamentally

1. Webster, "The Holiness and Love of God," 254.

2. Donald Bloesch writes, "The Holy, for Evangelicals, is not a place or object, but a Person. It is not sacramental substance but personal presence that is the primary medium of

about receiving Christ by the Spirit, and this is just as true for sanctification as it is for justification. A full account of sanctification, therefore, must speak of being holy as receiving Christ by the Spirit for life with Christ by the Spirit. Reducing sanctification to morality, spiritual growth, or spiritual practices fails to attend to the nature and ends of holiness, within which morality, growth, and practice find their proper mooring. Put differently, if our temptation with justification is to talk about righteousness and imputation in a way that seems mechanistic—replacing the self-giving of God in Christ with sterile accounts of ledger balancing—our temptation with sanctification is to shift away from God's self-giving in Christ and the Spirit to talk about morality.

As we unfold our doctrine of sanctification in this chapter, we emphasize three things. A doctrine of sanctification, first, focuses on the work of the Son and the Spirit to sanctify. It is ever mindful of sanctification's trinitarian character and does not focus primarily on its relation to other soteriological loci (e.g., how sanctification relates to justification). Therefore, second, it addresses what it means to be made holy in Christ and to be formed into that holiness by the Spirit (what are often called the "definitive" and "progressive" aspects of sanctification, respectively). Third, the whole life of a believer is then understood *within and for life with God.* It is tempting in constructing a doctrine of sanctification to move too quickly past the first two emphases to focus on the third. This unmoors sanctification from God's life, such that practical guidance overwhelms the doctrinal content. When this happens, the moral, spiritual, social, and ecclesial life of a Christian is often developed apart from the biblical construct of holiness, replaced by natural and pragmatic constructs alien to life in the Spirit.

In what follows we develop these three emphases in turn. But first we consider doctrinal categories in general and show how these help give shape to a doctrine of sanctification.

the Holy" ("Evangelical Spirituality," 169). Or, as he states elsewhere, "In biblical theology the Holy is none other than the presence of the living God who encounters us in Jesus Christ. The profane or the secular lies under the judgment of the Holy because of the sinful rebellion of the creature. Even the religious life of humanity stands under the judgment and censure of the Holy. The preaching of the Word and the sacramental acts of the church can be a vehicle of the Holy, but they themselves must never be equated with the Holy" (Bloesch, *The Crisis of Piety*, 46). Likewise, "the holy is revealed through personal encounter" (Bloesch, "Evangelical Spirituality," 170).

A *Doctrine* of Sanctification

Far too commonly, doctrines are treated as if they are simply categories of information. A good doctrine of sin, in this sense, would affirm true things about what sin is while naming potential errors in articulating sin falsely. But this would make correct information the goal of theology, rather than recognizing that theology is, to borrow a historic definition, "the doctrine of living for God through Christ."[3] On this more robust notion of theology, a good articulation of sin should name the truth about sin and potential errors *but also* cause the reader to repent. A *doctrine* of sin should cut to the heart and expose the truth of a life before the face of God. The goal is not getting a good score on a theology exam but walking faithfully with your God.

When we articulate a doctrine of *sanctification*, then, we are not simply making sure we understand Scripture, which of course is fundamental. Rather, we seek to discern the truth of Scripture in order to know the holiness that God calls us into; we know the truth so that we can live with him who is the way, the truth, and the life (John 14:6). Articulating doctrine is more than naming true things; it is establishing an architecture of mind and heart, helping to understand the revelation of God in Scripture and what it means to walk by faith in this present evil age.[4]

Speaking of sanctification faithfully requires that we have our minds reshaped according to the contours of the truth. It requires a renewal of mind around Christ. This renewal of mind helps avoid the temptation to reduce sanctification to morality by ingraining *a continual focus first on God in his gracious self-giving*, and only then moving to the calling entailed by God's presence.

This twofold move may appear at first to involve a tension. It is the doctrine of sanctification's foremost responsibility to hold these together without reduction. We have already articulated the biblical emphasis on the former; the focus on God's self-giving is revealed throughout Scripture, but perhaps most obviously in the Sabbath, tabernacle, temple, and festal

3. This is the definition Petrus van Mastricht uses for this theoretical-practical theology (*Theoretical-Practical Theology*, 1:64).

4. Along these lines, Michael Allen rightly emphasizes the proper focus that a doctrine of sanctification should order our minds and hearts to: "the transforming presence of the glorious God of the gospel" (*Sanctification*, 183).

calendar. The logic of Sabbath, in particular, emphasizes that God *is the one who sanctifies* (Exod. 31:13). Sanctification is never a personal project of moral, spiritual, or social development; it is about God's triune self-giving that necessarily entails *the creature's relationally reciprocal response*. This latter aspect of sanctification requires us to pay careful attention to the actions that receiving God's self-giving invites. It is true that sanctification is not our personal project, and we cannot generate, advance, or govern it ourselves, but we are *not passive* in the endeavor of holiness, as we have already emphasized.[5] To be called into God's life is to be reordered by that life; the life of God is not ineffective but brings order out of disorder. The reordering of lives by God (their *holying* by God), however, does not dismiss creatures but requires their relationally responsive participation with the Holy One.

When we focus on the Son and the Spirit and their action to save, we immediately feel the weight of the apparent tension between what is already true (i.e., we are made holy in Christ Jesus) and what is yet to be completed by the Spirit (i.e., perfection). These two emphases of sanctification have often been felt in the tradition, and reductions to one side or the other are not difficult to find.[6] Some Protestants developed the concepts of definitive and progressive sanctification in an attempt to navigate these two poles by advancing two aspects of a whole.[7] Definitive sanctification, by

5. There are aspects of being passive, however, that need to be clarified. Our focus here is the whole of sanctification, as not merely being made holy but living a life of holiness. The Reformed have at times sought to distinguish between passive and active aspects of conversion, and with it, sanctification. Francis Turretin, for instance, distinguishes between "habitual or passive conversion" and "actual or active conversion." Turretin writes, "Through the former, man is renovated and converted by God. Through the latter, man, renovated and converted by God, turns himself to God and performs acts" (*Institutes of Elenctic Theology*, 2:522).

6. David G. Peterson writes, "Sanctification is commonly regarded as a process of moral and spiritual transformation following conversion. In the New Testament, however, it primarily refers to God's way of taking possession of us in Christ, setting us apart to belong to him and to fulfil his purpose for us. Sanctification certainly has present and ongoing effects, but when the verb 'to sanctify' (Gk. *hagiazein*) and the noun 'sanctification' (Gk. *hagiasmos*) are used, the emphasis is regularly on the saving work of God in Christ, applied to believers through the ministry of the Holy Spirit" (*Possessed by God*, 27).

7. As far as we are aware, the first person to use this specific language was John Murray. He writes,

> When we speak of sanctification we generally think of it as that process by which the believer is gradually transformed in heart, mind, will, and conduct, and conformed more and more to the will of God and to the image of Christ, until at death the

focusing on sanctification as something offered in Christ, asserts the truth that God is the one who sanctifies. When the New Testament addresses sanctification, it is often a completed, past-tense reality, and this is what the definitive pole sought to secure. Progressive sanctification, on the other hand, named the developmental call of sanctification. The progressive was not meant to be set against the definitive but was thought to advance it.

To be sure, there is something right and helpful about these terms and the realities they indicate. But distinguishing between definite and progressive sanctification can lose sight of Christ. Instead of talking about Christ and the Spirit, the terms lead us to talk about a state of sanctification and a progressive development of that *state*.[8] That shifts attention dramatically away from God the Holy One and his holying proximity—the proper focus of sanctification. Holiness in creation is God's personal presence, such that being made holy is being called into God's presence for the sake of life with him. Thus, the doctrine of sanctification needs to order us to God in Christ by the Spirit, not merely construct true statements about the state of sanctification. Likewise, when focusing on the development (or progression) of holiness, we need to maintain the locational dynamics of *proximity to God* that are woven through the Old and New Testaments.

These are the potential downsides of doctrinal constructs such as definitive and progressive sanctification. The distinction does name true and helpful things, and it can be useful in explaining what is going on doctrinally in salvation. However, clarifying the issue this way can actually muddy what the doctrine of sanctification seeks to make clear—namely, what it means to both receive God's life in Christ by the Spirit and to have that

---

> disembodied spirit is made perfect in holiness, and at the resurrection his body likewise will be conformed to the likeness of the body of Christ's glory. It is biblical to apply the term "sanctification" to this process of transformation and conformation. But it is a fact too frequently overlooked that in the New Testament the most characteristic terms that refer to sanctification are used, not of a process, but of a once-for-all definitive act. (Murray, *Collected Writings of John Murray*, 2:277)

8. J. C. Ryle, in his classic text on sanctification, recognizes this error and writes, "I have no desire to make an idol of holiness. I do not wish to dethrone Christ, and put holiness in his place" (*Holiness*, 64). He goes on to explain this more methodologically: "You must *begin with Christ*. You will do just nothing at all, and make no progress till you feel your sin and weakness, and flee to him. He is the root and beginning of all holiness, and the way to be holy is to come to him by faith and be joined to him. Christ is not wisdom and righteousness only to his people, but sanctification also" (67).

life reorder one's own. One could easily use definitive sanctification as a place to store biblical passages that talk about God's action to sanctify while still advancing pragmatic and self-centered accounts of progressive sanctification, decoupling Christian practice from Christ's presence by the Spirit. Doctrine must do more than name the truth; it must *shepherd us into the truth*, constructing a frame of mind and heart conformed to God's presence in Christ.

There are two major errors that emerge when sanctification becomes unmoored from God's action by the Son and the Spirit. The first, which shows up in various ways in the tradition, and most clearly in radical forms of Lutheran and Reformed thought, is to focus so fully on the fact that *God is the one who sanctifies* that the idea of holiness as a relationally responsive calling is lost. There is no calling of sanctification, only a declaration of God's act. The other error is often more seductive because it is closer to the truth. By focusing on the calling *to be more holy*, the completed nature of sanctification and its location in and through Christ and the Spirit ends up having no role. Practical discussions of Christian ethics, transformation, and individual and social morality are advanced without being grounded in God's continued action in Christ by the Spirit to sanctify. Sanctification, in this sense, becomes the bucket in which Christians locate discussions about growth, a growth that often differs little from general morality or personal development.

With patient attention to the biblical witness, we see how these two realities are united in Christ and known in the Spirit as a person's whole self is restored and renewed by sharing in God's life—ever more deeply and responsively. We are working hard throughout this volume to emphasize that all soteriological loci find their primary theological location in the *action of the Son and the Spirit*. This means remembering that our constant temptation is to turn away from the Son and the Spirit to something else, divorcing their benefits from their continued action and mission. This temptation shows up most practically in the doctrine of sanctification, which, unlike election, regeneration, or justification, is often directly associated with matters of Christian living. These practical matters, of course, are deeply significant, but they can easily come to *replace* sanctification rather than be articulated from within a doctrine of sanctification.

Therefore, we focus first on sanctification by Son and Spirit. We will then advance this material to consider how our biblical and historical discussions help govern a constructive proposal. To close the chapter, we turn to how sanctification needs to order and govern the practical matters that fall in its purview.

Sanctification by Son and Spirit

As the biblical material of chapter 2 highlighted, the spatial aspect of holiness points ahead to its fulfillment: God present in Christ through the incarnation as the personal presence of God able to be accessed through the Spirit (Eph. 2:18).[9] God and his presence are really known here—in *this one*. To see Christ truly is to see the Father (John 14:9), precisely because Jesus is "the image of the invisible God" (Col. 1:15). The spatial construct of Eden, tabernacle, and temple has been advanced in the humanity of the Son so that the presence of God can be known personally, just as one stands face-to-face with another. The face-to-face knowing of God that Moses experienced is actually available to the regenerate in greater and deeper ways than it was before Christ (2 Cor. 3:17–4:6). Furthermore, God's presence established in Christ is not a past-tense reality, focused only on the completed work of Christ.[10] While the Son really did establish a new holy place within humanity through the incarnation, that wasn't a short-lived reality. (See the sidebar "Jesus Takes Our Humanity into the Heart of God," p. 110.) He has brought that humanity beyond the veil to the right hand of God (Heb. 6:19). Christ's present reign is just as much a feature of sanctification as his earthly ministry. Jesus is the one who sanctifies, as he is our sanctification, making it available through union with himself by the Spirit of holiness. Unlike Moses, Jesus is no mere mediator but is the presence of God *himself*. To be present to God is to know the personal

9. Aaron Riches notes, "The result of the Chalcedonian formulation was to realize very clearly that 'the proximity of the divine' does not threaten or compromise 'the integrity of the human,' but in fact establishes it" (*Ecce Homo*, 61).

10. Our emphasis is similar to Allen's discussion of "evangelical holiness" when he states,

> My suggestion is that an evangelical account of the holy requires a steady focus upon the holiness of God, that is, the holiness of the inner triune life, so that its communication to creatures can be registered as truly gracious, that is, miraculous and free. In addition, to appreciate the christological context of the holy and of the ethical life requires attention not only to the past tense of the gospel but also to its present and future tenses, which are the continuing ministry of the risen Christ by his Spirit and its promised completion in glory. (Allen, *Sanctification*, 23)

Jesus Takes Our Humanity into the Heart of God

Jesus takes our human nature—yours and mine—to the very heart of God, and he speaks in a human voice. . . . He doesn't let go of us and he doesn't lose sight of us when we seek to lock ourselves up in the dark. Jesus hears all the words we speak—words of pain and protest and rage and violence. He hears them and he takes them, and in the presence of God the Father he says, "This is the humanity I have brought home. It's not a pretty sight; it's not edifying and impressive and heroic, it's just real: real and needy and confused, and here it is (this complicated humanity) brought home to heaven, dropped into the burning heart of God—for healing and for transformation." . . . Jesus picks up the cry of the hungry and the forgotten. He hears the human beings that nobody else hears. And he calls to us to say, "*You* listen too."[a]

a. Rowan Williams, *Being Human*, 107, 108, 110.

presence and revelation of God, to see him and share in his glory, and to be called into his holiness through the means he provides (John 17:22).

Following the patterns in the Old Testament concerning divine presence and holiness, one's holiness in Christ is both completed (i.e., definitive) and entails a deepening relational responsiveness to God (i.e., it is also progressive). The typologies of the tabernacle point forward to the realities of life in union with Christ by the Spirit. An object, for instance, can become *more* holy depending on its location in the tabernacle. A person's holiness, however, requires both *a state* (location) and *a way*. The *state* is a person's union with Christ—their deepest and most fundamental location—and the *way* is a life of relational responsiveness to the Spirit by which the holying of God *deepens*. *The way*, of course, is Jesus himself (John 14:6).

Too often, unfortunately, the details of the Old Testament blind us to the broader picture they paint, so we can miss the import that books such as Leviticus and Exodus have for understanding sanctification. Michael Morales, in contrast, writes, "The first half [of Leviticus] deals primarily with the approach to God through blood, while the second half is taken up with life in God's Presence through increasing holiness, the overall goal being fellowship and union with God."[11] It is through Christ's blood that we draw near for the sake of fellowship and union with God. In the light of the incarnation, we can discern that Leviticus points to Christ as the true fulfillment of sanctification and the true path to drawing near. Along these lines, Morales affirms that "it is preferable to discern holiness not as an end in itself but rather as a means to an end, which is the real theme, the abundant life of joy with God in the house of God."[12] Hebrews picks up on these themes, and we discover that Jesus inhabits the true tabernacle (not made with hands) so that we can draw near to God through his self-giving love. Christ is the ground and foundation of our life in God (Col. 3:3), and because of this, the believer can be transformed and purified as they draw near to him and abide in his presence.

The Two Poles of Sanctification

The unity of Christ helps us recall the unity of salvation, as we saw with Calvin. Advancing this emphasis, we can also say that the unity of the Son and the Spirit—their oneness in essence and action—refuses a separation between them in soteriology. In this sense, a doctrine of sanctification must reflect this unity of Son *and* Spirit and must not emphasize one at the expense of the other. Nonetheless, in this era of redemption we may feel a tension between the two emphases of how we know and experience sanctification.

The first emphasis is that Christ is our sanctification (1 Cor. 1:30). This focus on Christ must not be lost when attention shifts to the work of the Spirit, as if the third article of the creed were somehow divorced from the second article's emphasis on Christ's present rule and reign. Attending to the Spirit continues to narrow our vision on the fact that Christ sanctifies himself for our sake so that we might be sanctified in him who is true (John 17:19).[13] However else we talk about the Spirit at work in the believer, it is

11. Morales, *Who Shall Ascend the Mountain of the Lord?*, 29–30.

12. Morales, *Who Shall Ascend the Mountain of the Lord?*, 30.

13. Picking up on the theme that Jesus is the truth, Augustine notes that in John we hear that the truth will deliver us and that if the Son sets us free, then we will be free indeed (John 8:32, 36). Likewise, in John 17 we are told that we are sanctified in the truth and that Christ has sanctified himself for our sakes. Christ, who is "the way, and the truth, and the life" (John 14:6), is the space of our sanctification. Augustine declares, "The Father does indeed sanctify

never a work removed from the work of Christ. By the Spirit we grow up "into him who is the head" (Eph. 4:15), so that "Christ is formed in you" (Gal. 4:19). To be in Christ is to share in his sonship with the Father as "sons" of God (Gal. 4:4–7), so that Christians are called to the life of sons in the *Spirit of the Son*.[14] To be in the Son is to be a part of his body, and there is "one body and one Spirit" such that, to round out the trinitarian emphasis, there is "one God and Father of all, who is over all and through all and in all" (Eph. 4:4, 6). Attention to the action of Son and Spirit in the economy of salvation is fundamental for discerning how Old Testament themes of holiness and divine presence are fulfilled.

It is by this united work of the Son and the Spirit that we are drawn into the holying presence of God. In the Spirit we stand before Christ as those who know "the light of the knowledge of the glory of God in the face of Jesus Christ" (2 Cor. 4:6). This face-to-face presence with God in Christ is known now by faith (1 Cor. 13:12), but it will be known in full when "we shall be like him, because we shall see him as he is" (1 John 3:2). In and through the Spirit, we are to hold "fast to the Head, from whom the whole body, nourished and knit together through its joints and ligaments, *grows with a growth that is from God*" (Col. 2:19). But likewise, Christ is giving us *his* Spirit, who pours forth love into our hearts (Rom. 5:5). We have both a new foundation (the Spirit of love in our hearts) and a new telos (Christ as the image of the invisible God, in whom we access the Father, Col. 1:15; Eph. 2:18). We do not merely have a new path set before our feet, but we have *a person* before whom we stand face-to-face, and it is his Spirit in our souls that binds us to his life and empowers us to be conformed into his likeness.[15] We are already at home with God even as we pilgrimage toward the fulfillment of our at-home-ness.

---

in truth—that is, in his Word, in his Only-Begotten—his heirs and coheirs" (*Homilies on the Gospel of John 41–124*, 433–34).

14. Christopher Holmes writes, "In sum, we are baptized into Christ by the Spirit, and it is the Spirit who clothes us not with the Spirit's self but with Christ. The Spirit does not work by the Spirit's self but rather in the name of another, so that we too may cry out to his Father who is now, by virtue of our being adopted in his Son, *our* Father. Such knowledge is of course too deep to comprehend, and so the way in which it works its way into us is by 'faith working through love' (5.6)" ("The Perfecting God," 85).

15. Herman Bavinck rightly avers, "For our spiritual life is to be in conformity with God's life, an imprint of his life, which must be the archetype, the example, for ours. God's life consists in that perfect activity of God through which he perfectly knows and loves himself

Unlike Moses at the burning bush, afraid to look at God, we are sanctified in Christ to "set [our] minds on things that are above" and are formed before the face of Jesus Christ (Col. 3:2; see 2 Cor. 4:6). Our focal points thus far continue to form our doctrine of sanctification: First, *increasing* holiness is not synonymous with acquired virtue formation. Instead, with Calvin, Aquinas, and Wesley we must continually start with God's action *for us* and *within us* to reimagine virtue formation around his act. Second, in light of this, we must consider the nature of the internal work of the Spirit in the soul, which helps us understand how supernatural virtue formation differs from its natural counterpart. Third, the telos of Christian supernatural formation is not the formation of the person but is their *abiding in Christ*. God is the proper end of all Christian action, reordering all other ends around himself.

Our emphasis thus far has been on God's act to sanctify rather than on our relationally responsive action, and this emphasis follows the biblical witness as we discern it. We are thus led to do exactly what Scripture does: focus on the completed nature of sanctification *in Christ*. But if we stopped here we would fall short of a complete doctrine of sanctification. Stopping here would be seeking to tear Son and Spirit apart, separating the sanctification secured in Christ from his ongoing work in and through the Spirit. Christ is our sanctification, and in him we receive *his* Spirit, such that his Spirit descends into our "inner being," working with power to strengthen us (Eph. 3:16). The Spirit groans and prays for believers, searching their hearts according to the truth (Rom. 8:26–27). As the Spirit of holiness, the Spirit sanctifies believers for life in Christ, who is their sanctification, *so that they can draw near* to the Father in Christ and through Christ (Eph. 2:18). We can assert that, by the Son and the Spirit, God will "sanctify you completely," because he "who calls you is faithful; he will surely do it" (1 Thess. 5:23–24).

The Spirit is *the power and presence of God in the soul*, such that in receiving the Spirit one receives the Father and the Son. This Spirit who pours forth love into the soul is the Spirit of God's holiness (Rom. 5:5), ushering the Christian into the presence of God to stand face-to-face with him in Christ (2 Cor. 3:18). Sanctification is about the Son and the Spirit

---

and lives according to his holy nature in blessedness." Furthermore, "our spiritual life is similar to and an image of that blessedness" (*Reformed Ethics*, 1:263).

because sanctification is about *presence and access*. The Spirit's work of empowerment is always tied to Christ and to embracing Christ as life. For instance, in Ephesians 3, the Spirit works with power in our inner being "so that Christ may dwell in your hearts through faith," which is what leads to being rooted and grounded in love (Eph. 3:17). In Romans 5 the focus is on receiving the access given by grace for the sake of persevering in difficulty, precisely because the Spirit's work is a work of love, which is why our hope in Christ does not put us to shame. When focused on the Son and the Spirit, a doctrine of sanctification has a proper theological ground to address progressive sanctification.

In attending to the Son and the Spirit, a doctrine of sanctification must navigate the tension between what Christ has accomplished and what the Spirit applies. On one hand, to focus solely on Christ without the Spirit would be to name the space of sanctification without the way of its deepening and intensification. On the other hand, to focus solely on the Spirit apart from Christ is to focus on our formation without the grounding in Christ's accomplished and present work. Sanctification, as a doctrine, must hold together these poles without reduction and without gravitating away from the tension. *We are sanctified for God in Christ, to be shaped increasingly into his likeness and perfection by the Spirit.* Sanctification is life in the presence of God for the presence of God. The Spirit pours forth love into our hearts, but love is never abstracted away from a personal union with another. In fact, love "binds everything together" (Col. 3:14), Paul asserts, such that God's love sent in the heart of the believer binds them to God in Christ so that they are truly one spirit with him (1 Cor. 6:17). As Wesley emphasized, the holiness known in Christ by the Spirit is always a holy love, because God has given himself in love to his own and has called them in love to himself.[16]

This is God's gracious movement of self-giving that calls us to relationally respond by receiving Christ and the Spirit and rebounding that grace

16. Bavinck writes,

> God's love does not remain outside us, stirring our feelings and moving them only from the outside; rather, he enters us: "So we have come to know and to believe the love that God has for us. God is love, and whoever abides in love abides in God, and God abides in him" (1 John 4:16). The Holy Spirit who comes to live in us is the Spirit of love (2 Tim. 1:7) and thus works in us mutual love, not as a fleeting mood or sentiment, but as a lasting principle of the heart, so that the person loves God above all with one's whole heart and strength. (*Reformed Ethics*, 1:354)

in our own self-giving response. (See the sidebar "On Grace," p. 116.) To receive the self-giving of another—to truly *receive it*—is to respond by offering yourself. The proper response to grace in faith is to offer yourself to God. This relationally reciprocal response is always in the Spirit, which is what it means for the Spirit to grant us freedom; freedom is never merely freedom *from* things but is freedom *to another*. Furthermore, our action in supernatural formation is never merely *reactive*. Rather, in giving himself to his own, God's presence and action become the relational context for our presence and responsive action—the truest and most real *relational fellowship*. This is exactly what the doctrine of sanctification secures.

As the passages overviewed emphasize, there is no growth in holiness that is not growth *from God* (Col. 2:19). We do not generate supernatural growth. We are purified as we come into contact with the purifying fire. Proximity to the Holy Father is secured by union with Christ, which transforms us as we are formed by the Spirit within us in relationally responsive *withness*. This establishes the contours of Christian growth and transformation and affirms this growth as *within the agency of the Spirit*. Christians bear fruit as they abide in Jesus as branches abide in the vine (John 15:1–5). Likewise, to walk in the Spirit and to be led by the Spirit are to bear the fruit of the Spirit (Gal. 5:16–25). The Spirit who pours forth love into the soul offers the love that is the true fruit of the Spirit's life—a love that refracts through a soul as "joy, peace, patience, kindness, goodness, faithfulness, gentleness, self-control" (Gal. 5:22–23). As with sanctification as a whole, these virtues are not the end but are *the fruit* of the end. Even self-control, importantly, is not the fruit of a person's ability to wield fortitude and habituate a character. Rather, *self*-control is a fruit of the Spirit—a fruit of another—and as a *spiritual* fruit is a formation in and through love (Eph. 4:16).

The focus on redemption accomplished and applied helps explain why the biblical language can *seem* paradoxical.[17] We are told that we have died with Christ *and* are commanded to consider ourselves dead with Christ (Rom. 6:8, 11). We are told that we are adopted *and* that we await our adoption (Rom. 8:15, 23). We are told that we have put off the old *and* are commanded to put off the old (Col. 3:9; Eph. 4:22). This dynamic is simply naming what *has been accomplished* (the indicative) and the *calling*

17. See Sanders, "Wesleyan View."

On Grace

In the New Testament, *grace* (Latin *gratia*; Greek *charis*) appears 155 times and mainly in the writings of Paul. Depending on the context, it can mean "favor," "beauty," "thankfulness," "gratitude," "delight," "goodwill," "benefit," or "gift." "Gift" is what Paul most often names with the word *grace* (*charis*): the gifts that are given by churches, gifts from the Holy Spirit, and what God has done in time and space for us through his Messiah, Jesus. *The Christ-gift is grace* (e.g., Rom. 3:23b–24).

When we employ the word *grace* in this book to describe the realities of the Christian life and God's saving economy, we hold four theological and hermeneutical convictions:

1. *Grace* specifically names the Christ-gift and the related effects of the Christ-gift when received. What God freely does in time and space to heal and restore the created order we call *grace*. This includes the incarnation of the Son and the sending of the Spirit as well as their effects, such as the illumination of sin, forgiveness, justification, calling, and so on. The latter are *graces* in the sense that they relate directly to or orbit the Christ-gift in God's saving economy.

to a particular way inherent in applying this to the life of a believer (the imperative). Importantly, however, we do not leave behind the indicative on our way to the imperative, but we hear the command in light of what is now true of us in Christ Jesus. What Christ has accomplished for us specifies how we hear the command upon us, and it further specifies where we go to bear the fruit of that command—namely, Christ himself. The indicative-imperative paradigm is not a call to work hard to become what is already true of you, as it is sometimes articulated. Rather, it is a call to *abide in the one who defines you*. This is walking in the Spirit (Gal. 5:16). It is the Spirit who brings us to Christ, illumines the truth of who he is and who he is *for our sake*, and empowers us to embrace his life. This presence of the Spirit is what Scripture calls the *spiritual* life.

2. *Grace* is not a thing, ever. Affirming that "God gives his grace" to us does not mean that some *thing* moves from God to us but rather that *God freely acts* toward us in such a way that our reality changes. "God gives his grace" can theologically mean God the Father *sends* his Son, or that God *forgives* sin, or that God *makes righteous*, or that God *sends* his Spirit, or that God *illumines* sin, or that God *heals*, or that God *sanctifies*, and so forth. Grace is not a thing but rather *theological shorthand* for God's free actions that enable and invite our response.
3. *Grace* as the Christ-gift or its related effects is always radically underserved and awakens our relational response and participation. We can never earn or merit God's grace, but that does not mean that God's grace does not enable and invite our relational responses. Perhaps most simply, "Here I am, Lord."
4. *Grace as God's undeserved gift that awakens our relational response* is woven throughout the entire arc of Scripture even when the word *grace* and its cognates are absent (e.g., the creation of reality, the calling of Abraham, the exodus, and so forth).[a]

a. See Barclay, *Paul and the Power of Grace*; Barclay, *Paul and the Gift*; Barclay, "Grace and the Transformation of Agency in Christ"; Eilers, "The Grammar of Grace"; Eilers et al., *The Grammar of Grace*; Eilers and Strobel, *Sanctified by Grace*; Oden, *The Transforming Power of Grace*; Whitley, *The Doctrine of Grace*.

Sanctified for Spiritual Life

As the Spirit illumines Christ, awakening faith and hope in the soul, the Christian is ordered to and united to God in Christ by the Spirit through that faith. The fruit of this union is love, which is the visible manifestation of the Spirit's work to pour forth love into the soul and to meet the Christian in forgiveness, mercy, and grace (Luke 7:47). The redeemed life bears witness to God's action to save and manifests the fruit of that salvation in and through love. This is not a perfect life but one that knows God's power in and through our human weakness (2 Cor. 12:9). As with creation, where the Spirit hovered over the chaos to bring order out of disorder, the Spirit now dwells in our hearts to bring order to lives wrought in disorder. The realm of the Spirit's presence is centered on the presence of God in Christ; this field of action is truth, love, and holiness and is where the spiritual life is given its shape.

As we saw with our biblical exposition, God sanctifies forks, bowls, altars, and even unbelievers at times, so we have to be more specific about the sanctification of a *believer*. Furthermore, it is one thing for a bowl to be sanctified for God's presence and action in the temple, but another entirely for a Christian to be sanctified in Christ by the Holy Spirit. In this latter case, *a person* is sanctified as they are caught up in God's self-giving to stand face-to-face with God in Christ Jesus by the Spirit (1 Cor. 13:12; 2 Cor. 4:6). In eternity, Christians will be like him because they will see him as he is, standing face-to-face with the God of love who offers himself to them (1 John 3:2). This sanctification of persons reveals that God is doing more than simply ushering objects into the space of his action; God is calling persons to *partake in God's life* (2 Pet. 1:4). To be caught up in God's action to sanctify is to know *as you have been known* and to draw near to God in the truth of who he is in light of the truth of who you are. This sanctification does not leave behind any aspect of the person—body, soul, spirit—and calls the whole of one's self to him. (See the sidebar "Restoration of Our Whole Humanity.") It is this sanctification that requires a renewal of the mind (Rom. 12:2), the renovation of the will (Phil. 2:13), and the captivation of one's desires and affections in the Spirit (Gal. 5:17).

The field of the Spirit's action, in other words, reveals that God sanctifies a person only *as a person* and does not bypass or undermine their humanity in doing so.[18] Grace really does perfect nature, but what fallen nature cannot fathom is that the center (or ground, to use a different image) of one's self is outside oneself. To borrow Søren Kierkegaard's imagery, a self always stands before another that serves as its ground—either a mutable other that leads to the self's *dis*integration or an immutable other that leads to one's integration in love.[19] The true end of human beings is to find themselves hidden with Christ in God in such a way that they are *integrated into who they are in Christ by the Spirit*. Attempting to establish oneself is the path

18. Jonathan Edwards articulates this kind of vision, writing explicitly, "Christianity is not destructive of humanity" (*Ethical Writings*, 254).

19. For a profound exposition of this theme, see Hefner, *Kierkegaard and the Changelessness of God*.

Restoration of Our Whole Humanity

Gregory of Nazianzus (329–90) responds here to the teaching of Apollinaris, who claimed that the person of Jesus did not have a rational soul (i.e., mind). On Apollinaris's view, where we should expect to find the human mind of Jesus we find instead the eternal divine Logos. This is a deeply problematic understanding of the incarnation, for reasons that Gregory and others were quick to refute, and the christological grammar was eventually voiced in the Creed of Chalcedon (451). Gregory's response mirrors the logic of Hebrews 2: To save our whole humanity, the Son of God became *like us* "in every respect" (v. 17). No aspect of our humanity is left aside in the person of Jesus, and this is a constitutive feature of Christian soteriology. No aspect of our humanity remains unsavable, unredeemable, or unhealable, because God *takes it all to himself.*

> If anyone has put his trust in him as a man without a human mind, he is really bereft of mind and quite unworthy of salvation. For that which God has not assumed, he has not healed; but that which is united to his Godhead, is also saved. If only half Adam fell then that which Christ assumed and saves may be half also; but if the whole of Adam fell, he must be united to the whole nature of him that was begotten, and so be saved as a whole. Let them not then begrudge us our complete salvation, or clothe the Savior only with bones and nerves and the portraiture of a man. . . . Keep then the whole man, and mingle Godhead therewith, that you may benefit me in my completeness.[a]

a. Gregory of Nazianzus, "Criticisms of Apollinarius," 123–24.

of death, but to discover oneself in Christ is the path to life. This is the proper end of being made in God's image for the sake of imaging God to the world. Before his face, by the Spirit, we can be captivated by the love of God that reorders our whole lives to him so that we bear witness to his truth, goodness, and beauty.

This vision of sanctification appears counterintuitive because the foundation of the self is found outside oneself and in another, as noted above, but the vision bears witness to the full range of biblical revelation, which reveals our true life in relation: *We are called to image another* (Gen. 1). We know freedom only within the sphere of the Spirit's redemptive action (2 Cor. 3:17). We lose our lives in order to find them, and we no longer live in ourselves; we live in and through Christ in us (Gal. 2:20). Human creatures are given the value of being able to receive God's self-giving in Son and Spirit to share in his life and glory to rebound it back to him.[20] This is often known as God's self-giving *exitus* for the sake of *reditus*—God pours forth his life and love, and we receive it and rebound it to his glory in response.[21] To be made in God's image, in other words, is not primarily a claim about our constitution as creatures (although it assumes this); rather, it is a claim about *our vocation to image God back to him and the world he has created*.[22] Being made in God's image reveals that any attempt to self-image is beneath our humanity and erodes our humanity. We are fully ourselves only when we image him in the truth. The life of sanctification, therefore, is one of bearing witness to him through his presence and action as we draw near to him in truth and love, walking with him and in him by the Spirit.[23]

20. Bavinck writes,

> The believer experiences the life of God himself: *from* the Father *through* the Son *in* the Spirit and, conversely, *in* the Spirit *through* the Son *to* the Father. The spiritual life is therefore a life of God (Eph. 4:18), a life that originates from God, is granted by grace, unites us with God, is worked in us immediately through the Holy Spirit, and has the spiritual life of God himself as model and example. The spiritual life of believers is a shadow, an impression of the most perfect life of God himself, so that it is said that they share in the divine nature (2 Pet. 1:4). (*Reformed Ethics*, 1:250)

21. This theme is found throughout the tradition. In contemporary ethics, Jennifer Herdt utilizes it as well, writing,

> As bearers of agency, human beings are capable of knowing and loving God, of participating as finite embodied creatures in the uncreated friendship of the divine life. And they are capable of activity glorifying God by knowing and loving, appreciating and caring for, all things as created and loved by God. In so doing, they give voice to all of creation's glorifying of God, thereby participating in the *reditus*, the response of creation to God. This, as Karl Barth puts it, involves "participation in the life of God in a human existence and action in which there is a representation and illustration of the glory of God Himself and its work." (*Assuming Responsibility*, 12)

22. We are following Ryan Peterson's important study, *The Imago Dei as Human Identity*.

23. Augustine is characteristically insightful as he reflects on Jesus as the way to the Father:

> But why did he have to say, *I am the way and the truth and the life*, since, once the way was known by which he was going, what remained was to know where he was going,

Importantly, while the spiritual life is never *merely* a moral life, it is never *less than* a life of moral formation.[24] Moralism is always a temptation for the Christian, because it is closest to the truth. Christians are called to walk in obedience to the truth. The difficulty is that doing so might actually become a way *not to abide*. Morality can serve as a way, not to draw near, but to try to placate God in and by the flesh (Gal. 3:3). Christians are called instead to the *spiritual* life, which is, asserts Herman Bavinck, "a life *from*, *through*, and *in* the Holy Spirit of God."[25] This is always a holistic calling to have the whole self ordered to God in Christ. Along with moralism, there is also a temptation to segment aspects of our self to secure God on our own terms, often arising through reductions such as rationalism or various kinds of emotionalism (making the intellect or the emotions what really matter). Instead, it is the *whole person*, seen as an integrated and organic unity, that must draw near to God in Christ Jesus to know God and to be known by him (Gal. 4:9). This reality is depicted in biblical anthropology as the heart, the abiding center of the person and the core integrated fountain of their life.

To be sanctified as a person, therefore, is to be caught up in God's movement to reveal himself as he offers himself in love to his creatures, so that they share in his life and know the flourishing that can only come from knowing Christ as our center. But to be called into God's presence in Christ by the Spirit is to stand before God *in another*. We don't stand before God in ourselves, any more than we pray in our own name rather than in the name of Jesus. We stand before God in Christ to know as we have been known, which means that we must draw near in order to abide according to the life we have been given. Importantly, to share in God's life is not a call to move to some deeper or unknown depths beyond what has been revealed. Rather, to share in God's life is to be adopted as his

if he wasn't going to the truth or going to the life? Therefore, he was going to himself by way of himself. We are going to him by way of him; or rather, both he and we are going to the Father. For elsewhere he also says of himself, *I am going to the Father* (Jn 16:10), and in this passage he says for our sake, *No one comes to the Father except through me* (Jn 14:6). And thus he is going through himself both to himself and to the Father, and we are going through him both to him and to the Father. (*Homilies on the Gospel of John 41–124*, 239)

24. See Bavinck, *Reformed Ethics*, 1:240–52.

25. Bavinck, *Reformed Ethics*, 1:244.

children, to know God as Father, and to participate in the Son's imaging of the Father. This gives a certain shape to sanctification: We *are sanctified* in Christ for a life of *continual sanctification* in Christ. Notice that after Paul articulates the adoption one knows in Christ (Gal. 4:4–7), he writes, "my little children, for whom I am again in the anguish of childbirth *until Christ is formed in you*!" (Gal. 4:19). In adoption, we are simultaneously in Christ and therefore sharers of his sonship with the Father, and we are also *increasingly having Christ formed in us*. This is sanctification accomplished and applied in Christ in and through the Spirit.

While there are many images of the spiritual life in Scripture, we will focus on *two* sets of images in order to explicate our vision of formation in Christ that centers on proximity to God. The first is family-oriented and includes adoption, sonship, marriage, and the household, all of which orient Christian formation after the pattern of Jesus and within the imaginative frame of family.[26] The second is dying and rising to life, also known as mortification and vivification. Mortification and vivification may not be familiar language in many circles today, so we should emphasize that this image set is irreducibly connected in Christ. He is the obedient Son of the Father who walked to his death and trusted his Father for resurrection. We too, as children of our heavenly Father, walk in ways of *mortification* and seek him for *vivification*—we put off the old and put on the new by grace alone. Bavinck rightly proclaims that imitating Jesus "is the only form of the spiritual life. Therefore, our lives can be directed *to* Christ only when

26. Biblically, the term εὐσέβεια (*eusebeia*), particularly in the Pastoral Epistles, has similar contours to what we are suggesting here. Typically translated "godliness," *eusebeia* is a term related to household formation. *Eusebeia* refers to knowing God as Father in Christ Jesus by the Spirit of adoption, who shapes us into the image of Christ's sonship. Godliness, therefore, just like sanctification, follows the shape of the economy such that the space God has sanctified to be known and received by us is in his Son, to be sons and daughters of God in the Spirit of adoption. Thomas Aquinas, meditating on 1 Tim. 4:7, claims that Paul's use of godliness here "is the virtue by which we pay the debt of good will to our parents and native land, just as religion is the virtue by which we render worship to God. For godliness suggests affection directed to one's principle" ("Commentary on 1 Timothy," 297–98). He goes on to justify the translation of εὐσέβειαν (*eusebeian*) as "godliness," writing, "The principle of generation is one's country and one's parents. Therefore, it is required that a man have good will toward these principles. But the principle and father of all things is God: *if I be a father, where is my honor*? (Mal 1:6). This is why the name godliness is applied to the worship of God. . . . Hence *eusebeia* is another name for godliness" (298). We appreciate Matthew Lee Anderson pointing out this interpretation and pointing to Aquinas to consider the translation of *eusebeia* in these texts.

they proceed *from* him and abide *in* him. The mystical union with Christ is the foundation of the imitation of Christ."[27] We must not separate our imitation of Christ from our union with him, and likewise we should not separate being children of our heavenly Father from mortification and vivification. But just because we must not separate these things does not mean we should not order them. As Martin Luther admonishes, "The chief article and foundation of the gospel is that before you take Christ as an example, you accept and recognize him as a gift, as a present that God has given you and that is your own."[28]

What Christ offers to us as a divine gift (by grace), he has by nature: sonship. Christ enlarges his sonship to us such that, by faith through the Spirit, we are united to him as sons or daughters of God. We never leave the gravitational center of his life in order to advance ourselves on our own resources, nor do we turn his life into a commodity we can employ to further ourselves. Rather, it is always *from* him, *through* him, and *to* him that we live the Christian life (Rom. 11:36). Furthermore, knowing God as Father, and walking before him as his children, defines the shape of life as one of laying down our lives and having him raise them up in Christ. (See the sidebar "God's Incarnate Love," p. 124.) A generic account of union with God or participation in God will miss this or seek to ascend to a divine reality apart from Christ rather than one given shape by him (as Paul warns against in Col. 2:8). Instead, Christ is the model of Christian existence because his life is what gives shape to ours in and through union with him. In other words, Christ can never be reduced to *a* way, because he himself is *the* way. The Christian life can make sense only if he is present and active and forming his life into our own.

As we have seen, the acts of the Son and the Spirit are not separated in the economy of God, and sanctification cannot be moved from the Son to the Spirit as if their action were divisible. Rather, the sanctification of the Spirit simply is the life of the Son at work in the believer as they share in God's life. The Spirit does not communicate any life other than the life of God known in Christ, therefore enacting a *filial formation*. That is, the sonship offered to Christians is specified biblically through images of

27. Bavinck, *Reformed Ethics*, 1:339.
28. Luther, "A Brief Instruction on What to Look for and Expect in the Gospels," 72.

God's Incarnate Love

Rather than ask why God wants Jesus to *die* the way he did, we should ask why God wants Jesus to *live* the way he did and why this way of life led us to want to *kill* him. God wants Jesus to live the reality of God's kingdom, to live the kindness that is at the core of the divine identity while also living as one among us, facing all of the trials and troubles that fragile human flesh must face. God wants Jesus to live this way so he can show us what life in the kingdom of God—truly human life—is all about. And not simply to show us but also to forge a path into that kingdom, to give us a way to be what God created us to be. . . . God desires that divine love be incarnate in Jesus, even knowing that this will be too much love for a grasping, frustrated, frightened world to bear. God desires that love be incarnate, even if that love must be crucified.[a]

a. Bauerschmidt, *The Love That Is God*, 34–35.

adoption and marriage. Thus the predominant language after the book of Acts for followers of Jesus is familial terminology such as *brother* and *sister* (along with *saint*, the title of holiness). We could say that to be a saint, "sanctified in Christ Jesus" (1 Cor. 1:2), is to be a child of the Father in Christ. A child is a saint because they are one with Christ in the Spirit, sharers in God's holy life, which is why we have received "not . . . the spirit of slavery" but "the Spirit of adoption" (Rom. 8:15).

In Romans 8 we see this focus on adoption and the contrast with slavery. This is also where Paul claims, "For those whom [God] foreknew he also predestined to be *conformed* to the image of his Son, in order that he might be the firstborn among many brothers [and sisters]. And those whom he predestined he also called, and those whom he called he also justified, and those whom he justified he also glorified" (Rom. 8:29–30). To be sanctified is to be *relocated* before God in Christ by the Spirit, so that we can be conformed to the image of the Son of God as sons and daughters within the sonship of Jesus. (See the sidebar "Romans 8:12–17.") The restoration and recharacterization of Christians to their true self is always in Christ by the Spirit, who conforms us to Christ. To become a child of another is to embrace them and their way of life. To know God as a new *Father* is to *be* and *become* his child (one's *state* and *way*). A child of a father should

Romans 8:12–17

[12]Therefore, brothers and sisters, we have an obligation—but it is not to the flesh, to live according to it. [13]For if you live according to the flesh, you will die; but if by the Spirit you put to death the misdeeds of the body, you will live. [14]For those who are led by the Spirit of God are the children of God. [15]The Spirit you received does not make you slaves, so that you live in fear again; rather, the Spirit you received brought about your adoption to sonship. And by him we cry, "Abba, Father." [16]The Spirit himself testifies with our spirit that we are God's children. [17]Now if we are children, then we are heirs—heirs of God and co-heirs with Christ, if indeed we share in his sufferings in order that we may also share in his glory. (NIV)

become like their father, not merely partaking in his benefits but being conformed to his life.

Christian prayer conforms to the familial shape of the Christian life, as it is primarily prayer to the Father, in the name of the Son, and by the power of the Spirit. To pray in the name of the Son is to know the sonship he has with the Father and to be ushered into the life and love of the Father for the Son (John 17:26). Furthermore, having the Spirit of the Son is having the Spirit of adoption, who immediately begins calling out from the Christian's soul: "Abba! Father!" Paul narrates this salvation in Galatians 4:4–6, proclaiming that "when the fullness of time had come, God sent forth his Son, born of woman, born under the law, to redeem those who were under the law, so that we might receive adoption as sons. And because you are sons, God has sent the Spirit of his Son into our hearts, crying, 'Abba! Father!'" Christians are called to pray "Abba, Father" in Christ by his Spirit, because this is Christ's relation to the Father and because his Spirit is always already praying this from within the soul of a Christian (Rom. 8:15). Christian prayer in the Son's name reflects the basic shape of the Christian life. Christians are called into the presence of the Father *as Father*, as they share in the life of the Son and his relation to the Father, through his Spirit of love, adoption, and holiness. The path that Christians walk has already been laid down before them by the Son and the Spirit, who call them to walk only in ways they have walked themselves.

Christians pray "Abba, Father" because that is already the prayer of Son and Spirit *for* them, *through* them, and *from within* them.

The formation of a child before the Father is central to the New Testament witness. This reaches deep into the life of a person, where God establishes family relations to be primal psychological relations, for good or for bad, refusing to ignore these natural formations but seeking to redeem brokenness, failure, and pain.[29] God has us call him "Father," knowing that this is an already established relation in our lives. God does not ignore this relation but seeks to redeem it. Likewise, it is this familial formation of life with God as Father that helps establish the necessity of the communion of saints. The communion of saints is never less than a community of brothers and sisters in Christ whose relation to God is equal to our own. This is why Peter begins his second epistle by writing it to "those who have obtained a faith of equal standing with ours" (2 Pet. 1:1).

The sanctification offered in Christ, therefore, far from being generic, is *specified by Jesus's sonship*. To have access to his life is to have access to the fatherhood of God in the Son, which is why images of adoption and marriage are the predominant biblical motifs of salvation. Even the language of *godliness* points to a familial ethic—a household code—that is about being formed into the life of God by partaking in the life of *that family*. Thomas Aquinas seems right in his reading of *eusebeia* as focused on one's originating principle, such that the emphasis in the Pastoral Epistles on being "godly" is to be "like one's Father."[30] The First Letter to Timothy focuses on household virtues and relations, establishing the context for children to become like their heavenly Father as they stand in differing relations to their siblings in Christ (as an obvious example, see 1 Tim. 5:1–16).[31] Children first learn

29. Angela Carpenter narrates this theme across three generations of Reformed theologians (John Calvin, John Owen, and Horace Bushnell) in her helpful book *Responsive Becoming*.

30. See above, note 26. Thomas also claims, "But as to earthly godliness, its characteristic is to make a man have good will toward his compatriots; as to Christian godliness, it requires that a man have good will toward all men, because all of us belong to the same country" (Aquinas, "Commentary on 1 Timothy," 300). Importantly, when considering the Decalogue in relation to godliness, Thomas writes, "For in the precepts of the decalogue there is but one which refers to godliness, namely, to honor your father and your mother; but under it are contained all the precepts that are concerned with bestowing benefits upon one's neighbor" (299).

31. In 1 Tim. 5:4, Paul uses εὐσεβεῖν, typically translated as "godliness," to talk about widows' ongoing care for their own families. This discussion leads right into his discussion of elders.

"to show godliness" (εὐσεβεῖν, *eusebein*) in their own household, which is a kind of training for the household of faith (1 Tim. 5:4). In other words, the shape of holiness, as depicting the sphere of God's presence and our relationally reciprocal response, is understood through adoption as one increasingly images the truth of God in one's life: knowing God as Father through union with the Son by the Spirit. God saves individuals to partake in the life of a people. The parallels between human families and the family of God are significant, and this should guide how sanctification governs ethics, ecclesiology, and spiritual formation. In this sense the formation of sanctification is one of sonship and family life; the individual is never able to be separated from the communal (and vice versa).

In being adopted as children of the Father, we are being ushered into God's presence as his children, as those who are in Christ and therefore are sharing in his sonship. Both adoption imagery and marital imagery emphasize this, using the relation Christ has to the Father *qua* Father as the grounding for the relation available to believers in him (i.e., his sonship). To be united to Christ by faith is to share in his familial relation with the Father (as Jesus emphasizes in John 14–17, as we have seen). One might imagine a scenario where Christ achieved this through his incarnation, ministry, death, resurrection, and ascension but left his earthly ministry behind and created a path of ascent to the Father that bypassed these realities. But this is not what we find in the New Testament. Paul, in particular, is a bit shocking in this way. Paul, who was not a follower of Jesus when he was crucified, could have secured his vision of Christian faithfulness in the power of Pentecost rather than through the cross of Christ. But in Paul these are one. Paul knows no Christian power that is not power *in and through the weakness of the cross*, and he even warns that paths of ministry built on human ability and savvy can *empty the cross of its power* (1 Cor. 1:17). There is no participation in Christ's sonship without receiving his death and resurrection as well.[32]

32. John Webster writes, "The definitive setting aside of the old nature and the institution of the new are to be confirmed in the lives of regenerate creatures. The Son's death and resurrection are the wholly sufficient, perfect work of divine grace from whose accomplishment creatures are excluded: they are 'not your own doing' (Eph. 2:8). Yet they also provide the pattern of regenerate living as, by the moving power of the Holy Spirit, those who are in Christ appropriate the condition in which they have been placed by divine grace" ("Communion with Christ," 122).

This cruciform shaping of sanctification is what leads us to our second image set: mortification and vivification. The Reformed tradition followed the general trajectory we have focused on, orienting salvation in Christ, centering adoption as children of the Father, and then turning to mortification and vivification as the shape of that sonship. This is clearly seen in Calvin's *Institutes*, for instance. Bavinck, similarly, articulates a parallel impulse:

> Sanctification is also God's work. Spiritual growth is therefore a process of dying and being resurrected in communion with Christ (Rom. 6; Eph. 2). Dying with Christ is not a destruction of our personal self but only pertains to the sin in the self, in one's soul and body, insofar as they serve sin; we have died to sin (Rom. 6:2, 10). This dying is therefore the separation of the self from sin and its fellowship—that is, it is a dying-*off* (Col. 2:20; 1 Pet. 2:24).[33]

It is true that our personal self is not destroyed in our death with Christ, but in sin the reign of the autonomous self does need to die, such that we must lose our lives to find them in Christ (Matt. 16:25). The self that is mired in itself needs to be lost so that the self in Christ can be found.

In sanctification, we are caught up in God's action and relocated within the space of God's own holy life. We lose our lives—lives lived in and by our selves—and we find our new lives in Christ. There is a displacement of the self—the "I"—that has to occur, in which we discover that we no longer define, secure, or establish ourselves but are defined, secured, and established by the Holy One. This is how humility was originally understood: as losing one's life to find it in Christ.[34] This is why true humility is contrary to the self attempting to function autonomously apart from God. This is the self that has to die to discover that true life is found only in Christ.[35] As Paul writes, "I have been crucified with Christ. It is no longer I who live, but Christ who lives in me. And the life I now live in the flesh I live by faith in the Son of God, who loved me and gave himself for me" (Gal. 2:20). The "I" is somehow simultaneously said to be crucified *and yet*

33. Bavinck, *Reformed Ethics*, 1:348.

34. Kent Dunnington makes this argument in his helpful and provocative book *Humility, Pride, and Christian Virtue Theory*.

35. Webster writes, "Like the first created nature before its fall into ruin, this new form of creaturely being and activity is not autonomous or separate from its author. Regenerate life means being 'alive together with Christ'; it is life 'in him'" ("Communion with Christ," 122).

alive; *I* have died . . . and yet *I* live.[36] In Galatians, the spatial reality of being "in Christ" is set in contrast to being "in myself." As sin has caused human persons to turn inward on themselves (*incurvatus in se*), the condition in Adam is one of self-generation, self-identification, and self-grounding. This is the condition confronted by Christ.

As we saw in chapter 2, holiness concerns the Holy One of Israel, who establishes his presence amid his people to reorder them to that presence. Israel's camp, after Sinai, was entirely structured around God at the center, giving order and establishing a new harmonic field of existence. At the heart of biblical anthropology is the truth that in sin we seek to be like God, grounding ourselves in and through ourselves. Salvation requires that we are *displaced* from the center of this narrative, pushed to the margins of our own lives precisely so that we can find them through union with Christ. Sanctification names the truth of being both displaced from the center and being *re-grounded in Christ*. Christ is our life, and by the Spirit we become *spiritual* beings. To be spiritual, in this sense, is not antithetical to any aspects of our humanity as given to us by God, but is receiving Christ so that our whole self is reordered, reshaped, and reoriented by and to him. Thus Paul writes, "The spiritual person judges all things, but is himself to be judged by no one. 'For who has understood the mind of the Lord so as to instruct him?' But we have the mind of Christ" (1 Cor. 2:15–16). The spiritual person has the *mind of Christ*. The "I" that once, in Adam, sought to establish itself now lays down its quest for self-creation to trust that the Lord offers new creation (2 Cor. 5:17).

The life of faith, therefore, really is grace perfecting nature, but that is not the *experience* of natural humanity. This requires some explanation. To fallen humanity, the gift of life with God through Christ (the grace of the gospel) does not sound like life; it seems to be death. But the grace of God that is the Christ-gift to us *requires* our death, which is precisely how it offers resurrection life to us. Grace stands against the human desire in the flesh to self-constitute and self-construct; it does so by offering life

36. Susan Grove Eastman writes, "Paul's astounding self-description is all about death and life. On the one hand, 'I died to the law'; 'I have been crucified with Christ'; 'I no longer live.' On the other hand, 'that I might live to God'; 'Christ lives in me'; 'I live in the flesh'; 'I live in the faith of the Son of God.' This language of death and life comes to a climax in reference to Christ's death, depicted as a kind of gift: 'who loves me and gave himself (or delivered himself over) for me'" (*Paul and the Person*, 153).

through death and power perfected in weakness (2 Cor. 12:9). This is why humanity can be separated into two categories in Scripture: those "in Adam"—everyone outside of Christ—and those "in Christ." To be "in Adam" in this sense is to try to be like God and live a life generated and established in and by oneself.

This is why Paul, in Romans 5:12–21, uses Adam and Christ in contrast, addressing sin, death, law, and the possibility of justification, only to claim that our "old man" (i.e., Adam) was crucified with Christ so that we can live to God. What was crucified with Christ is what Adam sought to establish in himself. Ironically, Adam was seduced by the desire to be like God, whereas likeness to God is what is freely offered in creation as well as our new creation by faith. Unlike our failed attempts to be like God, in Christ we gain his likeness by grace. Called into his holy presence by being made holy in and through Christ by the Spirit, the Christian is now called to walk in the Spirit to abide in the Son for life with the Father.

This reveals why the Reformed tradition rightly turned to mortification and vivification in the doctrine of sanctification as a structure to understand Christian formation. Unmoored from our previous discussion of ordering sanctification around Christ and not his benefits, however, this notion could be easily commandeered by the flesh, once again turning Christ into a pattern of the flesh (the flesh longs to remake the gospel into law). But when kept in their proper order, mortification is putting off Adam, and vivification is, by the Spirit, putting on Christ.[37] Vivification is not simply the advancement of virtue but is having Christ as the telos of our action with the Spirit's work in the soul as the animating power of spiritual formation (Eph. 3:16–19). Furthermore, the love of Christ poured out by the Spirit establishes the character of Christ in the person, not abstracted from Jesus's person but known in and through communion with him. There is no true Christian formation outside of Christ through his Spirit, and mortification and vivification *point to that reality*.

This is why in Ephesians 4, after narrating how the gentiles are missing out on God's *life* (Eph. 4:18), Paul admonishes the Ephesians and reminds them that they did not learn Christ in a way that would lead to sinful lives.

37. Webster rightly notes, "As with any topic in the theology of the Christian life, a treatment of mortification and vivification talks about these human undertakings by talking about *God* and *God's work*" ("Communion with Christ," 122).

Rather, he tells them to "put off the old man, which is being corrupted and deluded by its lusts," and to "be renewed in the spirit of your minds, and to put on the new man, created after the likeness of God in true righteousness and holiness" (Eph. 4:22–24, our translation). The "old man" is the self in Adam, the "I" in sin that does not want to be defined by something or someone external to itself.

The call to put on the new man is the call to put on Christ, who is the ground, source, and image of our formation. This is also why Paul, in Colossians 3, says the Christian's life is "hidden with Christ in God" (3:3) and admonishes the Colossians to put off the old man and put on the new, which is "being renewed in knowledge after the image of its creator" (3:10). "Christ is all, and in all" (3:11), Paul declares, which is the foundation for his ethical imperatives that follow. The shape of ecclesial ethics, what is sometimes called "social holiness," is formed by this displacement of the self and relocation in the life of God, because being called into Christ is a new and all-defining reality. The passage in full states, "Here there is not Greek and Jew, circumcised and uncircumcised, barbarian, Scythian, slave, free; but Christ is all, and in all" (3:11). When *God relocates a people within his presence*, the social orders of the fallen world do not define the community; only God does. By faith, his creatures recognize a new order of reality where life is found through death, power found in weakness, and newness discovered only when the old is laid aside.

Mortification and vivification, as acts of faith, establish a pattern of life begun in conversion. We are saved *out of* death to life but also *through* death to life. Likewise, Christian activity and formation entails laying aside what has been judged by God in Christ to seek the life available in Christ. This is what it means to "walk by faith, not by sight" (2 Cor. 5:7) as we "set our minds on things that are above" (Col. 3:2). This is also why, removed from Christ, Christian formation, ecclesiology, and ethics are incomprehensible: "Has not God made foolish the wisdom of the world?" (1 Cor. 1:20).

A doctrine of sanctification in the wisdom of God is one that rests on the sonship of Christ before the Father and receives life in and through death. That is why it is incomprehensible and offensive in the flesh. This life is available only through the *presence of another*. We cannot simply habituate ourselves to this life, because the Christian life is *Christ's life*, which becomes our own only as we abide in him to know the growth that comes from God. The life of holiness is what it is because the holy life is

Christ's life; he has sanctified himself for our sake, that we might know the holiness by which God himself is holy. This is what is available in Son and Spirit and is the form of virtue, love, and community that is given shape in the life of Jesus.

Summary

Christian teaching about life with God should first and foremost attend to God and God's gracious self-giving that calls us into his life for the purpose of reordering our lives around him. For the sake of clarifying one's sanctified state and development in sanctification, Protestant doctrines of sanctification often trade in the categories of "definitive" and "progressive," but dependence on these categories risks losing the centrality *of Christ and the Spirit*. A doctrine of sanctification is about the sanctified person only in a derivative sense; the doctrine's primary focus is *God and God's gracious self-giving*. Jesus sanctifies us, for he *is our sanctification*—a reality made available to us through union with himself by the Spirit of holiness. One's holiness in Christ is both *a state* and *a way* (definitive and progressive). The *state* is one's union with Christ—a person's deepest and most fundamental location—and the *way* is a life of relational responsiveness to the Spirit by which the holying of God deepens, purifies, and perfects. Sanctification is *life in the presence of God for the presence of God.*

DOXOLOGICAL INTERLUDE

Ford Madox Brown, *Jesus Washing Peter's Feet*

> During supper, when the devil had already put it into the heart of Judas Iscariot, Simon's son, to betray him, Jesus, knowing that the Father had given all things into his hands, and that he had come from God and was going back to God, rose from supper. He laid aside his outer garments, and taking a towel, tied it around his waist. Then he poured water into a basin and began to wash the disciples' feet and to wipe them with the towel that was wrapped around him. . . . When he had washed their feet and put on his outer garments and resumed his place, he said to them, "Do you understand what I have done to you? You call me Teacher and Lord, and you are right, for so I am. If I then, your Lord and Teacher, have washed your feet, you also ought to wash one another's feet. For I have given you an example, that you also should do just as I have done to you. Truly, truly, I say to you, a servant is not greater than his master, nor is a messenger greater than the one who sent him. If you know these things, blessed are you if you do them."
>
> John 13:2–5, 12–17

Invitation

The scene is uncomfortably intimate. Everyone in the room would have been offended for Jesus to do menial servant's work—but still more uncomfortably, *they have nowhere to hide*. He will be just inches away as he holds their feet. As Ford Madox Brown portrays in this painting, Peter has nowhere to hide as Jesus clasps his feet, his arms flexing as he pulls soil and sweat into the basin. Those at the table behind Jesus know their turn will eventually come, and their eyes and posture reveal the truth that Brown invites the viewer to personally engage: *How can this be—even me?*

Brown places Judas just above the crown of Jesus's head so we would contemplate him and *ourselves* in him. Judas can only look sideways at the scene as he grasps his head in desperation and maybe terror, fingers splayed across his scalp as his elbows clench together on the tabletop. It's as if he intends to disappear between his forearms, but there's nowhere to go. *How can this be—even me?*

In this intensely embodied prophetic teaching, like Ezekiel's symbolic actions, Jesus pictures the meaning of God's presence for the world. God shares his life as a servant so that we can share our lives with God as his children. We are left to contemplate the extravagance of God's generous proximity: *How can this be—even me?*

Pause for a moment and prayerfully contemplate the story while holding the painting in mind. Too easily the wonder of God's extravagant welcome fades after seasons of faith. The miracle that God would become a servant so we would become children dims. Yet wasn't Judas's place at the table once ours? And don't we still slip into that chair again and again? Invite the Spirit to meet you in the question, *How can this be—even me?* What could this mean for your life with God and with others?

Notes

CHAPTER FIVE

Holiness, Virtue, and the Infusion of Love

Hope does not put us to shame, because God's love has been poured into our hearts through the Holy Spirit who has been given to us.

Romans 5:5

It is the Father's nature to love, and therefore the coming of the Father is marked by an infusion of love.

Bernard of Clairvaux[1]

NOW THAT WE HAVE ATTENDED to the proper location of the doctrine of sanctification, we must consider how sanctification can order what is often called a doctrine of the Christian life. In this chapter, we first consider how the biblical material shapes the doctrine, then discern how this governs Christian virtue formation, and finally turn to a case study on infusion. The case study is important because infusion is often misunderstood and maligned by Protestants. Aside from that, however,

1. Bernard of Clairvaux, *On the Song of Songs IV*, 28.

the case study also brings the current conversation about virtue ethics into contact with our proposal for the doctrine of sanctification.

Before turning again to the scriptural material, we should briefly pause to summarize four interrelated tensions we've seen thus far related to Scripture and the perceptions we hold about holiness. First, we've seen that for a thing or person or place to be holy does not mean for it "to be separate," even though for something to be made holy its separation is required. Second, holiness is not primarily an ethical category, but it cannot be sequestered from ethics. Third, holiness has its own constitution as a description of the divine life: *Holy* first and foremost refers to God the Holy One. As a description of God's *unified* life, the holiness of God cannot be understood apart from God's love and his justice; at the same time, we must remember that holiness must not be reduced to God's love or his justice. Fourth, we've seen how easily the doctrinal content of sanctification can be overtaken by its doctrinal neighbors. In most cases it is merely coupled with justification in such a way that our understanding of sanctification loses its scriptural shape. On a popular level and even in academic discourse, we too often find reductions on one side or the other of these tensions.

When it comes to virtue formation and habituation, there are still more problematic tendencies in contemporary discourse around spiritual formation, spirituality, and the Christian life. For instance, it is common for people to assume that virtue ethics is solely the domain of either secular ethics, on the one hand, or Roman Catholic moral theology, on the other.[2] There is likewise the tendency, prevalent in philosophical circles and the discussion of spiritual disciplines, to equate Aristotelian habituation with Christian spiritual formation. Both discussions are missing—much to their detriment—a doctrinally ordered account of Protestant virtue ethics, governed by the doctrine of God through an account of sanctification. We can say this another way: To address virtue, we must attend to God in his perfection (chap. 1) and then holiness and sanctification (chaps. 2–4). This approach enables us to speak into the present discourse on virtue ethics and spiritual formation. This chapter will conclude with some reflections on

2. Whereas this narrative is being overturned, it is still prevalent in more popular-level theological discourse. For two important works correcting these misinterpretations, see Sytsma, "John Calvin and Virtue Ethics"; Svensson, "Aristotelian Practical Philosophy from Melanchthon to Eisenhart."

how our ordering of sanctification and its relation to virtue can contribute to conversations about virtue and formation.

The Biblical Theme of Presence

Our reading of the biblical material concerning holiness and sanctification gives us a certain framework to consider the question of virtue. The central element of this framework is the notion of *presence*. The holy space of God's availability, resecured at Sinai (after the loss of Eden), is where God establishes his presence in the midst of his people to meet with them. The presence of God experienced at Sinai required a particular form of communal and personal approach, which is developed in and through the tabernacle and the temple's forms, symbology, and procedures. Thus the psalmist declares, "Sinai is now *in the sanctuary*" (Ps. 68:17). The presence of God known at Sinai is mediated in and through the tabernacle/temple system. Now, because of the incarnation, we know God's presence in the tabernacling of Christ and the descent of the Spirit. Christ is the "space" where God is known and understood; Christ is the archetype of which these former realities were mere shadow.

Divine presence is not a form of generic presence—the sort of personal presence available with other persons. God's presence is unique, as it is a presence within, around, and upholding his people. The intensive presence of the triune God establishes the *true source of life* in our midst. Furthermore, God's intensive personal presence is such that it *orders all of life around himself*, and it does not leave his creation unaffected. God always comes near to give order to what is unformed and broken for the sake of God and for life with him. This was seen in the camp, where Israel was organized by tribe around the tabernacle, the center, where God dwelled among them. It is this presence of God that is the defining feature of his people. Laws concerning Sabbath, land, feasts and the festal calendar, and the various ethical imperatives were all focused on God's presence with his people.

Archetypally, the notion of rest in Scripture signified this unique presence and availability of God, such that Sabbath was, in the words of Ezekiel 20:12, "a sign between me and them, that they might know that I am the Lord who sanctifies them." Those who have believed have entered this rest (Heb. 4:3), "for whoever has entered God's rest has also rested from his works as God did from his" (Heb. 4:10). God's rest on the seventh day serves as a thread woven throughout Scripture signifying that we must lay down our works to embrace the sanctification God provides. Or, as Paul articulates, "For by grace you have been saved through faith. And this is not your own doing; it is the gift of God, not a result of works, so that no one may boast. For we are his workmanship, created in Christ Jesus for good works, which God prepared beforehand, that we should walk in them" (Eph. 2:8–10). We are called to lay down our works so that we can embrace good works known in and through Christ.

The Christian is one who has died in the death of Christ and has been made alive together with him by faith (Col. 2:12–13). With Calvin, we can focus on locating salvation in Christ himself, such that salvation is receiving Christ by the Spirit, forming Christians into the shape of Jesus's death and resurrection through mortification and vivification. With Aquinas we could focus more on the internal dynamics of human psychology, considering how habituation of grace differs from the habituation of nature. While it is theologically important to attend at the broad, doctrinal level to how sanctification is located within an overarching soteriology, there is a danger that this could drown out a more phenomenological inquiry into the lived *experience* of the Christian. It is significant that our own Protestant tradition is filled with phenomenological accounts of the Christian life, attending carefully to various ways God acts in the soul and how we tend to misinterpret those acts (this is especially true in conversations concerning spiritual desertion).[3]

When it comes to training, formation, and ethics, the obvious historical location for these topics is the family, and is governed by the maturation into familial ideals. We are tempted to shift these things into different registers in our engagement with the biblical material, perhaps thinking that learning is primarily about finding a teacher or rabbi. But learning is a task located primarily in the family, which is no doubt one of the reasons why the church is most thoroughly described with familial imagery. In other words, to think about training we are not merely in the realm of virtue ethics, and we must distance ourselves even more from the academy as the place of formation. It is life in the family of God as "members of

3. For more on spiritual desertion, see Strobel and Coe, *When God Seems Distant*.

the household of God" (Eph. 2:19) where the theoretical description of presence comes home.

The Home of God

Miroslav Volf and Ryan McAnnally-Linz have recently argued for the theme of home as the center of biblical theology. This theme deeply resonates with our focus on God's holying presence as the organizing center of sanctification, and it has the added benefit of solidifying God's presence as a lived reality rather than an abstraction. While we all long for presence, Volf and McAnnally-Linz are right to note that the theme of home better attends to the even deeper longings of the heart. They write, "Beneath or alongside or mingled with the disquietude, perhaps you have felt an amorphous but insistent longing—a yearning for the truer modes of belonging, for fulsome forms of resonance that do not depend for their depth or intensity on the thrill of novelty, fascination with the forbidden, or the gravity of violence. In a word, a longing for *home*."[4] We all long for something we name "home," even if we cannot put words to what that entails. Put in a more traditional framing, but connected with our themes, all created things have an innate disposition to *move to repose*.

The telos of all created things is rest, imaging the truth that in God all things come from his rest, a rest that is simultaneously the fullness of his life. This is the holy God whose life is the infinite act of presence, an act so full that we can only point toward it and cannot begin to fathom its depths. We can only glimpse this holiness as the divine self-repose that is the fullness of his knowledge and love known as the divine blessedness (1 Tim. 6:15). It is in embracing the rest of God as life in his presence that we begin to understand the integrated, wholehearted life of sanctification.

In the creation account of Genesis 1 we find chaos—what was formless and void—and the Spirit hovering over the waters to bring order out of disorder. This account establishes rest as a *harmony ingrained in creation around God's presence*. Creation's harmony was both an established reality and *a calling* (a "way"). The harmony was real, but it had to be maintained, cultivated, and consented to. This is the harmony of home. This is the reality of Augustine's famous claim from his *Confessions*, "Our hearts are

4. Volf and McAnnally-Linz, *The Home of God*, 1.

restless until they rest in you."[5] What the image of home does well is to show that not all cultures have to look alike, and yet there is a profound phenomenology to home that is innately human. We might not even be able to describe it, but we know it when we experience it. There is an organic nature to Christianity that allows this repose to look different in different contexts, communities, and cultures, all the while being connected to this presence of life, love, and revelation.

Whatever else home might be in nature or in our personal experience, sanctification establishes that, in grace, *home is the presence of God*, known in Christ by the Spirit. In Christians, the Spirit is hovering over and within the chaos of their soul to bring order out of disorder. Likewise, in Christian communities the Spirit establishes an order in and around the crucified Lord of glory. This is a presence that is simultaneously for us and yet against us; it declares peace even while it calls us to put to death what is earthly in us (Col. 3:5). This is a harmony that rejects the human propensity to cultivate the community, culture, and economies of our desires, something already revealed in the churches of the New Testament era (e.g., 1 Cor. 1:10–17; James 2:1–9). This is a harmony defined by the beauty of the cross; it refuses to remain in sterile isolation from the ugliness and mess that can define this world, instead revealing a path of reconciliation from within the truth of human sin, strife, and brokenness.

The harmony we are talking about—the harmony called home—has internal and external features. In the history of theology, the internal has perhaps been more emphasized, always ordered to the perfection of eternity in the beatific vision. The telos of human flourishing is the beatific vision, which is a sight-intensive way of rendering what it is to share in the divine presence and intimacy of knowing as we have been known and loving as we have been loved. This age, however, is not the age of sight but the age of faith and hope (2 Cor. 5:7; Rom. 8:24). Therefore, faith, hope, and love are the virtues of this harmony—serving to judge the economies of the world, the flesh, and the devil (James 3:13–17) and establishing a kingdom economy amid an evil age (Gal. 1:4). These virtues, as supernatural virtues, are grounded in *presence and intimacy*, and they fail to lead to wisdom without the abiding presence and action of God, which gives them meaning. In other words, these virtues are not schemes of survival

5. Augustine, *Confessions* 1.1.1 (p. 39).

or flourishing but forms of relational responsiveness to who God is and how God has given himself to be known.

By situating Christians in the presence of God, in Christ, and by the Spirit (known in faith), a doctrine of sanctification establishes that the promised flourishing and reconciliation of all things is perfected only in him and through him (grounding our hope). Faith and hope, as precursors to sight, serve as the logic by which a Christian is rooted and grounded in love for the sake of uniting all things in love. "Faith, hope, and love abide, these three; but the greatest of these is love" (1 Cor. 13:13). Love is greater because it is of the realm that never fades, whereas faith and hope dissolve upon sight. Love defines the economy of eternity, because God's life, presence, and love are the abiding rhythm that unites all things in harmony in that place. Faith and hope are what ushers this eternal harmony into creation, as the right and left hands of a person embracing grace. As we stand face-to-face with the Father who has embraced his own, faith and hope are the way we "close upon him" in Christ by the Spirit (to use the older explanation of faith as "closing with Christ").[6]

By configuring salvation around the familial language and imagery given to us in Scripture, such as adoption, marriage, and the household, we are trained to never forget the essence of soteriology: We are saved for God's personal presence, known in faith and hope *for love*. If this is salvation, then sanctification is, as we have been saying, *life in the presence of God for the presence of God*. We are home with God already for the sake of being home with God forever, and for all that being home with God entails then *and now*: the recharacterization of our whole self after the image of the Son, our reorientation toward others and the nonhuman world, and our participation in the mission of the Son and the Spirit.

While the idea of home can be deeply meaningful, it is also true that the internal and external dynamics of home are messy. We often know how meaningful an institution is based on how deeply it can hurt us. The

6. With Volf and McAnnally-Linz's helpful articulation of home, Volf's earlier construct of *inclusion* and *embrace* also parallels our doctrine of sanctification. He writes, "To describe the process of 'welcoming,' I employed the metaphor of 'embrace.' The metaphor seems well suited to bring together the three interrelated themes that are central to my proposal: (1) the mutuality of self-giving love in the Trinity (the doctrine of God), (2) the outstretched arms of Christ on the cross for the 'godless' (the doctrine of Christ), (3) the open arms of the 'father' receiving the 'prodigal' (the doctrine of salvation)" (Volf, *Exclusion and Embrace*, 19).

reframing of God's presence as home, therefore, is not the formation of an already virtuous life but the formation of a life veined with vice. To address the fullness of this dynamic is beyond the bounds of this book; it would require addressing not only the various faculties of the soul but also what is required for them to be purified in love and for love. In other words, to address internal dynamics would entail talking about how the rational features of personhood (understanding, will, and affection) are ordered to contemplating the beauty of the Lord, to loving the Lord and our neighbor as ourselves. This is the cry of the psalmist:

> One thing have I asked of the LORD,
> that will I seek after:
> that I may dwell in the house of the LORD
> all the days of my life,
> to gaze upon the beauty of the LORD
> and to inquire in his temple. (Ps. 27:4)

This is the presence of God that orders all things around himself, bringing the heart in harmony with the crucified, risen, and ascended Lord. This is how a rational agent is drawn to repose, resting in the beauty, harmony, and glory of God.

The harmony of the Lord is not, however, isolated to individuals. The growth Christians are called to is a communal one. Paul calls the church of Colossae to hold fast to Christ, their head, "from whom the whole body, nourished and knit together through its joints and ligaments, grows with a growth that is from God" (Col. 2:19). This, of course, includes individuals, but this ordering is always for life *together* in the presence of God. Home signifies the truth that Christians are called into a body defined by a new and heavenly Father, such that we are now siblings to one another in faith. All of the callings of the Christian are now read through this familial dynamic, such that we learn not as mere students but as children of the Father and members of his household (Eph. 2:19). We are saints as we are children of his family, as those given access to God in Christ by the Spirit of holiness (Eph. 2:18). We are followers of Jesus as we are being built into him who is our head.

There is a significant temptation of the flesh to leave our home in God's presence to seek goodness apart from him. The moralistic temptation is one that rightfully recognizes God as judge, and even understands that all should be done *for* him, but misses the truth that true virtue is virtue known *from* him.[7] In this sense we are called into the presence of the purifying fire, and we must seek his presence to be formed in and by him. There is not a direct line from our action to our virtuous formation, in other words; *the line to virtue formation always goes to and through Christ.* We bear fruit as we abide in him, so Christ is the telos of our action, in whom and by whom we are formed. It is important that in one of Jesus's most explicit teachings about abiding to bear fruit, he also explicitly states that without him we can do nothing (John 15:5). This notion of abiding can be understood in parallel with the image of God as a purifying fire. As we abide in him, we are caught up in the presence of the purifying fire. It is only as we remain in his presence—only as our action and contemplation move us to him—that we know the fruit of his work in our lives. On a practical level, this means that accounts of virtue formation through mere habituation (i.e., acquired virtue) are not sufficiently Christian, although these accounts should have a place within a Christian understanding of natural virtue. Instead, Scripture pushes us to recognize that God is not merely the first mover of Christian virtue; he is *always its immediate efficient and formal cause.*[8]

7. Recent discussions in New Testament studies have raised questions about more traditional accounts of legalism, articulating a view of the Pharisees and their understanding of the law different from that of classic Protestant accounts. Grant Macaskill accepts some of this reinterpretation but argues, in contrast, that

> the performance of obedience as something that generates symbolic capital by which our status as "insiders" is affirmed to ourselves, to our peers, and to God. This may not be the result of deliberate or conscious effort on our part. Rather, it is wrapped up in our constitution, our flesh as Paul calls it, and operates deep in our psyche. Such social capital is acquired by the one who acts: it is a righteousness that is "mine." This assumes that I am both competent to act in such a creditable way and am the one who should be so credited, because "I" am the moral agent. Paul's account of righteousness in Christ opposes this entirely by recognizing that "I" can never be credited with righteousness, because that "I" no longer lives; it is now the I-in-Christ who lives, and it is Christ-in-me who works. The righteousness is his; I enjoy it because I share in him. (*Living in Union with Christ*, 138)

8. Calvin articulates Aristotle's four causes in relation to salvation this way, in a discussion about good works: "The efficient cause of our salvation consists in God the Father's love; the material cause in God the Son's obedience; the instrumental cause in the Spirit's illumination, that is, faith; the final cause, in the glory of God's great generosity" (*Institutes* III.xiv.21 [1:787]).

New Testament Virtue and Formation

We have seen that creaturely holiness is about *God's action* to make space in his personal presence; our holiness is not won but derived from the holiness that is uniquely God's life, known by virtue of our proximity to God in union with Christ. Our holiness is received in and through God's act to sanctify creatures for himself. Old Testament depictions of the holiness of things, people, and spaces show all such things being cleansed and sanctified *for* God's presence. In the New Testament we see, in light of the incarnation, that God's presence *as such* cleanses and sanctifies. The potent holiness of Jesus prevails against the powers of all that is unclean and unholy. The incarnation clarifies our vision of divine holiness, for in the life of Jesus we discover that God's holiness *entails the restoration and transformation of anything drawn into its presence*. The call to draw near to God in his dwelling place—known through the tabernacle/temple and sacrificial system—is now the call to draw near through the blood of Jesus and his sanctifying Spirit. God and his self-giving presence make us fit for life in him and with him. God's overabundance of life and fullness abounds to us in Christ and the Spirit such that we are sanctified *in* Christ Jesus and *by* the indwelling Spirit, whose work in our "inner being" is for the sake of Christ dwelling in our hearts through faith (Eph. 3:16–17).

However else we articulate an account of *Christian* virtue formation, it must follow these scriptural contours of divine and creaturely holiness. While holiness cannot be reduced to virtue, we must avoid separating them. The reason is that one is made holy *for a new end*; the creature made holy has a new indwelling presence and is oriented to God, who has provided access to himself in Christ by the Spirit (Eph. 2:18). This access to God is access that leads to reordering all things around himself through the relational responsiveness of the one united to Christ. To be made holy means that "I have been crucified with Christ. It is no longer I who live, but Christ who lives in me. And the life I now live in the flesh I live by faith in the Son of God, who loved me and gave himself for me" (Gal. 2:20). This reordering of the person in and around Christ displaces the "I" from the center and *locates the foundation of the self in Christ*. (See the sidebar "The Self in Relation to Christ.") Jesus's teaching proves true: "For whoever would save his life will lose it, but whoever loses his life for my sake will find it" (Matt. 16:25).

The Self in Relation to Christ

Susan Eastman notes that when Paul addresses the human person in Galatians 2:19–20 and Romans 7:15–18, 20, there is a pattern: "I no longer (verb) but (subject plus verb) in me."

> In each case, the speaker says, "I no longer am acting, but someone or something else inhabits my person as the subject of my actions." The difference between the constructions of the self in the two passages consists in the difference between distinctly other and yet personally indwelling actors—in the first case, "Christ who lives in me," and in the second, personified "Sin that dwells in me." These two actors could not be more opposed to one another. Yet the *structure* of these opposing constructions of the self is remarkably similar. In both cases the self is a self-in-relation-to-another, suggesting that . . . the person is shaped in relationship to a separate entity that is both external and indwelling. . . .
>
> These realities may be personal, in an "I-Thou" relationship, such as that between Paul and Christ, or they may be impersonal and indeed depersonalizing, as in the "I-It" relationship between the self and "sin" in Romans 7:17–20. For Paul, these opposing relational loci are the only alternatives in human existence; there is no place where an autonomous "individual" can stand aside and evaluate, let alone choose, between different possible identities. There is no freestanding "self" in Paul's cosmos, nor is there a neutral environment within which human beings may act out their personal lives. Rather, Paul's anthropology is participatory all the way down. It does not mean, however, that there is no "self."[a]

a. Eastman, *Paul and the Person*, 6–9.

In this reordering of the self in and around God, there is a new foundation, a new center, and a new telos for the one who is in Christ. This way of presenting sanctification resonates with Bonaventure's claim about the original state of humanity, that we were meant to accomplish our works "with God as [our] source, in accordance with God's norms, and with God as [our] end."[9] An account of sanctification needs to explain God's new creation of human persons for his presence as a reformation

9. Bonaventure, *Breviloquium*, 100.

by grace through faith, as it is a reconstitution of their person in Christ. The scriptural language secures this through images of death and resurrection, losing one's "I" to be replaced by Christ (i.e., Gal. 2:20) and having one's life "hidden with Christ in God" because one has died and risen with Christ (Col. 3:2–3). *The presence of God that makes holy* must also be shown to explain how a creature is now reconstituted as a person *in* him, *with* him, and *for* him. Furthermore, with Bonaventure, we need an account of human action and virtue formation that is *from* God, based on his norms, *for* him as our true end. This is one of the most significant roles for the doctrine of sanctification in a theological system.

We enter God's holiness by means of the space God creates for us. As we have seen, this space is made available in Christ, and communion with God entails our relational responsiveness to the Spirit, who lives within us. Scripture names the creaturely counterparts to God's extravagant welcome—our relational responsiveness—as faith, hope, and love. Faith, hope, and love specify the supernatural *responses* to the presence and activity of God for us and within us. Importantly, these are not general, one-size-fits-all responses to the presence and activity of God. Rather, they are *for us personally*; they are *not* relational responses merely to the idea of God but responses *within intimate divine fellowship with* God who is for us. Virtue then, as a fruit of God's action in the soul, requires an inward work of God that serves as the foundation of a new form of habituation. (See the sidebar "Habituation.") We find this in both the Old Testament and the New Testament, but the latter describes with greater clarity following the incarnation how God's inward work is *now available in Christ by the indwelling of the Spirit*. As Paul claims, highlighting how our own action is predicated on God's prior action in the soul: "Therefore, my beloved, as you have always obeyed, so now, not only as in my presence but much more in my absence, work out your own salvation with fear and trembling, *for it is God who works in you, both to will and to work for his good pleasure*" (Phil. 2:12–13). God works in us *to will and work*. It is this willing and working that is addressed when we talk about Christian virtue. God does not work *against* our willing and working but *in us for our willing and working*. The Western tradition that stems from Augustine through the medievals into Protestant theology presents this vision with differing emphases but the same overall focus.

Habituation

In virtue ethics, the process whereby stable states of character (virtues) are formed in a person through repeated virtuous actions is known as *habituation*. Who you become is directly related to what you repeatedly do. The origins of this theory of moral formation are commonly traced to ancient Greek philosophy and to Aristotle in particular: "For one swallow does not make a summer, nor does one day; and so too one day, or a short time, does not make a man blessed and happy" (*Nicomachean Ethics* 1.7). On Aristotle's view, "excellence is not an act, but a habit."[a]

a. Durant, *The Story of Philosophy*, 87. On the significance of Aristotle's moral philosophy for virtue ethics, see Hursthouse and Pettigrove, "Virtue Ethics."

God's action, and our relationally responsive obedience and formation, must always be kept in view as the context within which we understand biblical imperatives. We do not shift to *mere* habituation when we come across commands in Scripture, as if we were called to simply generate obedience by exciting our wills.[10] Likewise, however, we must not allow God's action to so overshadow our own that it leads us into a sort of passivity. We need to understand how our action flows from God's action—perfected only by his activity and presence—if we want to understand habituating supernatural virtue.

We see this overarching vision in the teaching of Jesus, who grounds our life and activity in himself and through his Spirit for the sake of his glory. It also appears clearly in passages on virtue such as 2 Peter 1, which begins by affirming that the reader's faith is of "equal standing" to Peter's

10. Luther, in his lectures on Galatians, writes,

> Therefore "doing" is one thing in nature, another in philosophy, and another in theology. In nature the tree must be first, and then the fruit. In moral philosophy doing means a good will and right reason to do well; this is where the philosophers come to a halt. Therefore we say in theology that moral philosophy does not have God as its object and final cause, since Aristotle or a Sadducee or a man who is good in a civic sense calls it right reason and good will if he seeks the common welfare of the state and tranquility and honesty. (*Lectures on Galatians: Chapters 1–4*, 262)

own because it is grounded on the righteousness of Christ (2 Pet. 1:1). Following this, Peter continues to ground supernatural virtue in God's action: "His divine power has granted to us all things that pertain to life and godliness, through the knowledge of him who called us to his own glory and excellence" (1:3). Life and godliness are available through knowledge of Jesus, a theme that reverberates throughout 2 Peter.

Calvin reflects on the gift of godliness and life through the power of God in 2 Peter, writing, "Peter does not speak here of the natural gifts of God, but only mentions those things which he confers peculiarly on his own elect above the common order of nature."[11] God's gifts to his own are what raise them up to a supernatural formation by faith for the sake of love.[12] This is what Calvin calls "the peculiar endowments of the new and spiritual life, which derive their origin from the kingdom of Christ."[13] Calvin, expositing Peter's epistle with its call to virtue, notes the emphasis we have already seen in our biblical exposition: Supernatural virtue is from God by his grace, calling his people to a life funded and governed by God's own presence and life.[14]

In 2 Peter, the emphasis is on the power of God for his people, such that through God's gifts we become "partakers of the divine nature" (2 Pet. 1:4). Paralleling our engagement with the Gospel of John and the creeds, Calvin argues that *nature* here should be understood not as essence but as *life*.[15] God has communicated his life in the Son by the Spirit to his people. As we share in his life, we bear the fruit of his life.[16] In doing so, Calvin

11. Calvin, "2 Peter," 368.

12. Calvin argues that Scripture "expressly declares that wisdom, love, patience, are the gifts of God and the Spirit. When, therefore, the Apostle requires these things, he by no means asserts that they are in our power, but only shews what we ought to have, and what ought to be done. And as to the godly, when conscious of their own infirmity, they find themselves deficient in their duty, nothing remains for them but to flee to God for aid and help" ("2 Peter," 373–74).

13. Calvin, "2 Peter," 369.

14. Calvin writes, "But since everything necessary for godliness and salvation is to be deemed among the supernatural gifts of God, let men learn to arrogate nothing to themselves, but humbly ask of God whatever they see they are wanting in, and to ascribe to him whatever good they may have. For Peter here, by attributing the whole of godliness, and all helps to salvation, to the divine power of Christ, takes them away from the common nature of men, so that he leaves to us not even the least particle of any virtue or merit" ("2 Peter," 369).

15. Calvin, "2 Peter," 371.

16. Luther writes, "For here we work nothing, render nothing to God; we only receive and permit someone else to work in us, namely, God" (*Lectures on Galatians: Chapters 1–4*, 5).

writes, God restores his holiness and righteousness to us "that we may at length be partakers of eternal life and glory as far as it will be necessary for our complete felicity."[17] This is the context that leads Peter directly into a call for virtue: "For this very reason make every effort, by your faith to produce virtue, by virtue knowledge, by knowledge self-control, by self-control steadfastness, by steadfastness godliness, by godliness brotherly affection, and by brotherly affection love" (2 Pet. 1:5–7).[18] This list begins with the virtue of faith and ends with love.[19] It is not a progression, as if we should start with faith and through much effort and discipline *achieve* love.[20] Rather, it is as the Christian has received God himself in Christ by his love that they are able to walk in and for love, such that there is a kind of progression from the love of God that *culminates with love*.[21] Founded on God's love for us, a properly *Christian* life is shaped by God through faith. If these qualities increase in a person, the person will not be unfruitful in their *knowledge* of Jesus.

Colossians 2–3 is a very different sort of passage, but an important one in light of Paul's critique of self-made religion and worldly asceticism. Before criticizing the worldly spirituality that troubles him, Paul affirms the Colossians: "Therefore, as you received Christ Jesus the Lord, so walk in him, rooted and built up in him and established in the faith, just as you were taught, abounding in thanksgiving" (Col. 2:6–7). For those having received Christ, Paul's call to walk *in* Jesus sets up his critique of any way of life (i.e., "philosophy," Col. 2:8) that is not built on Christ. The truth and the life are *in Christ*, such that any failure to find life and goodness

17. Calvin, "2 Peter," 371.

18. This translation is from Bauckham, *2 Peter, Jude*, 172. Darian Lockett explains, "Because everything pertaining to life and godliness is freely given in Christ, Peter exhorts his readers to a new life of moral progress in 2 Peter 1:5–10. The phrase 'For this very reason' at the beginning of 2 Peter 1:5 marks the flow of thought from the knowledge and promises given in 2 Peter 1:3–4 to the ethical characteristics outlined in the next phrase" (Lockett, *Letters for the Church*, 104–5).

19. See Bauckham, *2 Peter, Jude*, 176; Lockett, *Letters for the Church*, 105.

20. Calvin makes a similar point: "This is not here, however, properly a gradation as to the sense, though it appears as to the words; for love does not in order follow patience, nor does it proceed from it. Therefore the passage is to be thus simply explained, 'Strive that virtue, prudence, temperance, and the things which follow, may be added to your faith'" ("2 Peter," 372–73).

21. Lockett writes, "Love is the climactic or the crowning virtue that encompasses all the previous virtues" (*Letters for the Church*, 105).

in him leads away from where life is found. Worldly spirituality focused on visionary experiences or rigorous asceticism does not hold "fast to the Head, from whom the whole body, nourished and knit together through its joints and ligaments, grows with a growth that is from God" (Col. 2:19). The growth of holiness that Paul articulates—the vision of virtue formation that animates his theology—is one that is a growth from God. This is growth *from* him and *to* him.

When Paul criticizes misguided spirituality, it is not only because it is false but also because it simply won't work. He claims that worldly forms of spirituality "have indeed an appearance of wisdom in promoting self-made religion and asceticism and severity to the body, but they are of no value in stopping the indulgence of the flesh" (Col. 2:23). This spirituality is no help against the flesh, because only holding fast to Christ can mortify the flesh. To "hold fast" to the ascended Christ is to seek him who is above. So Paul admonishes, "If then you have been raised with Christ, seek the things that are above, where Christ is, seated at the right hand of God. Set your minds on things that are above, not on things that are on earth. For you have died, and your life is hidden with Christ in God" (Col. 3:1–3). In a similar way to Peter, Paul grounds Christian formation in Christ, growing into him and contemplating him by faith to know him as our proper end. This is why Paul turns to mortification (i.e., "putting to death") and vivification (i.e., "putting on") as the proper response of faith. To put on virtue is to put on Christ, and in embracing his self-giving life and righteousness we gain access to the Father. This is why his imperative is to put on "the new man"—Christ—so that we can bear the fruit of his life.

These two passages illustrate the logic of the New Testament's emphasis on virtue and depict how that logic follows the contours of one's holiness in Christ. Virtue is not something *merely* habituated, because the virtue of holiness is the fruit of the divine life. Christ is the head from whom the whole body grows, with a growth that is from God (Col. 2:19). Far from allowing for passivity or inactivity, God's work in the person is that they "will and work" (Phil. 2:12–13); God's presence and action awaken the person to a life of relational responsiveness to the Spirit that leads to virtue.[22]

22. The Reformed tradition is probably seen as the tradition that focuses too much on God's action, such that human action is undermined. It is important to note, however, that

What we have articulated thus far is exactly what the Western theological tradition has emphasized, albeit in differing ways, through a focus on the *grace of God and infusion*. The primary work infusion does is to secure the supernatural life *from without*, reconstituting the person in the grace, holiness, and love of God. In other words, infusion advances an account of virtue by grace. It establishes God as the primary cause of supernatural virtue, not as a mere first mover but as the one whose *presence and act of love is continually necessary for Christian maturation*.

Sanctification, Virtue, and Reconstructing Infusion

One of the problems concerning the doctrine of sanctification, as seen in the last chapter, is that it rarely does significant doctrinal work in theological systems. It is common to move from justification to a generic account of the Christian life, with sanctification merely serving previously assumed accounts of formation or, more often, continuing to serve as another mechanism to protect justification. But the account we offer throughout this volume provides a different avenue. We argue that a key theological function of the doctrine of sanctification is that it governs accounts of moral and spiritual theology. This means that moral and spiritual theology need to be ordered *by the Holy One in our midst*, focusing on God's presence and activity as the proper mooring for relationally responsive human activity. To return to the imagery of home, God creates a path for life with him as his children—from within the sonship of Jesus—to know God as Father in and by the Spirit, who helps secure life in his presence.

We must, therefore, differentiate our "moral grammar" from our "theological grammar" (to use Luther's terminology) as we address ethical

---

this was never the goal and that all traditions struggle to make sense of how God's work in us to *will and to do* (Phil. 2:12–13) does not undermine human action while upholding the prior and undergirding action of God. Calvin advances Augustine on this, claiming,

> We agree that labour and striving are needed on both sides. Nor do we deny that the struggle is of such a kind as both to involve the utmost difficulty and to require the greatest efforts and the whole of a person's dedication. The question is only whether we fight for God with our own strength, or he supplies from heaven the skill, the courage, the hands, the strength, and the weapons. . . . It is not that we ourselves do nothing or that we without any movement of our will are driven to act by pressure from him, but that we act while being acted upon by him. (Calvin, *The Bondage and Liberation of the Will*, 152)

questions.[23] D. Stephen Long helpfully articulates the difference between what he calls "Christian ethics" and moral theology along these lines.[24] Christian ethics, on his reading, seeks to develop ethical theory from outside a theological system, whereas moral theology is grounded doctrinally and ordered by that doctrinal framework. In the account of holiness that we have articulated above, *holiness is the proper sphere of Christian virtue*, and therefore, as such, follows the doctrinal call to a robust moral theology. John Webster articulates this call well:

> Christian moral theology is in part the depiction of the moral field of the gospel. The gospel sets out the order within which human moral reasoning and action occur, an order which is properly understood as the history of the encounter between the God who graciously creates, saves and perfects, and the creatures who receive these graces and respond to them with grateful action. . . . The moral field is thus defined as the arena of God's activity as creator, reconciler and perfecter, the one who brings all things into being, upholds them against all threats and enables them to attain their proper end.[25]

23. Luther writes,

> As I have said, true "doing" is a doing in faith and a theological doing, which someone who seeks righteousness on the basis of works does not have. Therefore every doer of the Law and every moral saint who wants to be justified through human will and reason is under a curse, because he comes before God in the presumption of his own righteousness. In "keeping" the Law he does not keep it. This is what Paul calls "relying on works of the Law," namely, that the hypocrites keep the Law, and yet in keeping it they do not keep it, because they understand this "doing" according to the moral grammar, which does not apply in theology. (*Lectures on Galatians: Chapters 1–4*, 268)

Likewise,

> Thus if the statement from Dan. 4:24, "redeem your sins by giving alms," is produced, one must immediately consult the grammar—not the moral grammar but the theological grammar. This will show that "redeem" here is a matter not of morality but of faith, that it includes faith. For in Sacred Scripture a work presupposes a good will and a right reason, not in the moral sense but in the theological, which means faith. In this way you can easily stop the mouth of the sophists. For they themselves are forced to grant, as they teach on the basis of Aristotle, that every good work proceeds from choice. If this is true in philosophy, it is much more necessary in theology that a good will and a right reason based on faith should precede a work. (Luther, *Lectures on Galatians: Chapters 1–4*, 294)

24. Long, "Moral Theology."
25. Webster, *Word and Church*, 234.

As we consider the nature of virtue in relation to the doctrine of sanctification, we are articulating the moral field of the gospel. Creaturely formation is ordered from within God's gracious presence, never leaving behind his presence and action.

Virtue, Habituation, and Holiness

There are several well-established axioms broadly assumed by Protestant Christians concerning virtue. First, Christian virtue begins and ends with God, such that it is first and foremost *received*.[26] What is received is often deemed infused grace, supernatural principles, or, at times, principles of holiness in the soul. This is what many traditionally called "habitual grace."[27] Second, while the *habituation* of Christian virtue might look like natural virtue, Christian virtue habituates something from *without* (outside the self), and therefore the notion of habituation needs to be adapted given its unique telos and mode. In short, the mode of supernatural virtue is faith, hope, and love, ordered first and foremost *to* God and only then to realities other than God. These penultimate realities are not simply "second" to God but are ordered to God as their proper telos in God's creation. While God does not take our eyes off creaturely goods, his goodness frames and locates these in relation to himself in such a way that allows us to focus on them properly. Supernatural virtue, therefore, requires the reorientation of all human capacities to God through the continued activity of faith, hope, and love. However, an articulation of the reception of Christian virtue, and the habituation of what is received, is still not enough for a full-fledged Christian account of supernatural virtue. Directly related to this, third, is the work of the Spirit forming the soul for his presence and action according to the fruit of God's life in our lives (through the gifts

26. Angela Carpenter titled her book on Reformed sanctification and formation *Responsive Becoming*, which signals the responsive (and therefore received) nature of formation.

27. For instance, in his account of regeneration, John Owen claims that a "new spiritual principle, an infused habit of grace, or gracious abilities, to be required in and unto regeneration" (*Pneumatologia*, 220). This "new spiritual principle or nature" is "wrought in us by the Spirit of God" (220). Owen uses the language of new dispositions, power, and abilities for renewed human faculties. This is a divine and spiritual principle of operation, "namely, an habitual holy principle of spiritual actions and operations" (221). Importantly, Owen does not think that this habitual grace can function in the soul without the continued action of God. See *Pneumatologia*, 475.

of the Spirit for Aquinas, the "illapse" of the Spirit for John Owen, and so forth).

To summarize, we now have three axioms:

Axiom 1: Christian virtue begins and ends with God.

Axiom 2: The mode of supernatural virtue is faith, hope, and love. The telos of these realities is first and foremost God, and within that primary telos, second, all other ends are ordered according to the economy of God's kingdom.

Axiom 3: The Spirit forms the soul for his presence and action to bear the fruit of God's life in ours.

Admittedly, one can affirm these and come up with different accounts of grace, infusion, virtue, and much else. Here we want to take our account of holiness and advance a way to take these three axioms in a slightly different direction from the accounts provided thus far.

To do so, we need to consider the category of infusion as such. At first glance, infusion may not seem to mesh with our biblical depiction of holiness. Infusion seems to function in a mechanistic register, and it can carry with it, no matter how much qualification to the contrary, the sense of receiving *something* into the soul. There is a temptation to see infusion as something handed over, such that someone who was not virtuous (e.g., does not have patience) becomes a Christian and is now immediately healed of that vice. The problem is that formation tends not to work this way, and the idea that God simply heals us of vice runs contrary to the biblical language of maturation (e.g., 1 Cor. 3:1–3; 13:11; 1 John 2:12–14; Heb. 5:12). The Christian tradition has tended to follow the biblical language of growth as maturation from childhood to adulthood, instead of advancing the idea that God heals vice like he heals broken limbs or blindness in Jesus's New Testament ministry. Furthermore, in contrast to how infusion sounds in some contemporary discourse, the language of holiness is deeply connected to *relational* presence. So how does relational presence relate to infusion?

When infusion is understood in concert with the gift of the Spirit, it is deeply connected with God's indwelling. Several in the Christian tradition have developed their account of infusion this way, such as Bonaventure,

Bernard, Turretin, and Edwards.[28] For each of these figures, the Spirit's personal, indwelling presence is the controlling theological reality, and infusion is an explanatory tool for specifying aspects of the Spirit's indwelling. In this sense, the Spirit's indwelling is directly connected to the initial act of infusion and the preservation of what is infused. Whatever we take infusion to mean—and the tradition includes more than one understanding—it can't mean something contrary to what we believe about the Spirit's personal and intimate indwelling and all its effects in the believer. Thus, the Spirit of God illuminates Christ in faith and hope (2 Cor. 4:6), pours forth love into the heart (Rom. 5:5), and ushers the person into God's presence in such a way that the whole person is called before God in Christ to be reordered around him as the center (Eph. 2:18).

By mooring infusion language to indwelling, we can contrast our position with more mechanistic accounts of infusion, maintaining a focus *on the work of the Son and the Spirit*. That has been the overarching emphasis of our soteriology at every step. Consider Ephesians 3:16. Paul implores that the Father would strengthen the Ephesians "with power through his Spirit in your inner being." What is the Spirit's work in the "inner being" for? Paul explains: "so that Christ may dwell in your hearts through faith—that you, being rooted and grounded in love, may have strength to comprehend with all the saints what is the breadth and length and height and depth, and to know the love of Christ that surpasses knowledge, that you may be filled with all the fullness of God" (Eph. 3:17–19). The Spirit works internally so that Christ will more fully dwell in a person, so that they can be further established in and by love for the sake of love. Rather than functioning in a mechanistic register, infusion is a personal indwelling of God calling persons to draw near to himself to know and be known, and to love and be loved.

The Spirit's work in the soul has a christological orientation to it, such that Word and Spirit can never be divided. The "love of Christ" received through the work of the Spirit is not just love in general (as if love could be abstracted from persons-in-relation). Jesus indicates a more profound

28. Bonaventure, *Breviloquium*, 97; Bernard, *On the Song of Songs II*, 129; Turretin, *Institutes of Elenctic Theology*, 2:523; Edwards, *Writings on the Trinity, Grace, and Faith*, 195. To situate Edwards's claim that creatures partake of the holiness by which God himself is holy, see Strobel, "True Grace Is Divine," in Peppiatt and Strobel, *Virtue Ethics, Grace, and a Protestant Doctrine of Infusion*.

horizon when he prays to the Father, asking him that "the love with which you have loved me may be in them, and I in them" (John 17:26). In this section of John, Jesus anchors the believers' relationship to him directly to his own relation to the Father. The love he shares with the Father is *enlarged* to internalize believers. This is the love that the Spirit pours forth in the soul of the Christian as it is received from within the Spirit's work to unite them to Christ. Faith, hope, and love are the proper response to Christ's establishing the person within himself before the Father, and they are enacted from within the Spirit's work upon the soul (his working with power in the "inner being"). To be "filled with all the fullness of God" is to have the Spirit of the Son, who illumines Christ and establishes his presence, and to know the love he pours into the hearts of believers. The Spirit indwells Christians so that these realities are infused in them as abiding dispositions of the heart.

To summarize, the language of infusion should be scrubbed of its mechanistic overtones by focusing on the personal nature of the Father's love for the Son and the Son opening his life to internalize his own people into himself by the Spirit. (See the sidebar "Metaphor in Theology.") When given a solid trinitarian footing such as this, what is often just called "indwelling" is given further specification by the language of infusion. We can further clarify the relation between these two realities this way: The Spirit indwells the person such that his personal nature of love and holiness is now present within the human heart. The Spirit is not inertly present to the soul, as if the Spirit were inactive. Rather, the Spirit takes what is Christ's—namely, the love of the Father upon him—and infuses this into the soul of the believer. *Love is infused* as it is poured forth into the heart by the Spirit, and *holiness is infused* as the Spirit communicates himself to the soul as the personal presence of God that unites a person to God's life in Christ.[29] In this sense, infusion relates to indwelling as, in some accounts, imputation relates to union. Instead of something being added, the use of infusion and imputation clarifies indwelling and union, respectively. *Infusion names the kind of work that the Spirit is doing in the soul* to establish the person as a "partaker of the divine nature" (2 Pet. 1:4). The goal is not to shift the focus away from the person of Christ and the Spirit to something else,

29. The infusion of love is a particular theme in Bernard's commentaries on the Song of Songs. See, for instance, Bernard, *On the Song of Songs II*, 238.

Metaphor in Theology

Metaphor is essential for theology. God *as God* is beyond the comprehensive reach of our intellect (a long-standing Christian conviction), so metaphors provide ways to talk about God and life with God by drawing on things we know from human experience. Thus, authors of the Old Testament liken God to a shepherd, rock, king, potter, father, fire, water, wind, and so on, because these are imagery-rich ways of describing what God reveals about his character and nature. The New Testament likewise overflows with metaphors for life with God, such as friendship, carrying one's cross, abiding, following, adoption, marriage, imitation, participation, and so forth. All such metaphors do not equate God or life with God to whatever *this-is-like-that* associations they offer. Rather, they engage our imaginations so that we can *really and truly know* what cannot be comprehensively grasped with our minds and explained with our words.

In theological writing and discourse, metaphors are profoundly important, for they turn our imaginations toward the imagery they employ in powerful ways. All theological metaphors are limited, but some are more effective than others at turning our imaginations toward the realities of God. Scripture can be our guide as we use metaphors in theology, for it provides a wealth of universally relevant metaphors. It also provides the meta-story that tests the resonance of our metaphors. We should thus avoid overly mechanistic metaphors that fail to evoke the *relational aspects of God's life in himself* and the *relational dimensions of God's saving economy*.[a]

a. On the use of metaphor in theology, see Soskice, *Metaphor and Religious Language*. For those who are wary of using nonscriptural metaphors, consider Sarah Coakley's metaphor of magnetized iron filings for prayer ("Prayer as Divine Propulsion") or Rowan Williams's evocative metaphor of the Christian life as being caught in a tide (*Being Christian*, 8).

which is always the danger of adding technical vocabulary. The language of infusion should help focus on the work of the Son and the Spirit in the soul for a reorientation to God in Christ by the Spirit.

Further, the language of infusion can help us specify what it means for one to *receive holiness and love* from the indwelling of the Spirit. To have these realities is to *have the Spirit*. Infusion articulates the Spirit pouring forth love *within* the heart and not merely upon the person from without. This action in the soul originates from without but is so internal to the person that God's action is not somehow outside the person's free act but establishes it (Phil. 2:12–13; see the sidebar "Philippians 2:1–13"). This is the kind of action of God that brings freedom and does not inhibit it; God's work is not *against* the person, because it is internal to their own willing (2 Cor. 3:17). This is pastorally important because the Spirit's presence to the soul awakens the conscience in important ways, such that the new believer responds to sin in ways that were not true prior to conversion. As we have seen, it is from within the sin, rebellion, and brokenness of the heart that the person needs to draw near to God, who is holy, pure, and stable in himself, such that he communicates his holiness, purity, and stability within the person. God's holiness brings purity and access within it, as it is the holiness known in Christ's reconciling work to make peace "in himself" (Eph. 2:15).

To locate infusion in the indwelling Spirit is to continually recall the personal and relational nature of Christian formation. The ultimate telos of formation—true supernatural formation—is that we will be like Jesus only when we see him as he is (1 John 3:2). All formation is a face-to-face knowing (1 Cor. 13:12) such that to habituate the love infused requires that one receive this love by faith. To habituate this love is to stand before the Father, in the Son, by the Spirit, as one made holy by being united to Christ for walking by the Spirit (Gal. 5:16). This holiness establishes the face-to-face presence of God known in Christ by the Spirit, which gives shape to the kind of habituation necessary to cultivate *supernatural* virtue. To habituate supernatural virtue, on this understanding, is to habituate something received because it is something relational; supernatural formation requires the habituation of God's life in our life.

Take our earlier example of patience. We might say that one could habituate patience naturally simply by seeking to be more patient, establishing disciplines or rhythms of life that prioritize patience, and rejecting actions of impatience while contemplating the goodness of patience. This would be to habituate a natural good. But the kind of virtue God calls his people to is virtue that is relationally responsive to his self-giving—not responsive in the sense of *reactive*, but responsive in the way that we receive and internalize the very realities that need to overflow in and through us

Philippians 2:1–13

1So if there is any encouragement in Christ, any comfort from love, any
participation in the Spirit, any affection and sympathy, 2complete my joy
by being of the same mind, having the same love, being in full accord and
of one mind. 3Do nothing from selfish ambition or conceit, but in humility
count others more significant than yourselves. 4Let each of you look not
only to his own interests, but also to the interests of others. 5Have this
mind among yourselves, which is yours in Christ Jesus, 6who, though he
was in the form of God, did not count equality with God a thing to be
grasped, 7but emptied himself, by taking the form of a servant, being born
in the likeness of men. 8And being found in human form, he humbled
himself by becoming obedient to the point of death, even death on a
cross. 9Therefore God has highly exalted him and bestowed on him the
name that is above every name, 10so that at the name of Jesus every knee
should bow, in heaven and on earth and under the earth, 11and every
tongue confess that Jesus Christ is Lord, to the glory of God the Father.
12Therefore, my beloved, as you have always obeyed, so now, not only
as in my presence but much more in my absence, work out your own
salvation with fear and trembling, 13for it is God who works in you, both
to will and to work for his good pleasure.

to be truly virtuous. This is why, as we have seen, New Testament ethics is often in an indicative-imperative form. God gives what he demands, as Augustine likes to remind us. Supernatural patience, in this sense, is founded on the patience of God and is cultivated in a life that comes to know and mature in God's patience *toward you*. At bottom, therefore, true supernatural virtue is virtue that overflows from what God has done, and more specifically what he has done for you, in and for love. We could make the same argument about gratitude or joy and the conviction that these are gateways to human flourishing. Natural joy is certainly a good, but supernatural joy requires that Christ's "joy may be in you, and that your joy may be made full" (John 15:11). This supernatural joy is received (i.e., infused) because it is Christ's, and it becomes internalized to overflowing.

The configuration of infusion that we advance invites an increasing knowledge of what God has done and who a person really is as one who stands before the face of the holy God. Luke 7:47 is a good example of this; we are told that the person who is forgiven little can love little, which implies that to love much one must be forgiven much. Knowing how much you need forgiveness involves an increasing knowledge of the depth of your sinfulness and rebellion, only to have that knowledge surpassed by God's grace and forgiveness. It is in knowing what God has given that you can begin to overflow in love and forgiveness. This is why, in Peter's description of virtue, failure to remember what you have been forgiven is the reason your life has become ineffective and unfruitful (2 Pet. 1:8–9). This kind of forgetfulness is a failure to embrace the kind of life offered in Christ and infused by the Spirit, which should always illumine our dependence on Christ and therefore our continual need of his mercy. None of this is true for the cultivation of natural goods, which simply requires the potentiality of virtue in a person and the fortitude to habituate goodness. But supernatural virtue requires that what is habituated be received in and through communion with God.

This emphasis on maturation in Christ, which requires seeing how much we need forgiveness to grow in love, solves a number of difficulties. For instance, if a convert has a lot of natural patience to begin with, one might assume that this is a supernatural virtue after conversion simply because the person is a Christian. Patience is patience, we might assume. But the model presented here resituates patience such that the person needs to relearn patience in and for love—not generic love but the love of the Father upon the Son that is offered in salvation. All our natural virtues need to be purified in light of God and his self-giving. Supernatural virtue, in this sense, is never simply *goodness*, precisely because "whatever does not proceed from faith is sin" (Rom. 14:23).[30] Faith, as a gift of the Spirit's work to illumine Christ, establishes a different form of virtue that

30. Calvin notes that faith provides the only proper end that makes virtues *right* before God:

> In short, when we remember the constant end of that which is right—namely, to serve God—whatever strives to another end already deservedly loses the name "right." Therefore, because they do not look to the goal that God's wisdom prescribes, what they do, though it seems good in the doing, yet by its perverse intention is sin. . . . Since they lacked the light of faith, they did not apply their deeds to the end to which they ought to have applied them. Therefore, true righteousness was not in them, because duties are weighed not by deeds but by ends. (*Institutes* III.xiv.3 [1:770])

cannot be reduced to goodness, as the Western tradition has never tired of emphasizing.[31] Likewise, there are not two orders of virtues functioning in parallel with a person (acquired and infused). Rather, each virtue has a foundation, form, and telos that establish a natural or supernatural *character* to the virtue.

In light of this focus on faith, reimagining natural virtues as kinds of vice is unnecessary (calling them "beautiful vices" or "glittering vices"). Nonetheless, these natural virtues are "nothing" (to borrow Paul's term from 1 Cor. 13) before the face of God. Outside of faith and the love of God, natural virtue is no virtue at all, because true virtue always stems from one's abiding in Christ. Furthermore, this explains why Christians can be less "virtuous" in appearance than their unbelieving neighbors. Love has been given to them, but not as a commodity that somehow immediately transforms them into virtuous people. They need to be re-Fathered in and by his love, given in the Son, such that they relearn all of their life as children of their heavenly Father.[32] The moral and psychological changes are not instantaneous but require maturation in relational response to God. This is why the traditional account of infusion was never understood as mechanical or completed. Infusion, for Bernard, Thomas, and the Protestant theological tradition, was always followed by active reception, habituation, and the continued work of the Spirit to preserve and guide creaturely action.

Furthermore, since supernatural virtue is the habituation of something alien to the person and therefore requires another's presence, it is not surprising that Scripture turns to *marriage* and *friendship* to model the relationship Christians have with God. Marriage and friendship require a kind of face-to-face knowledge that isn't available outside the self-giving

31. Luther is characteristic: "Everything that is attributed to works belongs to faith. For works must not be looked at in a moral sense; they must be looked at in a theological and faithful sense. Therefore in theology let faith always be the divinity of works, diffused throughout the works in the same way that the divinity is throughout the humanity of Christ" (*Lectures on Galatians: Chapters 1–4*, 266).

32. This is Angela Carpenter's emphasis when she surveys Calvin's understanding of sanctification. She summarizes, "The believer is adopted as God's child and this change in status transforms her moral agency from a posture of fearful servitude to one of joyful and willing love. This transformation, though in some sense immediate, must also unfold over the course of human life as the person continues to reject an old identity of independence from God, and to live within her new identity as God's child" (*Responsive Becoming*, 44).

of the person, and they both require a kind of formation that happens only within the relationship itself. The presence, love, and self-giving of the other person—including forgiveness when relationships break down—are all necessary for the relationship to grow and for one to grow within the relationship. There can be something instantaneous, as in the saying of "I do" at a marriage ceremony, but that only establishes the space for continued face-to-face knowing and growth.

The personal presence of the indwelling Spirit, illuminating Christ and establishing our union with him, must continually undermine attempts to turn Christian formation into moralistic frameworks of creaturely goodness. As Paul admonishes the Galatians, "Did you receive the Spirit by works of the law or by hearing with faith? Are you so foolish? Having begun by the Spirit, are you now being perfected by the flesh?" (Gal. 3:2–3). However we might understand the ways the Galatians were seeking to become perfected by the flesh, it was not centered on or founded on the work of the Spirit. Accounts of formation must maintain this focus on the presence and activity of God, and in doing so must bear in mind that creaturely perfection is addressed in Scripture through presence, love, and sight, which is known as holiness. This is why the telos of our formation is sight: "When he appears we shall be like him, because we shall see him as he is" (1 John 3:2). Presence and sight can often be glossed by just one of those terms or by other theologically rich descriptions such as *glory*. Perhaps most often, though, Scripture glosses these claims as *love*. Love is both the grounding of virtue and its end, because God is love and his life is the foundation and end of all holy action.

Summary

Our doctrine of sanctification *orders the doctrine of the Christian life* and *informs our understanding of virtue formation* by centering both of these on God's sanctifying presence. As it concerns the Christian life, we emphasize home as an especially potent and resonant metaphor for the Christian's relation to God in Christ and the Spirit. When oriented to the presence of God, sanctification unfolds the nature of being at home with God already for the sake of being home with God forever, and all that being home with God entails for us *then and now*: the recharacterization of our whole self after the image of the Son, our reorientation toward others and the nonhuman world, and our participation in the mission of the Son and the Spirit. As it concerns virtue formation, we accentuate and clarify its *supernatural* character over against merely natural accounts of habituation with an account of infusion. The language of infusion has a long history and can helpfully specify the meaning of the Spirit's indwelling when it has solid trinitarian footing: The Spirit indwells the person, such that his personal nature of love and holiness is now *present* within the human heart to *enable* our relationally responsive actions.

DOXOLOGICAL INTERLUDE

Rowan and Irene LeCompte, *Mary Magdalene in the Garden with Jesus*

> Mary stood weeping outside the tomb, and as she wept she stooped to look into the tomb. And she saw two angels in white, sitting where the body of Jesus had lain, one at the head and one at the feet. They said to her, "Woman, why are you weeping?" She said to them, "They have taken away my Lord, and I do not know where they have laid him." Having said this, she turned around and saw Jesus standing, but she did not know that it was Jesus. Jesus said to her, "Woman, why are you weeping? Whom are you seeking?" Supposing him to be the gardener, she said to him, "Sir, if you have carried him away, tell me where you have laid him, and I will take him away." Jesus said to her, "Mary." She turned and said to him in Aramaic, "Rabboni!" (which means Teacher). Jesus said to her, "Do not cling to me, for I have not yet ascended to the Father; but go to my brothers and say to them, 'I am ascending to my Father and your Father, to my God and your God.'" Mary Magdalene went and announced to the disciples, "I have seen the Lord"—and that he had said these things to her.
>
> John 20:11–18

Invitation

Mary weeps at the threshold of Jesus's tomb when angels meet her. They seem to bring little comfort, and having lamented the absence of Jesus's body, she turns in despair. Jesus is there. He is unmistakably present—probably feet away—but she mistakes him for the gardener (perhaps the Lord of new creation was gardening). Even when he addresses her obvious sorrow, "Why are you weeping?" she doesn't recognize him. Only when she hears *her name*, the one word that singles her out as a unique person—*this* person—does she recognize Jesus. "Mary," he says.

None capture the intimacy of their interaction better than Rowan and Irene LeCompte in this mosaic. Even as a tear rests on Mary's cheek, her exuberance at being in Jesus's presence is unmistakable. She is welcomed by Jesus, his shoulders and body turned toward her as he holds her wrist. Most portrayals have Jesus pushing Mary away with an outstretched arm, fixating on the words, "Do not cling to me" (v. 17). But the mosaic leaves us certain that it was their *embrace* that prompted those words. Is John subtly inviting us to see ourselves in Mary's experience? Is her progression from seeing to recognizing to embracing a process that John invites us to enter? Seeing is one thing; perceiving and then embracing are distinctly others. We struggle, like John's original audience, to progress from seeing to perceiving to embracing—and not merely at the origins of faith's pilgrimage but at every moment.

Pause and prayerfully invite the Spirit to help you consider your capacities for perceiving and embracing Jesus. Do you perceive Jesus as you once did, or does that capacity need to be awakened again? Are the fellowship and communion of embracing Jesus with your whole self still your experience of sharing life with God, or does it seem that Jesus holds you at arm's length? And could it be that the story also invites us to contemplate our life *with others*? Does your capacity for *recognizing others as Jesus does* call for the same awakening? What could such awakenings mean for your life with God and others?

Notes

CHAPTER SIX

Sanctifying Theology

> If anyone loves me, he will keep my word, and my Father will love him, and we will come to him and make our home with him.
>
> John 14:23

> In union with God, in being brought near to God, all the trials and sorrows of life—sufferings, loss, moral failing, the oppressive stunting of opportunities and vitality, grief, worry, tribulation and strife—are purified, remedied and reworked through the gifts of God's grace.
>
> Kathryn Tanner[1]

WE STARTED THIS VOLUME with a brief reflection on spirituality and theology and on the devastating divorce that has riven doctrinal reflection from the lived reality of our spiritual existence in Christ. The contrast, as it is sometimes described, is between a "theology at the desk" and a "theology at prayer." We highlighted these tensions early in the volume to frame our discussion of sanctification and interweave prayer and reflection throughout as doxological interludes, crafting space for the contemplation of God amid doctrinal construction. The goal was that

1. Tanner, *Jesus, Humanity, and the Trinity*, 2.

our form of reasoning would conform to our calling in Christ, holding together the intellectual and experiential dynamics of the Christian life. Here our goal is to recollect the various threads of our argument and weave them back together to articulate the distinctively *spiritual* task of the theological endeavor. Instead of advancing new material, we want to apply our discussion to cast a vision for the renewal of a distinctively Protestant spiritual theology.

Sanctification serves as a particularly important case study for theological methodology, because sanctification addresses what it means to exist in the presence of God. Therefore, it proves helpful to consider how a doctrine of sanctification can give guidance to the task of articulating a real *spiritual* theology. Spirituality, far from being a general human construct, concerns life in the presence of God as one uniquely indwelled by the Spirit of God. The theological task must always remain a spiritual one, never secluding itself into mere academic sophistication. Theology must always be ordered and governed by love and by the God in whose presence we reason. In this sense, spiritual theology is a task of sanctified reason caught up in God's self-revelation that both reveals and judges. God's revelation not only illumines but also weighs and evaluates—the Spirit searches not only God's depths but ours also (1 Cor. 2:10).

In light of our account of sanctification, then, we have to consider theological reasoning before the face of God as those sanctified in Christ by the Spirit. There is no other location in which sanctified reason can adequately theologize. This approach is not obvious in many academic and churchly spaces. For many, doctrine quickly devolves into summary statements of either biblical passages or the tradition, doing little more than mapping well-worn territory. At times this is necessary, but doctrinal reflection needs to stand under the guidance and judgment of Scripture as it seeks to bear witness to God. Recall the definition of the theological task noted earlier as "the doctrine of living for God through Christ."[2] Or, with Jeremy Taylor, "theology is rather a divine life than a divine knowledge," although it would be folly to set these in opposition.[3] Against the

2. Van Mastricht, *Theoretical-Practical Theology*, 1:64.
3. Taylor, "Sermon VI: *Via Intelligentiae*," 361.

prevailing assumptions of the modern academy, the theological task cannot be separated cleanly from Christian spirituality.[4]

There is an opposing temptation alongside the error of creating a sterile science of academic theology segmented from devotion and the spiritual dynamics of life with the Lord. This temptation is simply to assert that *theology is spirituality*, as though asserting the right doctrinal constructs will transform a soul. There is a similar impulse to describe theology as a task of contemplation, which still proves meaningless for the form of theological reflection. It is easy to make claims about theology as prayer or theology as contemplation, but these assertions rarely pierce the depths of what they entail. Our focus on sanctification as being caught up in the self-giving of God to stand face-to-face with God in Christ Jesus should, instead, govern and guide theological method. It should affect the material content, the form, and the telos of theological reflection.

Karl Barth serves as a helpful example of attending to the form of theological reflection. Barth's concern that theology should always be in the mode of prayer gave shape to his theological exposition such that his theology is meant to awaken prayer within the reader.[5] (See the sidebar "Theology with a Skylight," p. 174.) Or, along similar lines, a proper Christian doctrine of God should cause the reader to praise and stand in awe of who God is, just as a theology of sin should cause the reader to repent and to throw themselves on the mercy of God. Sanctified theology should spring from worship and lead us back toward it. To merely articulate true things would miss that the theological task is never divorced from life

4. Similarly, Richard Baxter defines theology using an interconnection between theoretical and practical dynamics: "Divinity is an affective-practical science: Knowing is not the ultimate or perfective act of man: but a means to holy love, and joy, and service. Nor is it clear and solid knowledge, if it do not somewhat affect the heart, and engage and actuate the life, according to the nature and use of the thing known" (*The Divine Life*, 166–67).

5. Ashley Cocksworth, in one of his expositions of Barth's theology of prayer, writes,

> However, if the emerging scholarly consensus is anything to go by, something has gone badly wrong in modern theology if prayer is no longer seen as central to the nature and task of Christian theology. Yet prayer is no less periphery to Barth's thinking as it is to Christian theology itself. While there are central sections in Barth's theology where he sets his sights on explicit theorizations of prayer, in a much more fundamental sense Barth thinks his theology *through* prayer. It could be said that Barth's entire theology is a form of prayer, an extended contemplative stretching to God undertaken in the obedience and humility of prayer. ("Karl Barth's Very Theological Theology of Prayer," 447–48)

Theology with a Skylight

Proper and useful theological work is distinguished by the fact that it takes place in the realm which not only has windows (which in themselves are admittedly good and necessary) facing the surrounding life of the Church and world, but also and above all has a skylight. That is to say, theological work is opened *by* heaven and God's work and word, but it is also open *toward* heaven and God's work and word. It cannot possibly be taken for granted that this work is performed in this *open* realm, open toward the object of theology, its source and goal, and in this way open toward its great menace and the still greater hope which is founded upon its object. If theological work should attempt to hide itself from danger and hope, it would soon find itself locked in a closed, barred, stuffy, and unlit room. . . .

Theological work can be done only in the indissoluble unity of prayer and study. Prayer without study would be empty. Study without prayer would be blind.[a]

a. Barth, *Evangelical Theology*, 161, 171.

with God but is a task of Christian wisdom. Sanctification is about life in the presence of God for the presence of God, which we have circled around throughout this book. This pushes us to locate the theological task—as a task of sanctified reason—before the face of God as those who are in Christ and indwelled by the Spirit. Theology is more than merely reasoning *about* divine things but is, by faith, reasoning in God's presence.

What does it mean, then, to engage sanctification Christianly? How should Christian wisdom shape our reflection on this doctrine? What is the proper response to knowing that one has been sanctified in Christ Jesus? Keeping the task of theology before our eyes in this final chapter, we turn first to a theology of presence, which helps answer these questions. To engage sanctification as a doctrine of living for God through Christ, we weave the threads of this book together into a tapestry of presence. This is what will allow us to articulate sanctification as a doctrine, which will, finally, help us consider what it means to be a theologian of sanctification.

Throughout this final chapter the question in our minds is this: Who can be a theologian of sanctification? The theological task is not reducible to mere academic achievement. To embrace the theological task as it was always understood in the Christian tradition is to embrace a certain way of life. What is that way of life? What does it mean to advance sanctified reason in the presence of God for the presence of God?

Holiness and a Theology of Presence

We have been confronted with a vision of sanctification that cannot be sequestered to human formation or ethics. This vision is about presence. There is, nonetheless, an "order" to salvation, such that justification can still be seen as "preceding" sanctification. But we must recall that the first move of soteriological reflection is focusing not on the benefits of Christ but *on Christ himself as our righteousness and sanctification*. Salvation is Christ, full stop. Centering a doctrine of sanctification on that soteriological conviction focuses it on the presence and life of God in Christ Jesus for our communion with God in Christ by the Spirit. What was foregrounded in our reflection on the Gospel of John in the first chapter is that God is life, and in Christ Jesus he is offering us access to his life (Eph. 2:18). *Presence*, therefore, is not generic presence, nor even omnipresence, but is access to the life offered to us in Christ Jesus by the Spirit of God. *Sanctification, in other words, is concerned with the saving presence of God.*

Christian soteriological reflection moves from Christ's incarnation through his sacrificial death, resurrection, and ascension to address how it is possible that the ungodly are justified and are now reconciled to God to share in this life. This is exactly what is seen in Paul's argument in Romans 5:10: "For if while we were enemies, we were reconciled to God through the death of his Son, much more surely, having been reconciled, will we be saved by his life" (NRSV). The movement here is from hostility to reconciliation, and to having access to his life for the deliverance that *his life* provides. This is why Christians are called to put off Adam and put on Christ for true righteousness and holiness (Eph. 4:22–24). It is his life of righteousness and holiness that becomes ours through our abiding in him.

The presence that sanctification articulates is the Son's entrance into humanity in and through his incarnation, where he has sanctified himself for our sake so that we can be sanctified in the truth (John 17:19). Through his life, death, resurrection, and ascension, he has sent his Spirit of holiness to establish his presence within us as members of his

Theology and Spirituality

Put as bluntly as possible, theology without spirituality becomes ever more methodologically refined but unable to know or speak of the very mysteries at the heart of Christianity, and spirituality without theology becomes rootless, easily hijacked by individualistic consumerism. . . . In other words, when a culture has grown used to the divorce between theology and spirituality, between doctrine and prayer, then the mutually critical function of the two breaks down. Neither is in sufficient dialogue with the other to keep it honest. And after a long period of such separation it becomes increasingly difficult to see what is missing in so much of the pale pretenders that pass fairly often for theology and spirituality today.[a]

a. McIntosh, *Mystical Theology*, 10.

body—uniting us to himself. The divine presence is no longer understood according to specific spatial locations, but instead according to relational and restorational images of persons drawing near to their Lord, who has called them to himself. This is why sanctification, in terms of theological method, pushes the task of theology into the register of contemplation and prayer. To be sanctified is to be made holy within the holiness of Christ, who is our sanctification. It is not to be made holy from afar but to have Christ enlarge his holiness for his own. Likewise with contemplation and prayer. (See the sidebar "Theology and Spirituality.") Contemplation and prayer are constant reminders that the theological task is a task of grace.

Contemplation and prayer are founded on the work of God in Son and Spirit to redeem. Contemplation is setting one's gaze upon the one who gazes upon you; contemplation is knowing as we have been known (Gal. 4:9; 1 Cor. 13:12).[6] Prayer, likewise, is not an independent response to God's action but is something the Christian enters. As we have seen, true Christian prayer is entering into the prayers of the Son and the Spirit. In prayer, the believer has the Spirit praying "Abba! Father!" from their depths. As Jesus prays to his Father, so too does the believer pray within the identity of Christ given to them in salvation (Gal. 4:6; Rom. 8:15–16).

6. See Strobel, "Contemplation by Son and Spirit."

Communion in the Spirit

Indeed, our reconciliation to God through Christ the Savior could have been accomplished in no other way than through communion in the Spirit and sanctification. That which knits us together, as it were, and unites us to God is the Holy Spirit. When we receive the Spirit, we are made participants and sharers in the divine nature, and we receive the Father himself through the Son and in the Son. The wise John writes to us concerning him, "By this we know that we remain in him and he in us, because he has given us of his Spirit." And what does Paul say about this? "And because you are sons," he says, "God has sent the Spirit of his Son into our heart, crying, 'Abba! Father!'"[a]

a. Cyril of Alexandria, *Commentary on John*, 2:298.

This is why the Christian does not pray in their own name but ascends to the Father in the name of his Son, Jesus.

The presence of God articulated in our doctrine of sanctification is the presence of God shared in union to God in Christ by the Spirit. (See the sidebar "Communion in the Spirit.") This union is one that we see anticipated in Moses, who is called into God's presence to radiate the glory of God. Moses steps onto holy ground and hides his face because he is afraid to look at God (Exod. 3:6). It is Moses's archetypal intimacy with God, as we have seen, that sets up Paul's claims in 2 Corinthians 3–4, where Moses serves as the overarching image of Christian formation.[7] Considering what life in God's presence entails, he writes, "And we all, with unveiled face, reflecting the glory of the Lord, are being transformed into the same image from one degree of glory to another. For this comes from the Lord who is the Spirit" (2 Cor. 3:18). Some, however, who do not know the Lord are blind to his revelation. They cannot see the "light of the gospel of the glory of Christ, who is the image of God" (2 Cor. 4:4). But the God who spoke creation into existence, Paul argues, has shone in the hearts of those with faith, "to give the light

7. Paul's use of Moses as the archetype of being in God's presence to radiate his glory is not lost on the early church. Gregory of Nyssa's *Life of Moses* is a good example. Moses, for Gregory, is the shape of a life ascending to God in virtue, and a proper articulation of his life will lead the faithful one to elevate this life into the form of Christian faithfulness.

of the knowledge of the glory of God in the face of Jesus Christ" (2 Cor. 4:6). Through this, the *life of Jesus* is being made manifest in the lives of believers (2 Cor. 4:11).

We find in Paul's comparison between Moses and Christians in 2 Corinthians 3–4 that God establishes spaces of his presence that he might be received and known. This reception and knowledge are often articulated in visual metaphors, highlighting that while faith is not sight, it is best described using the language of vision (1 Cor. 13:12; 2 Cor. 5:7).[8] The sight of faith in this age is perfected as the sight of the beatific vision in eternity. This use of the visual highlights presence, intimacy, and formation. These reveal that while we are made holy for God's presence through union with Christ and the infusion of his Spirit, we are also called to be conformed to that presence through relational responsiveness to God. The language of *glory* is often employed at this point. Holiness and glory work together to articulate the call to be centered in and on Christ while also reflecting his life back to him through the ways he conforms us to himself. To be conformed to Christ in this presence and intimacy is articulated through both *internal* and *external* dynamics.

The invisible and internal glory of God, which shines in our hearts through the Spirit, who brings us face-to-face with Christ (2 Cor. 4:6), does not remain invisible or internal. This glory gives shape to a life ordered in and on Christ. The visible and external glory of God in the Christian is the fruit of love, refracted through a person's life as the fruit of the Spirit (Gal. 5:22–24). In other words, the visible fruit of the invisible action of the Spirit is love, and love forms a life in humility, dependence, and faithfulness. Whereas Moses's glory transformed his physical appearance, Christian glory is transformative by faith, which is made visible not as light but by its fruit. In that imaging of God to the world, God's presence is "seen" by faith as the invisible center that upholds and governs the people of God. Scripturally, therefore, holiness names the divine presence and intimacy through God's availability in Christ, as it reorders the Christian to a life centered on Christ. This intimacy and presence is a purifying fire to the soul. This is why Christian formation cannot be established in an

8. Furthermore, throughout Scripture God's presence is depicted as either blinding or illumining, something perhaps best seen in the earthly ministry of Jesus. This ministry is applied to believers who are the "aroma" of God to unbelievers and believers alike, Paul argues, "to one a fragrance from death to death, to the other a fragrance from life to life" (2 Cor. 2:15–16).

Aristotelian mode of habituation and why theologians across the Western theological tradition have rejected that as an adequate mode of *supernatural* formation. Our formation requires another. We are not merely given *something* called grace or holiness, but grace and holiness signify God's self-giving and recentering in himself in love and for love.

Moses's desire to see God grasps deeply the basic human desire to stare into beauty, to be caught up in its harmony. Beauty is an important category to articulate Scripture's focus on images of light, sight, and glory that pervade expositions of creaturely perfection. Christian formation culminates in sight only because God's presence and availability are the central and necessary realities that make this formation possible: "We shall be like him, because we shall see him as he is" (1 John 3:2). Christian formation is always formation before the face of God, because we are like branches grasping the vine, knowing life only as we abide in another (John 15:4–5). Put in more traditional categories, we can say that the beatific vision of eternity orders the life of faith now. Our formation is never simply the habituation of natural potentialities, because Christians are called to more than mere *goodness*. As Bavinck declares, "There is, however, a life other than the moral one: a spiritual life."[9] This is the life of holiness.

The moral life, which is available by nature, is opposed to *vice*, whereas for the Christian, "whatever does not proceed from faith is sin" (Rom. 14:23). The opposite of sin is not simply goodness, therefore, but faith. As we have seen, faith is given its contours by its perfection in the sight of eternity. This is where we will know as we have been known, which is why Paul at times can switch between knowing God and being known by him as if they were synonyms (e.g., Gal. 4:9). This unveils the deepest core of our humanity and the path of our formation into the likeness of Christ, but it also reveals the temptation to choose less. The temptation is to choose a kind of self-construction—a formation of the flesh—rather than the formation available in the Spirit (see Col. 2:16–23). Again, Paul's language is helpful: "Are you so foolish? Having begun by the Spirit, are you now being perfected by the flesh?" (Gal. 3:3).

One way this emphasis comes to the fore in the Protestant theological tradition is through employing both the beatific vision and infusion to address the end and ground of spiritual formation, establishing a kind of

9. Bavinck, *Reformed Ethics*, 1:241.

harmony. These doctrines are harmonized by orienting the task of formation around God in his gracious self-giving. As seen in Thomas's development of infusion, although not unique to him, supernatural virtue could not be generated (i.e., acquired) through habituation like natural virtue, because we are called not merely to goodness but to holiness. Instead of being sterile or mechanistic, the categories of glory, beatific vision, holiness, and infusion *are given life in the intimacy of God's relational presence through the indwelling Spirit*. The command to "draw near" in Hebrews, for instance, recognizes that those made holy have been given access and that the entire call of the Christian life is a continual invitation to embrace that access in Christ. "Draw near!" is the command of love.

One advantage of correlating the doctrines of the beatific vision and infusion is that it makes sense of the ways in which the *experience* of the Christian often runs contrary to expectation. A reductive reading of Scripture may lead one to assume that, upon regeneration, a Christian continues to grow spiritually and experiences only growth and goodness in their life with the Lord. Orienting regenerate existence to its perfection in the beatific vision reminds us that we live not in the age of sight but in the age of faith. Rather than gazing with clarity into the face of love—standing face-to-face with God—we see through a *mirror dimly*. This dim mirror of faith recollects our hearts to the truth that we must set our gaze above—on Christ—and trust that our lives are hidden with him. Likewise, infusion reminds us that while we are called saints, having received his holiness infused into our persons as the Holy Spirit, we are still far from what we should be. Infusion does not signify the immediate transformation of our character but our receiving of the Spirit, whose holy presence and love remain external to our character until we receive and habituate this presence and love. To receive the infusion of love is to know, by faith, that you have received the love of God as a call to have your person recharacterized in and by that love.[10] Infusion, as a feature of grace known by faith, is an invitation to draw near to the source of life in God himself.

God and his self-giving determine the nature of presence that is articulated in a doctrine of sanctification. This includes both internal and

10. Bernard of Clairvaux is characteristically helpful: "When the Word therefore tells the soul, 'You are beautiful,' and calls it friend, he infuses it into the power to love, and to know it is loved in return" ("Sermon 45:8–10," in *On the Song of Songs II*, 238).

external dynamics of presence that we have glossed with the term *home*. In John 14:23 Jesus declares that loving him means that he and the Father will make their home in his people. This internal reality of God's life and presence in the soul of a Christian establishes the communal external space of believers as the home of God. We are called to be harmonized both inwardly and outwardly within the sphere of God's presence and activity. Infusion and the beatific vision together help name this ordering all of life before the face of God by faith as we know his presence internal to ourselves by that same faith. Christ truly is our sanctification, and so all of our drawing near to him is given shape by the holiness we know in union with him by the Spirit (as we have seen in prayer and contemplation). The Christian never draws near to God alone but is ushered into God's presence by the gracious knowing in which they come to know.

By articulating holiness through the lens of the presence and action of God, centering soteriology on the eternal identity of Jesus as the Son of the Father, and the Spirit as the Spirit of the Son, we come to see that presence has a distinctively familial shape. This is one reason why the language of "home" is fitting. To draw near to God is to draw near to God as Father and to draw near as his child. We present ourselves to God in the name of Jesus as one who belongs to him. We ascend in the very love the Father has for the Son because that is the love made available by grace (John 17:26). This framing of holiness, given shape in the economic movement of God, needs to establish the contours of the doctrine of sanctification. Too often it does not.

Framing Sanctification Doctrinally

Even if you have followed our argument and accepted our conclusions, you still might be wondering at this point: What is *the doctrine* of sanctification? In this section we want to attend to that question directly. How might we articulate a doctrine of sanctification?

If we assume a relatively standard ordering of salvation (*ordo salutis*), we have space after justification and before glorification where we typically slot in whatever material we develop under the heading of sanctification. (See the sidebar "*Ordo Salutis*," p. 182.) But matters are not so easy. If we follow this route, we are tempted to stop talking about God and his work in the Son and the Spirit to focus entirely on the benefits of that work.

Ordo Salutis

Ordo salutis (Latin) means "order of salvation" and refers to the temporal or logical sequence of God's saving work. It's one of the few Latin phrases still commonly used in English-language theology, and the order it signifies is often a touchpoint for disagreement between Calvinist theologians and those from other Reformation traditions (e.g., Lutheran, Wesleyan, and free church). Elements of God's saving work that are included in the *ordo salutis*, and debated as it concerns their sequence, are calling, regeneration, adoption, union with Christ, conversion, faith, justification, and so forth. Most Calvinists, for instance, have traditionally held that regeneration necessarily precedes conversion (to emphasize the graciousness of God's redemptive agency), and others disagree, ordering conversion and faith prior to regeneration (seeking to emphasize the integrity of human freedom). Even within Reformed theology there is no uniformity about the sequence (current debates center on the order of union with Christ and justification).[a]

a. See Allison, *Historical Theology*, chaps. 21–25; Miller, "The Debate over the *Ordo Salutis* in American Reformed Theology."

Sanctification, in this sense, is often hijacked to serve other ends. Instead, sanctification as a doctrine needs to articulate the nature of life in Christ by the Spirit, along with governing and guiding spiritual, ethical, and formational directives to give an account of a holy life. It needs to deliver on both sides of our definition: Sanctification is life *in* the presence of God *for* the presence of God.

This means that the doctrine of sanctification will address spiritual formation, but it will do so in a broader sense than is often conceived. Under the heading of sanctification would have to be the nature of holiness, supernatural virtue formation, Christian experience, ecclesial life, marriage and singleness, calling, mortification and vivification, and so forth. Instead, in older works, what is often found is a chapter on sanctification followed by a series of reflections on the Christian life that stand alongside the doctrine of sanctification but are not ordered by it. Important topics of Christian living are often addressed, but they are addressed unmoored from the doctrinal content of sanctification itself.

We can attend to this matter from a different direction by distinguishing between the content of sanctification as such and sanctification as a doctrine. Sanctification as such is life in Christ by the Spirit. To talk about sanctification in this sense is to address the lived reality of life in Christ by the Spirit and the nature of a truly *supernatural* life. But the *doctrine* of sanctification has to be fitted within a theological system where it affects other doctrinal content. (This issue is often considered under the rubric of doctrinal location.) Sanctification, in this latter sense, focuses on the accomplished work of Christ and the application of that work by the Spirit. What this ends up meaning practically, for the theologian articulating a soteriology, is that the material content one might normally put in a doctrine of sanctification has often already been developed under regeneration, union with Christ, or another category of participation or fellowship with God. What the *doctrine* of sanctification should do, in those cases, is articulate how to apply the material content of holiness to the practical dynamics of life in Christ and growth in and through the Spirit, refusing to allow pragmatic impulses to reign and rejecting any theologizing that fails to address the spiritual dynamics of life in Christ.

Working outward from our content on divine presence above, we argue that a doctrine of sanctification must articulate how God's life bears fruit through creaturely life. There is, by necessity, a developmental dynamic to the doctrine of sanctification, such that affirming the sanctified status of a person is not enough (the first half of the definition: "life *in* the presence of God"). One must also attend to how a sanctified person becomes more sanctified, just as one must articulate how faith grows in the life of a believer (the second half of the definition: "*for* the presence of God"). In this sense the doctrine of sanctification begins with God's work in Christ both to enlarge his life to believers, uniting them to himself, and to indwell them in and by the Spirit. Starting a doctrine of sanctification with the person and work of Christ and the Spirit to order and guide soteriology will be necessary, but the theologian of sanctification must also articulate *the reality* of life in Christ by the Spirit. This requires expositing the ways in which the presence and action of God give shape to discussions of spiritual formation, virtue development, and relational knowing. Each of these is necessary to talk about the formation of love, for example, as the nature of love is given shape by an account of God's presence and action in Christ by the Spirit (1 John 4:10).

Along with the content and exposition of life in the presence of God in Christ, we need to attend to the experiential form of the doctrine of sanctification. (See the sidebar "John 15:1–11.") If, as suggested above, a proper account of the doctrine of sin should cause the reader to repent, then what should a proper doctrine of sanctification do? As an articulation of the presence of God made available in and through Christ by the Spirit, a doctrine of sanctification should cause us to declare, "Without Christ, I can do nothing," while also affirming that if we abide in him we can bear much fruit. In this sense, *abiding in Christ* is the proper response to a doctrine of sanctification (John 15:4–5). To put this differently, and fitting with the spatial and relational dynamics of holiness, a doctrine of sanctification should *cause us to draw near to God in Christ Jesus, trusting that Christ truly is our righteousness and sanctification*. This means that the temptation in hearing a doctrine of sanctification is to turn elsewhere other than Christ—to moralism or antinomianism—and so dreadfully misunderstand the scriptural call to a holy life. The vision of sanctification affirmed throughout this volume is one of *drawing near* to God in

John 15:1–11

1 I am the true vine, and my Father is the vinedresser. 2 Every branch in me
that does not bear fruit he takes away, and every branch that does bear
fruit he prunes, that it may bear more fruit. 3 Already you are clean because
of the word that I have spoken to you. 4 Abide in me, and I in you. As the
branch cannot bear fruit by itself, unless it abides in the vine, neither can
you, unless you abide in me. 5 I am the vine; you are the branches. Whoever
abides in me and I in him, he it is that bears much fruit, for apart from
me you can do nothing. 6 If anyone does not abide in me, he is thrown
away like a branch and withers; and the branches are gathered, thrown
into the fire, and burned. 7 If you abide in me, and my words abide in you,
ask whatever you wish, and it will be done for you. 8 By this my Father is
glorified, that you bear much fruit and so prove to be my disciples. 9 As
the Father has loved me, so have I loved you. Abide in my love. 10 If you
keep my commandments, you will abide in my love, just as I have kept
my Father's commandments and abide in his love. 11 These things I have
spoken to you, that my joy may be in you, and that your joy may be full.

Christ by the Spirit. We have sought to captivate your heart with the one who has given himself to you in Christ Jesus and by his Spirit calls you to himself. The only proper understanding of sanctification is to seek, grasp, and embrace God by faith as the one who has done everything needed for you to draw near.

Being and Becoming Theologians of Sanctification

It is possible to affirm what we have said about sanctification while failing to feel the weight of that affirmation in one's theological method. Or, perhaps more troubling, it is possible to affirm this idea of sanctification while failing to embrace it in our lives. A theologian who attends to the theological task Christianly is one who embraces the fact that they are sanctified in Christ and that all proclamation of God is done in God's presence and thus before his face. We do not declare a God who is absent from or ambivalent about the human condition; instead, we declare one who has given himself to us in Christ Jesus. This is why we never leave God's presence and action in order to talk about intellectual, moral, or practical advancement. God's presence reorders all of life around him, and there are intellectual, moral, and practical features to that dynamic. Drawing near to God to live all of life before him, including to intellectually engage questions about sanctification, requires an openness of heart that can see and name the truth of one's life. The temptation, instead, is to look into the mirror of God's Word and forget what we look like (James 1:24), not sitting with the reality of our rebellion, brokenness, and pain long enough to stand before the Lord in the truth.

Theological method that is self-conscious of its call requires a theologian who embraces that he or she is holy in and through Christ. Holiness names not only the life of God in and of himself but also the consequence of being graciously caught up in the harmony of God's life by faith. Only God is holy in himself because only God is *of himself*. Only God is holy in himself because only God can be the foundation and end of his own existence. Created in the image and likeness of God but thinking that likeness to God is attainable in and through our own power, human persons collapse inward, seduced by the lie that we can live self-cultivated, self-sustaining, and self-generating lives. Curved in on ourselves, we seek the resources that only God can provide. Only God is the I AM who is of, from, and to himself; only God is fullness and life. Creaturely pride seeks to establish "I am who I am" in ourselves, saying things like, "You be you," or "Just be true to yourself." What holiness names, in contrast, is the truth that the Christian's life is hidden with Christ in God (Col. 3:3) and that flourishing is found only in the one who can say, "It is no longer I who live, but Christ who lives in me" (Gal. 2:20).

David's prayer in Psalm 24 helpfully confronts us:

> Who shall ascend the hill of the Lord?
> And who shall stand in his holy place?
> He who has clean hands and a pure heart,
> who does not lift up his soul to what is false
> and does not swear deceitfully.
> He will receive blessing from the Lord
> and righteousness from the God of his salvation.
> Such is the generation of those who seek him,
> who seek the face of the God of Jacob. (Ps. 24:3–6)

Who is the theologian who can stand in his holy place? The one with clean hands and a pure heart—the one regenerated by God's cleansing and purifying power—who ascends to God in Christ and draws near in the truth to live in his presence to be conformed to his life. These are the ones who seek the face of God.

In this sense the theologian of sanctification is one who, through regenerate rationality, stands before God by faith as one made new in him: born from above as he is from above (John 3:31). To be a theologian of sanctification is to be a theologian who is justified in Christ Jesus, who knows that Christ is their righteousness (1 Cor. 1:30). This is one who comes to Christ—the one from above who lives to the Father—to be born from above to live to the Father (John 16:28). The true theologian is one who knows that the Spirit groans with groaning too deep for words, and who in the Spirit draws near to God in righteousness, holiness, and truth to present themselves to him in humility (Rom. 8:26). Or, with Evagrius, "If you are a theologian, you will pray truly; and if you pray truly, you will be a theologian."[11]

11. Evagrius of Pontus, *Chapters on Prayer*, 199.

To ascend the mountain of the Lord to draw near to the Holy One is to stand in recognition of grace and one's desperate need for mercy. It is here, in this place, that theological rationality is purified, as it stands in contrast with the Tower of Babel of academic achievement. Academic advancement is not wrong or bad, but it can often replace the humble drawing near of prayer. When academic achievement becomes the goal, theology becomes a "theology at the desk" and ceases to be a "theology of prayer." At times these tasks might look identical, but the fruit differs. The fruit of a theologian in prayer who reasons before the face of God is love. This theologian is frequently reminded of Paul's words to the church at Corinth: "God chose what is foolish in the world to shame the wise; God chose what is weak in the world to shame the strong; God chose what is low and despised in the world, even things that are not, to bring to nothing things that are, so that no human being might boast in the presence of God" (1 Cor. 1:27–29). Before the face of God theological boasting falls silent.

In this form of sanctified reason, we present our body and life to God as a living sacrifice for the renewal of our minds (Rom. 12:1–2). The mind is renewed in God's presence as we present our bodies, lives, and rationality to God to be reordered in and by his presence. This presentation has traditionally been understood as contemplation, and theology understood as a contemplative act (i.e., a *theoretical* act).[12] Contemplation is not abstract gazing upon a disinterested object but is *receiving* by faith the self-giving of God who illumines, giving eyes to see and ears to hear. Such sight, importantly, does not set our hearts on Christ in such a way that blinds us to other things. Seeing God allows us to see others properly. This sight reveals that the things that feel solid and eternal are actually fragile and temporal. It is the invisible things that do not fade, Paul tells us, and the unseen things that are eternal (2 Cor. 4:16–18). This is why he admonishes us not to lose heart, because we can realize that "this light momentary affliction is preparing for us an eternal weight of glory beyond all comparison." Contemplation is setting one's mind on things above—drawing near to the Father, in the Son, by the Spirit—to locate the Christian in the truth of their life hidden with Christ in God (Col. 3:3).

12. A. N. Williams writes, "For Augustine . . . contemplation does not signify an advanced form of prayer. What it does designate is a form of knowledge of God" ("Contemplation," 137).

Although contemplation is a *rational* act, contemplation is not in tension with the affective capacities of the soul, because the heart is an integrated reality in Scripture. Rationality does not value the mind *over* the heart, or the mind and heart over the person as a whole. Rather, contemplation is the act of drawing near to God as one seen and known by God, to *know as we have been known*.[13] Contemplation is the ascent of a person to the God who has descended to embrace us in Christ, modeled after the pedagogy of holiness seen throughout the Old Testament and made manifest in Christ. In his call to "set your mind on things above," Paul starts by re-grounding believers in the work of Christ, reminding them that "you have been raised with Christ" (Col. 3:1). In being raised with Christ the believer raises their heart Godward. But this is the gaze of faith that always longs for its perfection in sight, knowing that "he who raised the Lord Jesus will raise us also with Jesus and bring us with you into his presence" (2 Cor. 4:14).

The sanctifying presence of God establishes the proper ground for theological reflection. Contemplation attends to who God has revealed himself to be and how he has called us to submit our rationality to him. We are called into his presence to be centered on Christ and to have our whole persons conformed to him (including having our minds renewed according to what is "good and acceptable and perfect" [Rom. 12:2]). Put differently, we are called, in the fullness of our humanity, to know our life entirely harmonized around the crucified, risen, and ascended Lord of glory. This harmonizing around Christ is the secret cadence of the Spirit's witness in the soul (Rom. 8:16)—as the Spirit of Christ—who reforms and transforms his people in and through himself.

In this sense, theological methodology is given shape by the three features of the sanctified life: presence, encounter, and order. Each can be reduced to abstraction, just as each can be diminished into pragmatism. What *presence*, *encounter*, and *order* provide, however, is a vision of sanctified existence that continually focuses on God as the Holy One who calls his creatures into his life to have their entire selves reshaped in and by his presence. Summarized, especially in Hebrews, as *the call to draw near*, this emphasis also must account for the fact that we can easily be present in body but absent in person. You can align your body devotionally without

13. See Strobel, "Contemplation by Son and Spirit."

that act reordering your affections; spiritual disciplines and liturgies do not have the power to transform a life. Similarly, one can seek to order one's affections in a kind of therapeutic self-gazing that does not align with the harmony of the kingdom, where love of neighbor and the fruit of the Spirit depict a certain trajectory of Christian maturation.

Pushing against these deviations, what *presence*, *encounter*, and *order* ultimately name is love, and the dynamic of God's self-giving love that establishes the contours of Christian existence. By naming this *love* we are not moving away from our focus on the sanctification available in the Son by the Spirit but are specifying the mission of God to redeem as a mission where "God so loved the world, that he gave" (John 3:16). It is in this gift of *himself* in his Son that we know the proper sphere of sanctification. Sanctification is not only located in the Son, however, but also finds its proper harmony, telos, and order in the Son. The economic movement of God is what helps establish sanctified Christian existence, because Christian formation is always bearing the fruit of God's life in our own. It is in abiding in the Son that we bear much fruit, precisely because salvation comes from without.

A theologian of sanctification, therefore, is judged not ultimately by the profundity of their commentary or the analytical precision of their distinctions but on the basis of love and the call of love. "The rule which governs teaching about the Trinity, and therefore about creation as one of its extensions" is love, writes John Webster. He continues: "Love alone restores knowledge. Love, furthermore, is the end of theological contemplation of the creator and his work. The goal of the redeemed mind's exercise in this matter is 'that [God] may himself be sought, and himself be loved.'"[14]

Love Never Ends

The formation of love, therefore, helps specify the nature of God's presence and creaturely encounter with God. We might be tempted to know God as an object—to have a speculative knowledge of God—but this, of course, is demonic knowing (James 2:19). We might be tempted to construct self-made religion that seeks to establish a generic account of human formation in and through our own spiritual discipline (Col. 2:20–23), but this misses

14. Webster, *God Without Measure*, 1:84, quoting Augustine, *On the Trinity* 2.1.

the fact that holiness, righteousness, and even God's love itself are sourced from outside us and only given over in the continual freedom of God's work in the Spirit (Rom. 5:5). What the formation of love recognizes is that we are formed in Christ, through Christ, and for Christ, as we stand face-to-face with Christ. We can put this differently, of course, by saying we are formed in the Spirit, through the Spirit, and for the Spirit; but as the Spirit is the Spirit of the Son, this would be the same assertion. To receive the Spirit is to receive the Spirit of the Son in Christ and to know Christ's very Spirit of holiness indwelling us.

This is also why talking about holiness is always talking about love. With Wesley, the call of holiness is the call of love, and with Aquinas, the call of love is the call for union. To be called into God's presence establishes an encounter with him by faith; this encounter reorders our lives before him, around him, and in him. This is what it means to know the love of God. But this requires reciprocity, such that we are open-hearted to God and others (2 Cor. 6:11–12). Love is the harmony that unites persons and orients the theologian to Love, himself (1 John 4:16).

God's movement of love is not God relating *at* or merely *toward* creation. Rather, he opens wide his own heart by internalizing his people into the Father's love of the Son in the Holy Spirit (John 17:26). God reaches his two hands into creation to embrace his beloved to draw them near to himself. It is *this love* that reveals the depth and direction of holiness, because holiness names the call to be present to God in his presence, to draw near to him in an encounter of faith, and to have all of life reordered around him. This means that God's self-giving establishes a framework and a model to have life reordered in him and through him.

In our account of sanctification, it is the finished dynamic of our sanctification, like the covenant commitment of marriage, that creates the context for the relational responsiveness of life with God in which we are recharacterized and transformed by the holying presence of God. God makes us holy for a life of holiness. To be sanctified in Christ Jesus is to have access, but access itself is not the proper end of sanctification. Rather, one must use that access to draw near to God in and through him. Having misordered loves leads people away from opening wide their hearts to God or others, and so, unsurprisingly, the summarization of the law remedies this neglect through the imperative to "love the Lord your God with all your heart and with all your soul and with all your mind. . . . And . . . love your neighbor as yourself" (Matt. 22:37, 39). The Lord has established this love in humanity in and through Christ, and he breaks that love open in Christ by the Spirit so that we too can receive him and walk in him. But this requires a whole life. This requires the reordering of the affections, but it also requires reordering the ways we navigate the world.

The holiness that God provides for his people is a presence that reorders life around him and establishes his image bearers before his face to reflect his glory (2 Cor. 3:18). It is from within this holiness that the people of God communally draw near to know the growth that is "from God" (Col. 2:19). It is within this holiness that we must grapple with our misordered affections and feel the penetrating mirror of the living Word demanding that we see what is actually true of us (James 1:23–24). In this sense, holiness establishes the contours of a properly *super*natural life in Christ that pushes against the ever-present temptation to reduce spiritual formation into its natural counterpart. Rather than gravitating away from Christ and the Spirit into a Pelagian account of self-construction, a doctrine of sanctification trains our focus on Christ, in Christ, and for Christ in the Spirit.

The doctrine of sanctification has wide borders; much falls within its range. To address the task of virtue formation, for instance, we need to relocate habituation into a supernatural modality that prefers *reception* over generation. To talk about spiritual practices requires more than encouraging a set of prebaptized spiritual acts; it necessitates a deeper form of wisdom—guiding a person to Christ and helping them navigate their temptations to seek something else. To preach is to do more than pass along information, however accurate and helpful; it is to shepherd a holy people into the presence of a holy God. Applying a text should never encourage someone to bypass Christ but should lead a people to the only place where holiness is found—in Christ. The doctrine of sanctification gives shape and guidance to every feature of Christian living, shepherding, and direction because it never moves beyond the Son and the Spirit's act to draw us out of ourselves and into the holying presence of the triune God.

To reason along the grain of this doctrine, and to declare not only its material content but also its supernatural form, is to be filled with the Spirit. This is the fullness of a holy life. One filled with the Spirit bears the fruit of love, as love refracts through their person as "joy, peace, patience, kindness, goodness, faithfulness, gentleness, self-control" (Gal. 5:22–23).

Against these things, we are told, "there is no law." Likewise, just as "those who belong to Christ Jesus have crucified the flesh with its passions and desires" (5:24), so too should the doctrine of sanctification crucify intellectual vice, passion, and desire. Spiritual theology is not simply addressing practical matters of life with God but is a task of sanctified reason to be conformed to God's self-giving in Christ. This is the task modeled in this volume, and we invite you into it.

Summary

Sanctification guides the theological task, orienting method and practice around life in the presence of God. More than merely reasoning *about* divine things, theology is reasoning *in God's presence*. Three implications follow for theologians, readers of theology, and theological method. (1) As it concerns the theologian: The presence of God has a distinctly familial shape that should orient a theologian's self-understanding. A theologian reasons from within the extravagant and abiding embrace of God as Father. (2) As it concerns the reader of theology: The doctrine of sanctification should cause one to draw near to God in Christ Jesus, trusting that Christ truly is one's righteousness and sanctification. Seeking, grasping, and embracing God by faith as the one who has done everything needed for one to draw near is the only proper understanding of sanctification. (3) As it concerns theological method: *Love* and *the call of love* are the tests of true theology. A theologian of sanctification joins God's gracious movement of love, in which God's own heart is opened wide in generous, extravagant, cross-shaped love.

Bibliography

Allen, Michael. *Sanctification*. New Studies in Dogmatics. Zondervan, 2017.

Allison, Gregg R. *Historical Theology: An Introduction to Christian Doctrine*. Zondervan, 2011.

Anderson, Gary A. *That I May Dwell Among Them: Incarnation and Atonement in the Tabernacle Narrative*. Eerdmans, 2023.

Aquinas, Thomas. "Commentary on 1 Timothy." In *Commentary on the Letters of Saint Paul to the Philippians, Colossians, Thessalonians, Timothy, Titus, and Philemon*, translated by F. R. Larcher, 241–341. Latin/English Edition of the Works of Thomas Aquinas 40. The Aquinas Institute for the Study of Sacred Doctrine, 2012.

Aquinas, Thomas. *Summa Theologiae*. Translated by Laurence Shapcote. Latin-English Opera Omnia. Emmaus Academic, 2018.

Aristotle. *Nicomachean Ethics*. Translated by Terence Irwin. 2nd ed. Hackett, 1999.

Augustine. *The Confessions*. Translated by Maria Boulding. Works of Saint Augustine I/1. New City Press, 1997.

Augustine. *Homilies on the Gospel of John 41–124*. Translated by Edmund Hill. Works of Saint Augustine III/13. New City Press, 2020.

Augustine. "Letter 187, To Dardanus (On the Presence of God)." In *St. Augustine: Letters 165–203*, translated by W. Parsons, 221–54. Fathers of the Church. Catholic University of America Press, 1955.

Barclay, John M. G. "Grace and the Transformation of Agency in Christ." In *Redefining First-Century Jewish and Christian Identities*, edited by Fabian E. Udoh, 372–89. University of Notre Dame Press, 2008.

Barclay, John M. G. *Paul and the Gift*. Eerdmans, 2015.

Barclay, John M. G. *Paul and the Power of Grace*. Eerdmans, 2019.

Barron, Robert. *The Priority of Christ: Toward a Postliberal Catholicism*. Brazos, 2007.

Barth, Karl. *The Christian Life: Church Dogmatics IV/4: Lecture Fragments*. Translated by Geoffrey W. Bromiley. Eerdmans, 1981.

Barth, Karl. *Church Dogmatics*. Vol. II/1, *The Doctrine of God*. Edited by Geoffrey W. Bromiley and Thomas F. Torrance. T&T Clark, 1957.

Barth, Karl. *Evangelical Theology: An Introduction*. Eerdmans, 1992.

Barth, Karl. *The Holy Spirit and the Christian Life: The Theological Basis of Ethics*. Translated by R. Birch Hoyle. Westminster John Knox, 1993.

Bauckham, Richard J. *2 Peter, Jude*. Word Biblical Commentary 50. Word Books, 1983.

Bauerschmidt, Frederick Christian. *The Love That Is God: An Invitation to Christian Faith*. Eerdmans, 2020.

Bavinck, Herman. *The Doctrine of God*. Translated by William Hendriksen. Eerdmans, 1951.

Bavinck, Herman. *Reformed Dogmatics*. Vol. 2, *God and Creation*. Edited by John Bolt. Translated by John Vriend. Baker Academic, 2003.

Bavinck, Herman. *Reformed Ethics*. Vol. 1, *Created, Fallen, and Converted Humanity*. Edited by John Bolt. Baker Academic, 2019.

Baxter, Richard. *The Divine Life: Knowing and Walking with God*. Lexham, 2017.

Bernard of Clairvaux. *On the Song of Songs II*. Translated by Kilian Walsh. Cistercian Publications, 1976.

Bernard of Clairvaux. *On the Song of Songs IV*. Translated by Irene Edmonds. Cistercian Publications, 1980.

Bloesch, Donald G. *The Crisis of Piety: Essays Toward a Theology of the Christian Life*. 2nd ed. Helmers & Howard, 1988.

Bloesch, Donald G. "Evangelical Spirituality." In *Christian Spirituality East and West*, edited by Jordan Aumann, Thomas Hopko, and Donald Bloesch, 165–203. The Priory Press, 1968.

Bonaventure. *Breviloquium*. Translated by Dominic V. Monti. Bonaventure Texts in Translation Series. Franciscan Institute Publications, 2005.

Brandt, Jared. "Growth in Infused Virtue in the Work of Thomas Aquinas." PhD diss., Baylor University, 2018.

Bromiley, G. W. "Presence, Divine." In *Evangelical Dictionary of Theology*, edited by Walter Elwell, 873–74. Baker, 1984.

Brown, John (of Haddington). *Systematic Theology: A Compendious View of Natural and Revealed Religion*. Reformation Heritage Books, 2002.

Calvin, John. *Acts of the Council of Trent with the Antidote*. In *Selected Works of John Calvin*, edited and translated by Henry Beveridge, 3:17–188. Baker Book House, 1983.

Calvin, John. *The Bondage and Liberation of the Will: A Defence of the Orthodox Doctrine of Human Choice Against Pighius*. Translated by G. Davies. Baker Book House, 1996.

Calvin, John. *Commentaries on the Epistle of Paul the Apostle to the Romans*. Translated by John Owen. Baker Book House, 1993.

Calvin, John. *Commentaries on the Epistles of Paul to the Galatians and Ephesians*. Translated by William Pringle. Baker Book House, 1993.

Calvin, John. *Commentary on the Epistles of Paul the Apostle to the Corinthians*. Translated by John Pringle. Baker Book House, 1993.

Calvin, John. *Commentary on the Gospel According to John*. Translated by William Pringle. Baker Book House, 1993.

Calvin, John. *Institutes of the Christian Religion*. 2 vols. Edited by John T. McNeill. Translated by Ford Lewis Battles. Westminster, 1960.

Calvin, John. "Reply to Sadolet." In *Calvin: Theological Treatises*, translated by J. K. S. Reid, 221–56. Library of Christian Classics. Westminster, 1954.

Calvin, John. "2 Peter." In *Commentaries on the Catholic Epistles*, translated by John Owen, 364–426. Baker Book House, 1993.

Canlis, Julie. *Calvin's Ladder: A Spiritual Theology of Ascent and Ascension*. Eerdmans, 2010.

Carpenter, Angela. *Responsive Becoming: Moral Formation in Theological, Evolutionary, and Developmental Perspective*. T&T Clark, 2020.

Charnock, Stephen. *The Existence and Attributes of God*. Updated and unabridged ed. Crossway, 2022.

Ciampa, Roy E., and Brian S. Rosner. *The First Letter to the Corinthians*. Pillar New Testament Commentary. Eerdmans, 2010.

Clements, R. E. *God and Temple: The Idea of the Divine Presence in Ancient Israel*. Wipf & Stock, 2016.

Coakley, Sarah, and SueJeanne Koh. "Prayer as Divine Propulsion: An Interview with Sarah Coakley, Part I." *The Other Journal* 21. https://theotherjournal.com/2012/12/prayer-as-divine-propulsion-an-interview-with-sarah-coakley.

Cocksworth, Ashley. "Karl Barth's Very Theological Theology of Prayer." In *T&T Clark Handbook of Christian Prayer*, edited by Ashley Cocksworth and John C. McDowell, 447–68. T&T Clark, 2022.

Cocksworth, Ashley, and David F. Ford. *Glorification and the Life of Faith*. Soteriology and Doxology. Baker Academic, 2023.

Collins, Kenneth J. *The Scripture Way of Salvation: The Heart of John Wesley's Theology*. Abingdon, 1997.

Colón-Emeric, Edgardo A. *Wesley, Aquinas, and Christian Perfection: An Ecumenical Dialogue*. Baylor University Press, 2009.

Cyril of Alexandria. *Commentary on John*. Vol. 2. Translated by David R. Maxwell. Ancient Christian Texts. IVP Academic, 2015.

Dalferth, Ingolf. *Becoming Present: An Inquiry into the Christian Sense of the Presence of God*. Studies in Philosophical Theology. Peeters, 2006.

Dunnington, Kent. *Humility, Pride, and Christian Virtue Theory*. Oxford Studies in Analytic Theology. Oxford University Press, 2019.

Durant, Will. *The Story of Philosophy: The Lives and Opinions of the Greater Philosophers*. Simon & Schuster, 1926.

Duvall, J. Scott, and J. Daniel Hays. *God's Relational Presence: The Cohesive Center of Biblical Theology*. Baker Academic, 2019.

Eastman, Susan Grove. *Paul and the Person: Reframing Paul's Anthropology*. Eerdmans, 2017.

Edwards, Jonathan. *Ethical Writings*. Edited by Paul Ramsey. Works of Jonathan Edwards 8. Yale University Press, 1989.

Edwards, Jonathan. *The "Miscellanies," 501–832*. Edited by Ava Chamberlain. Works of Jonathan Edwards 18. Yale University Press, 2000.

Edwards, Jonathan. *Writings on the Trinity, Grace, and Faith*. Edited by Sang Hyun Lee. Works of Jonathan Edwards 21. Yale University Press, 2003.

Eilers, Kent. *Faithful to Save: Pannenberg on God's Reconciling Action*. T&T Clark, 2011.

Eilers, Kent. "The Grammar of Grace." Forrester Lecture Series, April 2021. YouTube, 1:09:20. https://www.youtube.com/watch?v=nA2PE05NGyo.

Eilers, Kent, Ashley Cocksworth, and Anna Silvas, eds. *The Grammar of Grace: Readings from the Christian Tradition*. Cascade Books, 2019.

Eilers, Kent, and Kyle Strobel, eds. *Sanctified by Grace: A Theology of the Christian Life*. T&T Clark, 2014.

Evagrius of Pontus. *Chapters on Prayer*. In *Evagrius of Pontus: The Greek Ascetic Corpus*, edited by Robert E. Sinkewicz, 183–209. Oxford Early Christian Studies. Oxford University Press, 2003.

Gammie, John G. *Holiness in Israel*. Overtures to Biblical Theology. Wipf & Stock, 2005.

Gorman, Frank H., Jr. *Divine Presence and Community: A Commentary on the Book of Leviticus*. Eerdmans, 1997.

Gorman, Mark. "John and Charles Wesley on Deification." In *Transformed into the Same Image: Constructive Investigations into the Doctrine of Deification*, edited by Paul Copan and Michael M. C. Reardon, 166–83. IVP Academic, 2024.

Gorman, Michael J. "'You Shall Be Cruciform for I Am Cruciform': Paul's Trinitarian Reconstruction of Holiness." In *Holiness and Ecclesiology in the New Testament*, edited by Kent E. Brower and Andy Johnson, 148–66. Eerdmans, 2007.

Gregory of Nazianzus. "Criticisms of Apollinarius." In *Christian Doctrine: A Reader*, edited by Lindsey Hall, Murray Rae, and Stephen Holmes, 123–24. SCM, 2010.

Gregory of Nyssa. *Life of Moses*. Translated by Abraham Malherbe and Everett Ferguson. Classics of Western Spirituality. Paulist Press, 1978.

Hefner, Craig A. *Kierkegaard and the Changelessness of God: A Modern Defense of Classical Immutability*. New Explorations in Theology. IVP Academic, 2023.

Hellerman, Joseph H. *Jesus and the People of God: Reconfiguring Ethnic Identity*. Sheffield Phoenix, 2013.

Herdt, Jennifer A. *Assuming Responsibility: Ecstatic Eudaimonism and the Call to Live Well*. Oxford University Press, 2022.

Holmes, Christopher R. J. "The Perfecting God." In *Sanctified by Grace: A Theology of the Christian Life*, edited by Kent Eilers and Kyle Strobel, 75–88. T&T Clark, 2014.

Horton, Michael. *The Christian Faith: A Systematic Theology for Pilgrims on the Way*. Zondervan, 2011.

Hursthouse, Rosalind, and Glen Pettigrove. "Virtue Ethics." In *The Stanford Encyclopedia of Philosophy*, Fall 2023 ed., ed. Edward N. Zalta and Uri Nodelman. https://plato.stanford.edu/archives/fall2023/entries/ethics-virtue.

Jenson, Philip Peter. *Graded Holiness: A Key to the Priestly Conception of the World*. JSOT Press, 1992.

Jenson, Philip Peter. "Holiness in the Priestly Writings of the Old Testament." In *Holiness Past and Present*, edited by Stephen C. Barton, 93–121. T&T Clark, 2003.

Klawans, Jonathan. *Purity, Sacrifice, and the Temple: Symbolism and Supersessionism in the Study of Ancient Judaism*. Oxford University Press, 2006.

Knobel, Angela McKay. *Aquinas and the Infused Moral Virtues*. University of Notre Dame Press, 2021.

Koester, Craig R. *The Dwelling of God: The Tabernacle, Intertestamental Jewish Literature, and the New Testament*. Catholic Biblical Quarterly Monograph Series 22. Catholic Biblical Association of America, 1989.

Leigh, Edward. *Systeme or Body of Divinity: Consisting of Ten Books*. London, 1662.

Levenson, Jon D. *Sinai and Zion: An Entry into the Jewish Bible*. HarperOne, 1985.

Lindström, Harald. *Wesley and Sanctification: A Study in the Doctrine of Salvation*. Francis Asbury Press, 1996.

Lister, J. Ryan. *The Presence of God: Its Place in the Storyline of Scripture and the Story of Our Lives*. Crossway, 2015.

Lockett, Darian R. "Catholic Epistles." In *The Trinity in the Canon: A Biblical, Theological, Historical, and Practical Proposal*, edited by Brandon D. Smith, 311–42. B&H Academic, 2023.

Lockett, Darian R. *Letters for the Church: Reading James, 1–2 Peter, 1–3 John, and Jude as Canon*. IVP Academic, 2021.

Long, D. Stephen. *John Wesley's Moral Theology: The Quest for God and Goodness*. Kingswood Books, 2005.

Long, D. Stephen. "Moral Theology." In *The Oxford Handbook of Systematic Theology*, edited by John Webster, Kathryn Tanner, and Iain Torrance, 456–75. Oxford University Press, 2007.

Loyer, Kenneth M. *God's Love Through the Spirit: The Holy Spirit in Thomas Aquinas and John Wesley*. Catholic University of America Press, 2014.

Luther, Martin. "A Brief Instruction on What to Look for and Expect in the Gospels." In *Martin Luther's Basic Theological Writings*, edited by Timothy F. Lull and William R. Russell, 71–75. 3rd ed. Fortress, 2012.

Luther, Martin. *Lectures on Galatians: Chapters 1–4*. Luther's Works 26. Fortress, 2007.

Macaskill, Grant. *Living in Union with Christ: Paul's Gospel and Christian Moral Identity*. Baker Academic, 2019.

MacDonald, Rev. James Alex. *Wesley's Revision of the Shorter Catechism with Notes: Showing the Connection of Methodist Doctrine with That of the Reformed Church, the Ancient Faith, and the Word of God*. Simpkin, Marshall & Co., 1906.

Marshall, I. Howard. "Holiness in the Book of Acts." In *Holiness and Ecclesiology in the New Testament*, edited by Kent E. Brower and Andy Johnson, 114–28. Eerdmans, 2007.

Mattison, W. C., III. “Beatitude and the Beatitudes in the *Summa Theologiae* of St. Thomas Aquinas.” *Josephinum Journal of Theology* 17 (2010): 233–49.

McCormick, Steve. “Theosis in Chrysostom and Wesley: An Eastern Paradigm of Faith and Love.” *Wesleyan Theological Journal* 26 (1991): 38–103.

McIntosh, Mark. *Mystical Theology: The Integrity of Spirituality and Theology*. Blackwell, 1998.

Milgrom, Jacob. *Leviticus: A Book of Ritual and Ethics*. Continental Commentaries. Fortress, 2004.

Miller, Timothy. “The Debate over the *Ordo Salutis* in American Reformed Theology.” *Detroit Baptist Seminary Journal* 18 (Fall 2013): 41–66.

Miner, Robert. “Infused Virtue as Virtue Simply: The Centrality of the Augustinian Definition in *Summa theologiae* I/2.55–67.” *Scottish Journal of Theology* 71, no. 4 (2018): 411–24.

Moffitt, David M. *Rethinking the Atonement: New Perspectives on Jesus’s Death, Resurrection, and Ascension*. Baker Academic, 2022.

Morales, L. Michael. *The Tabernacle Pre-Figured: Cosmic Mountain Ideology in Genesis and Exodus*. Peeters, 2012.

Morales, L. Michael. *Who Shall Ascend the Mountain of the Lord? A Biblical Theology of the Book of Leviticus*. New Studies in Biblical Theology. InterVarsity, 2015.

Murray, John. *Collected Writings of John Murray*. Vol. 2. Banner of Truth Trust, 1977.

Norton, John. *The Orthodox Evangelist*. London, 1654.

Oden, Thomas C. *The Transforming Power of Grace*. Abingdon, 1993.

Owen, John. *Pneumatologia (The Holy Spirit)*. Works of John Owen 3. Banner of Truth Trust, 1994.

Payne, Don J. *Already Sanctified: A Theology of the Christian Life in Light of God’s Completed Work*. Baker Academic, 2020.

Payne, Don J. “Response to Steve L. Porter.” *Journal of Spiritual Formation & Soul Care* 13, no. 2 (2020): 300–309.

Peppiatt, Lucy, and Kyle Strobel, eds. *Virtue Ethics, Grace, and a Protestant Doctrine of Infusion*. Routledge, forthcoming.

Peterson, David G. *Possessed by God: A New Testament Theology of Sanctification and Holiness*. New Studies in Biblical Theology. IVP Academic, 2001.

Peterson, Ryan. *The Imago Dei as Human Identity: A Theological Interpretation*. Eisenbrauns, 2016.

Pinckaers, Servais. *The Sources of Christian Ethics*. Catholic University of America Press, 1995.

Pinsent, Andrew. *The Second-Person Perspective in Aquinas's Ethics: Virtues and Gifts*. Routledge Studies in Ethics and Moral Theory. Routledge, 2012.

Placher, William C. *The Domestication of Transcendence: How Modern Thinking About God Went Wrong*. Westminster John Knox, 1996.

Riches, Aaron. *Ecce Homo: On the Divine Unity of Christ*. Eerdmans, 2016.

Ryle, J. C. *Holiness: Its Nature, Hindrances, Difficulties, and Roots*. Banner of Truth Trust, 2014.

Sanders, Fred. "The Triune God." In *Sanctified by Grace: A Theology of the Christian Life*, edited by Kent Eilers and Kyle Strobel, 21–32. T&T Clark, 2014.

Sanders, Fred. *The Triune God*. New Studies in Dogmatics. Zondervan, 2016.

Sanders, Fred. "Wesleyan View." In *Five Views on the Extent of the Atonement*, edited by Adam Johnson, 164–85. Zondervan, 2019.

Schuele, Andreas. "The Spirit of YHWH and the Aura of Divine Presence." *Interpretation* 66, no. 1 (2012): 16–28.

Shanley, Brian. "Beyond Libertarianism and Compatibilism: Thomas Aquinas on Created Freedom." In *Freedom and the Human Person*, edited by Richard Velkley, 70–89. Studies in Philosophy and the History of Philosophy 48. Catholic University of America Press, 2007.

Sonderegger, Katherine. *Systematic Theology*. Vol. 1, *God the Lord*. Fortress, 2015.

Soskice, Janet Martin. *Metaphor and Religious Language*. Clarendon, 1987.

Strobel, Kyle C. "Contemplation by Son and Spirit: Reforming the Ascent of the Soul to God." In *Embracing Contemplation: Reclaiming a Christian Spiritual Practice*, edited by John H. Coe and Kyle C. Strobel, 166–84. IVP Academic, 2019.

Strobel, Kyle C. "The Sight of God." *Credo Magazine*, October 23, 2018. https://credomag.com/article/a-spiritual-sight-of-love.

Strobel, Kyle, and John Coe. *When God Seems Distant: Surprising Ways God Deepens Our Faith and Draws Us Near*. Baker Books, 2026.

Strobel, Kyle, and John Coe. *Where Prayer Becomes Real: How Honesty with God Transforms Your Soul*. Baker Books, 2021.

Stump, Eleonore. *Wandering in Darkness: Narrative and the Problem of Suffering*. Oxford University Press, 2010.

Svensson, Manfred. "Aristotelian Practical Philosophy from Melanchthon to Eisenhart: Protestant Commentaries on the *Nicomachean Ethics* 1529–1682." *Reformation & Renaissance Review* 21, no. 3 (2019): 218–38.

Svensson, Manfred. *The Aristotelian Tradition in Early Modern Protestantism: Sixteenth- and Seventeenth-Century Commentaries on the "Ethics" and the "Politics."* Oxford University Press, 2024.

Sytsma, David S. "John Calvin and Virtue Ethics: Augustinian and Aristotelian Themes." *Journal of Religious Ethics* 48, no. 3 (2020): 519–56.

Tanner, Kathryn. *God and Creation in Christian Theology: Tyranny or Empowerment?* Fortress, 1988.

Tanner, Kathryn. *Jesus, Humanity, and the Trinity: A Systematic Theology in Brief.* Fortress, 2001.

Taylor, Jeremy. "Sermon VI: *Via Intelligentiae.*" In *Jeremy Taylor: Selected Works*, edited by Thomas K. Carroll, 355–88. Classics of Western Spirituality. Paulist Press, 1990.

ten Klooster, Anton. *Thomas Aquinas on the Beatitudes: Reading Matthew, Disputing Grace and Virtue, Preaching Happiness.* Peeters, 2018.

Timmer, Daniel C. *Creation, Tabernacle, and Sabbath: The Sabbath Frame of Exodus 31:12–17; 35:1–3 in Exegetical and Theological Perspective.* Vandenhoeck & Ruprecht, 2009.

Turretin, Francis. *Institutes of Elenctic Theology*. Vol. 2. Translated by George Musgrave Giger. Edited by James T. Dennison Jr. P&R, 1994.

van de Walle, Bernie A. *Rethinking Holiness: A Theological Introduction.* Baker Academic, 2017.

van Mastricht, Petrus. *Theoretical-Practical Theology*. Vol. 1, *Prolegomena*. Translated by Todd M. Rester. Edited by Joel R. Beeke. Reformation Heritage Books, 2018.

Venema, Cornelis P. *Accepted and Renewed in Christ: The "Twofold Grace of God" and the Interpretation of Calvin's Theology*. Vandenhoeck & Ruprecht, 2007.

Volf, Miroslav. *Exclusion and Embrace: A Theological Exploration of Identity, Otherness, and Reconciliation*. Rev. and updated ed. Abingdon, 2019.

Volf, Miroslav, and Ryan McAnnally-Linz. *The Home of God: A Brief Story of Everything*. Brazos, 2022.

von Balthasar, Hans Urs. *Word and Redemption: Essays in Theology 2*. Herder & Herder, 1965.

Walton, John H. "Equilibrium and the Sacred Compass: The Structure of Leviticus." *Bulletin for Biblical Research* 11, no. 2 (2001): 293–304.

Webster, John. "Communion with Christ: Mortification and Vivification." In *Sanctified by Grace: A Theology of the Christian Life*, edited by Kent Eilers and Kyle Strobel, 121–38. T&T Clark, 2014.

Webster, John. *God Without Measure: Working Papers in Christian Theology*. Vol. 1, *God and the Works of God*. T&T Clark, 2016.

Webster, John. "The Holiness and Love of God." *Scottish Journal of Theology* 57, no. 3 (2004): 249–68.

Webster, John. "'It Was the Will of the Lord to Bruise Him': Soteriology and the Doctrine of God." In *God of Salvation: Soteriology in Theological Perspective*, edited by Ivor J. Davidson and Murray A. Rae, 15–34. Ashgate, 2011.

Webster, John. *Word and Church: Essays in Christian Dogmatics*. T&T Clark, 2001.

Wells, Jo Bailey. *God's Holy People: A Theme in Biblical Theology*. Sheffield Academic, 2000.

Wesley, John. "The Circumcision of the Heart." In *John Wesley's Sermons: An Anthology*, edited by Albert C. Outler and Richard P. Heitzenrater, 23–32. Abingdon, 1991.

Wesley, John. "The Great Privilege of Those That Are Born of God." In *Sermons I: 1–33*, edited by Albert C. Outler, 431–43. The Works of John Wesley. Abingdon, 1984.

Wesley, John. "An Israelite Indeed." In *Sermons III: 71–114*, edited by Albert C. Outler, 278–89. The Works of John Wesley. Abingdon, 1986.

Wesley, John. *John and Charles Wesley: Selected Writings and Hymns*. Classics of Western Spirituality. Paulist Press, 1981.

Wesley, John. "Justification by Faith." In *Sermons I: 1–33*, edited by Albert C. Outler, 181–99. The Works of John Wesley. Abingdon, 1984.

Wesley, John. "On Working Out Our Own Salvation." In *Sermons III: 71–114*, edited by Albert C. Outler, 199–209. The Works of John Wesley. Abingdon, 1986.

Wesley, John. "The Original, Nature, Property, and Use of the Law." Wesley Center Online. https://wesley.nnu.edu/john-wesley/the-sermons-of-john-wesley-1872-edition/sermon-34-the-original-nature-property-and-use-of-the-law/.

Wesley, John. "The Unity of the Divine Being." Wesley Center Online. https://wesley.nnu.edu/john-wesley/the-sermons-of-john-wesley-1872-edition/sermon-114-the-unity-of-the-divine-being/.

Wesley, John. "The Witness of the Spirit, I." In *Sermons I: 1–33*, edited by Albert C. Outler, 267–84. The Works of John Wesley. Abingdon, 1984.

Whitley, W. T., ed. *The Doctrine of Grace*. Student Christian Movement Press, 1932.

Williams, A. N. "Contemplation." In *Knowing the Triune God: The Work of the Spirit in the Practices of the Church*, edited by James J. Buckley and David S. Yeago, 121–46. Eerdmans, 2001.

Williams, Rowan. *Being Christian: Baptism, Bible, Eucharist, Prayer*. Eerdmans, 2014.

Williams, Rowan. *Being Human: Bodies, Minds, Persons*. Eerdmans, 2018.

Williams, Rowan. *Christ the Heart of Creation*. Bloomsbury, 2018.

Scripture Index

Subject Index